. . . .

Vital Mummies

. . . .

Vital Mummies Performance Design for the Show-Window Mannequin

Sara K. Schneider

Yale University Press   New Haven & London

Frontispiece photo courtesy of Patina-V.

Published with assistance from the foundation established in memory of Amasa Stone Mather of the Class of 1907, Yale College.

Designed by Nancy Ovedovitz and set in Bauer Bodoni type by The Composing Room of Michigan, Inc. Printed by Quebecor Printing, Kingsport, Tennessee.

The paper in this book meets the guidelines for permanence and durability of the Committee on Production Guidelines for Book Longevity of the Council on Library Resources.

10   9   8   7   6   5   4   3   2   1

Library of Congress Cataloging-in-Publication Data

Schneider, Sara K.
Vital mummies : performance design for the show-window mannequin / Sara K. Schneider.
p.   cm.
Includes bibliographical references and index.
ISBN 0-300-06039-4
1. Display of merchandise—United States.   2. Show-windows—United   States.   3. Mannequins (Figures)
4. Commercial art—United States.   5. Performance art—United States.   I. Title.
HF5845.S414   1995
659.15′7—dc20   94-40233
                                                          CIP

A catalogue record for this book is available from the British Library.

For Robert "Buddy" Hoskins

. . . .

Contents

Preface

Given that the vast majority of prominent New York display directors have been male and that both the figures they manipulate in the windows and the passersby whose desire they seek to rouse are predominantly female, this subject has considerable relevance for feminist critics researching the issues of silence, inanimacy, and agency. This study, however, takes the fact of the still body of the mannequin and treats it as a more or less unified genre of representation, a player within the larger frame of the show window as an environment for the design of behavior—that is, for theatre.

This adoption of some of the conventions of the representation of the female in mannequin form as givens permits an examination of several other issues of significance to cultural studies: the change in the locus of theatricality from a stage that is separate from the audience to one that includes the audience in an environment in which fashion figures, display directors, and passersby simultaneously act on each other; the altered size and scope of the self in a world in which altered bodies are treated as signs for dramatic characters; the refractability of the self in a mode of representation in which fake and real selves appear to be modeled on each other's shells, without either's seeming prior or discernibly more authentic; and the previously unexplored ways in which design of the physical world also embodies one means for designing human behavior and through it the very self.

Acknowledgments

This project owes its germination to William H. Burdick, my teacher and friend. Through our work in period dance forms I developed a strong interest in body stylizations across history and in choreographic visions. Robert "Buddy" Hoskins, the adjunct assistant professor of display and exhibit design at the Fashion Institute of Technology in New York, was the project's midwife. Both a scholar and a practitioner, Robert immediately saw where the project was going and pointed me in that direction. He was an invaluable interviewee, source of referrals, and interlocutor, and as a dear friend he is sorely missed.

Certain industry experts provided information so generously and so eye-openingly that I am especially grateful to Gene Moore, Tiffany & Company; Ralph Pucci, Pucci Manikins; Michael Southgate, Adel Rootstein; and Lloyd Squiers, Greneker.

I would also like to thank the display directors, mannequin manufacturers, and visual merchandising executives and their staffs who gave openly of their time, their observations, and their photo collections: George Alonso and Michelle DiChiara, Hindsgaul; Dan Arjé; Calvin Churchman; Edward T. Cranston and Leonard Bunch, E.T. Cranston-Almax; Bob Currie; Richard Currier, Bergdorf Goodman; Simon Doonan, Barneys; Robert Filoso; Nellie Fink, Adel Rootstein; Richard Gilbert, Steren Robotics; Victor Hugo; Martha Landau, Greneker; Robin Lauritano and Harry Medina, Bloom-

ingdale's; Sarah Lee; Robert Mahoney; Lou Mahr, George Dell; Jim Mansour, The Limited; George Martin, Patina-V; Philip Monaghan; Candy Pratts; Guy Scarangello; and Toshi. Model Rod McCray and display photographer Willo Font provided singular perspectives.

Performance artist Colette, robot mannequin Diane Everett, and multimedia artist Lynn Hershman shared work that helped me make vital connections between animate and inanimate window performance.

Marsha Bentley Hale and the Mannequin Museum, Los Angeles, provided a wealth of information and iconography on the history and aesthetics of mannequin design. I am also grateful for the resources of Saks Fifth Avenue; the Fashion Institute of Technology; the Film Studies Center, Museum of Modern Art; the International Center of Photography; the New York Public Library; and the New Museum of Contemporary Art.

I am, as always, thankful for the cut-the-crap advice of Richard Schechner. Cece Blake reminded me of Freud at just the right time. And I very much appreciate the good-spirited guidance of Barbara Kirshenblatt-Gimblett, Brooks McNamara, Charles Briggs, Marcia B. Siegel, Michael Taussig, and Peggy Phelan.

Many thanks to Rhea Lehman, Stuart Ewen, and David Goldblatt, who gave invaluable suggestions on the manuscript, and at Yale University Press to Dan Heaton, for his discriminating and compassionate editing, and Jonathan Brent, for his faith and enthusiasm.

. . . .

Vital Mummies

Introduction

In a Bloomingdale's store window, a conveyor belt carries Baggies filled with a white powdery substance through a gateway marked "Customs." Several suspicious-looking rattan attaché cases, labeled "Made in the Philippines," are placed significantly about the scene. In reality, the powder is rice and talc, but reality is trumped by appearance: even so, a figure in the window is a drug smuggler, and anyone who stops to gaze at the window is an accessory by association.

Members of the visual merchandising industry routinely talk about their work as theatre. Display directors speak of the mannequins as actors, among whom they circulate as authors of a total, three-dimensional vision. In fact, directors create a dramatic situation by placing the mannequins strategically—the static equivalent of stage blocking—and costuming them and propping their environment to maximize their impact. Display directors strive above all to control the ostensible emotional relation between mannequins and the impression their actors make on the public. Theatre directors and display directors are interpreters of a like nature—one makes the literary theatrical, the other makes the visual theatrical.

Live performances in windows underscore the charged relations between art and life, commerce and art, and stillness and animation represented in all window displays. Such performances also accent the double charge

"Flying Bride" window by Henry Callahan, 1958. Photo by Nick Malan Studios. Courtesy of Saks Fifth Avenue.

that *display* brings from ethology, where static and dynamic meanings converge. To attract the female, a male bird both fans his feathers (an action) and shows her his tail fan (a portrait).

Live window performances became quite common in the 1970s, when the Fiorucci boutique in New York, for example, captured media attention with its live windows, in which "models acted out deadpan plays in bizarre sets."[1] Model Pat Cleveland disco-danced in the windows, attached to a chain that was suspended from the ceiling; she transformed the chain into first a belt, then a sash, then a tie, then a tube top, as she danced. In Fiorucci's 1981 Christmas windows dedicated to Billy Boy, a famous Barbie doll collector, actors and models (including the well-known Dovima) wearing exaggerated evening gowns danced in a ballroom environment during the lunch hour. Madonna performed at Fiorucci in 1983. In another window, by set designer Calvin Churchman, pinup boys watered the grass and mowed the lawn in a backyard environment. For Valentine's Day 1980, Churchman staged a window entitled "Airplane Crash," which featured the interior of a plane, angled against the sidewalk. A "stewardess" (in reality the performer was a stripper) ran up and down the aisles screaming, a performance limited in duration by the performer's endurance.

Though they are usually still, window displays that

use mannequins as performers often also imply action over time yet are "performed" continuously during their "run." In fact, it may be the glamour of stillness that attracts viewers to the windows—even to the point of participation. Windows that encourage the participation of and performances by people on the street have been created both for the commercial store window and in the art world. For a 1991 installation by artist Perejaume at the New Museum of Contemporary Art in Soho, spectators were invited into the Broadway window, which was furnished with several rows of theatre seats intended to allow "visitors to become a 'display' at the same time that passersby [became] 'actors' to this audience." Both groups were simultaneously seen and seeing, and the challenge centered on who got to do the most looking.

For a July 1990 Macy's lineup entitled "New Faces on Broadway," shoppers were invited to enter the Broadway windows to receive makeovers at the hands of makeup artists representing six cosmetic companies.[2] Each window was staged as a different glamour set, into which the woman off the street would be cast as star. Several of the window environments were styled to look like theatrical settings, including a dressing room, an avant-garde photographic studio, and an art deco film set.

One of the window sets featured a bank of theatre chairs, as in the New Museum's window. Friends of the women being made over and women in line for their own appointments could wait in the windows, watching the loitering crowds—and watching themselves be watched. The stillness, the concentration, and the silence of the woman in the chair was designed to cause her living, breathing friends to appear fidgety, mundane, and unattractively "real" by contrast. The more the customer submitted herself to the situation of being a store-window performer, the more mannequin-like her glamour became.

The theatrical metaphor so familiar to display workers feels quite appropriate from the vantage point of recent theatrical history. For at least a century and a half,

display, commerce, and popular culture in general have shared striking commonalities with theatre in notions of persona, agency, and audience. As the twentieth century began, at least two theatrical traditions flourished. The dominant one is essentially humanistic in character, both prizing the virtuosity of and creating the aura surrounding individual performers, who symbolize for their audiences the elevation of the human spirit and will. The circus, the popular-music concert, the opera, and many plays celebrate talent the artist has plainly nurtured over years of labor. Everything else onstage—lighting, costumes, props and scenery, microphones, trapezes, even the circus elephants—are supporting players to the stage's star, the human performer, emblem of the wondrous limits of human performance. This humanistic tradition derives most recently from nineteenth-century theatre, which privileged the star actor to such an extent that he, as production supervisor, changed both his own and other actors' lines, costuming, and staging to showcase his own charms.

The alternative twentieth-century theatrical tradition can be characterized as a series of challenges to the unfettered and vainglorious actor—and to virtuosity for its own sake. In turn-of-the-century productions for the Moscow Art Theatre, Konstantin Stanislavsky staged meticulously detailed crowd scenes in which each performer, no matter the size of the part, painstakingly researched and prepared a life history and personality profile for his or her character. Stanislavsky demanded that each actor have a driving sense of purpose even for scenes in which he or she merely passed through an evening throng. Stanislavsky's naturalism emphasized the dynamics of the group in constant process and flux rather than spotlighting the individual. Fame mattered less than talent and the humility to submerge oneself within one's role; technique belonged not so much to the solo actor as to the production.

Darwin had struck at the root of humankind in suggesting that humans were patterned not directly on God but on "lower" life forms. Freud's blow came to rest a bit higher when he postulated that as much as human beings might be rational creatures, they were racked and thrown by forces of which they were unconscious—and which necessarily caused them shame. Perhaps even more threateningly, several twentieth-century theatre movements would be founded on the assumption that the living deserved no more exaltation than the inanimate.[3]

In some productions, the total work of art that Richard Wagner had called for in the 1870s was finally being attempted, as directors strove to integrate human and design aspects on stage so that the scenery and costumes, rather than remaining a stationary background for action, became an integral part of that action. Actors were forced to interact with their settings, to recognize them as part of the theatrical experience of the spectator. As early as the first decade of the new century, this development worked to equalize the importance of human and nonhuman elements of theatre. Max Reinhardt treated the stage setting as if it were an actor in his 1905 production of *A Midsummer Night's Dream*. A revolving stage permitted the forest setting to "turn and change" seductively before the audience's eyes, as elves and fairies danced in among self-transforming Nature.[4] The human had become one of a complex system of theatrical elements.

According to Aristotle's theory of tragedy, the action onstage must dramatize events and states of mind so terrible that, through empathy with the plight of the principal character, the audience would be spared the greater suffering of enacting similar events. The spectator's empathy with the protagonist and passive emotional catharsis seemed to serve both culture and the individual. Theatre informed by Aristotelian aesthetics ostensibly relieved a society of certain dangerous inclinations that its members might have, and it offered an escape valve for the individual, who was content to see things happen on a stage that was separate from his or her life.

Various theatre theorists—Bertolt Brecht the best known among them—radically reassessed the prevailing Aristotelian concept of the audience as those for whom the dramatic action is undertaken. Instead, Brecht demanded that the spectator become an active participant in deciphering the stage action and in determining his or her relation to it. Going to the theatre must no longer be an opportunity for the spectator to set himself or herself adrift from personal cares and awash in others' woes; it must become a chance for the intellect to exercise itself and to compare critically the world of the stage with that of experience. For Brecht, the two worlds were scarcely separate. His creative predecessor, Erwin Piscator, combined dramatic action with news material in his works during the 1920s to show audiences the links between the worlds portrayed and the worlds they themselves inhabited.

Complementing their efforts to train a more actively perceptive audience, Piscator and Brecht strove for a new "epic" playing style for the actor. Distanced from the role, the actor would *demonstrate* rather than *act as* the character, maintaining a clear distinction between his or her own personality and that of the character and indicating an attitude toward the character rather than merging completely with the role. Far from hiding behind a fourth wall that divided the stage and the audience into supposed separate entities, each private from the other until the final bow, actors would openly acknowledge the artificiality of the theatrical situation, simultaneously highlighting the theatricality of everyday life.

The occupation of director established itself in the twentieth century. No longer were productions managed and monkeyed with by their star players. Now the actor's job was defined as the organic and authentic development of character over the arc of the play—without reference to how others were playing their parts. Staging came to mean executing the vision of a single, more removed artist, the director, whose oversight extended not only to the actors' movements and interpretations of their roles but also to the visual expression of the play in theatrical design.

From this directorial perspective, the spectator's experience of the theatre took precedence over the script.

Many twentieth-century directors maintained that what triggered audience response in performance was the immediacy of the performer's body, not the playwright's words. These directors sought to enhance the visceral quality of theatre. Vsevolod Meyerhold, Antonin Artaud, and other twentieth-century theatrical innovators, influenced by Eastern stylized dance-drama forms, insisted that the performing body had to be expressive on its own terms rather than because it required a co-presence in time and space of actor and audience. The cornerstone of the art form was not the script but the actor's body and how he or she used it. Drawing on the Freudian sense of a divided self, expressionist productions of the early twentieth century parceled out roles among a number of actors, each of whom would play a grotesque of some isolated aspect of the self. All of these efforts to reconfigure the relation between the inside and the outside of performance have been reinforced for a popular audience—which has "bought" these images ideologically as it has bought them (at least visually) in the marketplace. Yet the clear evidence in front of the spectator was a *whole* person, though the actor might be playing a *part.*

In mannequin displays throughout the twentieth century, however, bodies themselves are regularly fragmented, withheld, or supplanted by inanimate objects in displays that carry the theatrical experiments of the twentieth century even further. Although these body fragments often are simply visually arresting ways of referring to whole selves, they may also suggest that the splinters, shards, and traces of bodies in the window displays are *all there is,* even in the world beyond the window frame, that they do not refer to a larger self but are themselves a self-sufficient self that we fear to acknowledge.

Such fragmentation suggests that human agency—a reassuring sense of the whole, fixed, regal human self—is neither as dignified nor as privileged as we have cared to think. We come to doubt both the psychologized interior and the whole, undamaged exterior of a person, even as we depend on them to make sense of the world, for the partial exterior may be a self, as may the empty interior. And, as with the "outside-in" acting style typically associated with the British school, it may be the outside—the design elements, the costume, the accent—that define the persona, rather than any feelings, intentions, or perceptions.

Or worse, perhaps, for the humanist—the inside and outside may be related only in passing, if at all.

Mannequin-personae are as frequently represented as the objects of dramatic action as they are the subjects. The street theatre windows of the mid-1970s suggest that characters may be defined by what is done to them as much as by what they themselves do, forcing us to radically reassess our notions of the dramatic hero or heroine. Of course, neither mannequin displays nor avant-garde art nor theatre movements operate in a vacuum. All are part of larger tides in Western culture, tides that in turn permit linguists, for example, to study conversation as interactive chains of simultaneous feedback between speaker and listener rather than as a ping-pong match in which the only action is on the speaker's side.

A tacit assumption of this book is that the display world and the fashion world—the inanimate and the perambulating—mutually create each other, that neither is prior. In one line of descent, the fashion model apes the "character" of the clothes a designer creates, a mannequin is often built on the inspiration of a model, and the consumer buys into the image of the mannequin. In another equally valid declension, the mannequin, the model, and the fashions themselves take their lead from what consumers are doing "on the street." This idea of co-creation is like what the linguists have suggested about conversation; what social scientists depict when they characterize violence and poverty not as individual failings but as "social problems"; and what playwright Caryl Churchill is getting at in *Top Girls,* where dialogue is "scored" so that overlappings, interruptions, and other simultaneities show how characters *A* and *B* act and react all the time.

With mannequin displays and consumers, the case is

even more complicated. For even though they act on each other simultaneously, the real action is concealed and implicit, as in a confession booth. Passersby see the *signs* of what the display director has committed on the mannequin and its surroundings, but usually not the act of commission itself. Display directors—particularly in the slim good cheer that characterizes modern retail—are held in check by the sales figures, the trace of the buying behavior of the passerby/customer. Each player is in a ghost town, tracking the other's footprints.

Gene Moore at work with his "girls." Courtesy of the artist.

1 Spawning an "American " Display

"People are looking different lately, maybe you've no-
ticed. The dummies must be changing."

"The dummies," said Kleinzeit. "Oh."

"First the dummies in the shop windows change," said
Flashpoint, "then the people."

"I didn't think anybody'd noticed that but me," said
Kleinzeit. "God makes the dummies maybe. Man makes the
people." He crossed his legs, kicking the flex that led to
Flashpoint's monitor. The plug came out of the wall, the
last blip faded and went down in smoke, the screen went
dark.

"Oh God," said Flashpoint. "I'm gone."

Kleinzeit plugged in the machine again. "You're back,"
he said. Together they watched the blips moving across the
screen.

—Russell Hoban, *Kleinzeit*

How can we speak about window dummies as performers, on a par with humans—or at least as part of
the same spectrum? Mannequins are inanimate, the
scenes in which they are placed usually as un-"event"-
ful as paintings on a gallery wall. If Gauguins are not
"performative," why should mannequin displays be?

Mannequin displays link the image of a body to a
tacit action: a realistic mannequin, though still, often
appears to be about to act or to have just acted. And
both realistic and abstract mannequins simultaneously
display and are displayed. Appearance is in fact a form
of action.

Mannequin displays may be the "purest" form of
commercial theatre: what is produced is literally what
sells. The primary purpose of a mannequin display is to
promote buying, whether of the specific clothing or
products displayed or of the image of the store, and
whether the passerby comes in and becomes a customer
this minute or a month down the road. Images and displays that don't sell, either directly or indirectly, bring
ignominious consequences for their creators. Implicit in
the gambit of window display is therefore a mandate for
behavior: customers must undergo the kind of emotional change that makes them desire things and crave
to buy them. "Appearing" works only if it is closely
linked with particular actions that inspire buying.

Novel in the range of performer-audience relationships in contemporary performance, the characters of
this drama are split into viewer and viewed: the role of
the viewed is as a goad to action; the viewer carries the
drama through the next two acts, the reception of the
message and the observance of the imperative to consume. The display designer functions as absentee-
director, anticipating and staging this transaction between mannequin and viewer. Predicting what will
touch off the possessive urge in the spectator, the de-

signer crafts an environment that will invite expression of that urge.

History of American Display

The "origin" of window display is debatable, depending upon the select criterion of the term; it is perhaps more useful to say that display has had several seed moments. In the 1880s the availability of plate glass (first manufactured in the United States in 1868) led to the widespread installation of large pane windows in commercial venues, making it possible for passersby to see the goods available for purchase; the filament lamp, invented in 1879, further amplified the visual experience of shopping. By the end of the nineteenth century, L. Frank Baum—the soon-to-be author of *The Wizard of Oz*—could write about window trimming as a distinct specialty. Some historians say display as an art form began shortly before World War I, when goods were first glamorized in window displays; others argue for 1925, when cluttered "variety" windows began to give way to window design that relied on pictorial composition to bring individual items into focus. In fact, all of the alternative histories work together: in the design business, technical innovation goes hand in hand with aesthetic change, and aesthetics evolve in relation to the professionalization of the designer.

Merchants conceived of placing goods close to the windows in the early nineteenth century. Although the original purpose of the windows had simply been to admit more light into the store, pedestrians could view beckoning goods as they passed by, just as they might in an open-air bazaar. By the 1830s goods were commonly styled to increase their selling appeal, and in that decade "the term *design* assum[ed] a modern definition, describing the superficial application of decoration to the form and surface of a product."[1] The dissociation between the function and the style of a consumer product evolved along with changes in strategies for attracting customers. As stores grew and had—in relation to their total selling volume—much less surface area than

before with which to lure passersby, they shifted from employing primarily environmental and tactile appeals to relying on seductive visual ones.

Although the term did not become current until the 1890s, the American department store was birthed between 1860 and 1910, at least in part out of economic necessity. According to the historian Susan Porter Benson, the early founders of department stores in the United States never "consciously [strove] toward a new type of firm, but simply [made] a series of tactical decisions for the immediate health of their businesses."[2] Taxes fell and capital was freed up during the mid-nineteenth century. The increasingly dense, mobile, and well-off city populations of the Industrial Revolution demanded more and higher-quality goods from shopkeepers; as "cutthroat competition" shrank profits to be made from traditional product lines, merchants began to search for ways to diversify their offerings.[3]

Department stores, which grew gradually over this fifty-year period, distinguished themselves from smaller urban shops with promises of reliable products, guaranteed satisfaction, and, perhaps most important, the new mantle of respectability and dignity that they placed on the act of shopping. In contrast with the smaller shops, where customers and clerks bargained over prices and where "customers were routinely badgered to make a purchase as the price of leaving the store," the new department stores openly displayed their prices (whose fixity was a matter of pride) and pledged uniform quality, critical in the new urban lifestyle, where buyer and seller were not acquainted and opportunity for fraud was increased.[4]

While the new store windows both sated and tempted the hunger of the urban middle class for heavily styled goods, they may also have fed mistrust of the marketable beautiful by displaying and reinforcing the disjunction between form and matter that had already been characteristic of industrial design for several decades. Victorian culture's "aesthetic of abundance" helped create the desire that was necessary to sell goods in quantity, goods that were sometimes displayed in polyisomorphic configurations: smaller items arranged in the shape of a larger version of themselves. The first display windows in the United States drew on the opulence and the exaggerated fondness for symmetry that were characteristic of Victorian visual culture, as well as on the icons of early Egyptian, Persian, and Greek art. Displays freely employed temple imagery, columns, urns, vines, mahogany, and other exotica. Early windows, which lacked the adaptability that display artists now demand, served primarily as heavily laden tables for the goods and decor within. Miles Orvell has traced the nineteenth-century popular fascination with such encyclopedic forms as the panorama, the diorama, the exhibition hall, and the gallery—and we might extrapolate to the Victorian show window as well—to a single organizing principle: "the containment of an infinitely expandable number of parts in an encompassing whole."[5] The all-embracing character of these window displays spoke to a universal interest in the array of objects that Euro-American ingenuity could produce or procure.

World's fairs and exhibitions had a marked impact on the development of styles for both museum and commercial displays. These expositions both disseminated the most forward-looking developments in design and provided representative displays rather than merely relying on verbal or two-dimensional expressions. Walter Benjamin counted the world's fairs as the origin of the "pleasure industry"; the fairs "refined and multiplied the varieties of reactive behavior of the masses." In Benjamin's view, the world's fairs conditioned urban crowds to the "principle of advertisements: 'Look, but don't touch,' and taught [them] to derive pleasure from the spectacle alone."[6]

The Great Exhibition of 1851 in London reveled in a style of display that overpowered the objects featured and "ushered in a tradition of World Fairs that have been vehicles for experiments in architecture and design ever since." At this first great international show, "much of the display material was arranged in the form of altars, or monuments, with the products of industry in a subordinate role, providing the components for

elaborate patchwork-like patterns," which were arranged in a rectangular grid. The Great Exhibition was not only a precursor of the modern museum but also a theatrically charged event, which added "to the original loot . . . the organisation of the fair, the entrepreneurial skill of the showman, the simulation of the waxwork tableaux, and the right of the general public to access."[7]

The late nineteenth century and the first quarter of the twentieth were marked by a realistic display style that was free of the coming terrors of surrealism. New York's Museum of Natural History was dedicated during these years to the preservation of existing resources and ways of life; it strove "to produce permanence," which served not only to show objects but also to hint at a moral "articulation of natural order."[8] In both museum and commercial window, displays attested above all to artifacts' existence and abundance. Show windows were filled with objects of every description, arranged without regard for visual composition.

An 1883 display manual, *Warehousemen and Drapers' Trade Journal*, treated the display of costumes only in terms of the visibility and quality of the goods and the symmetry of the window. The idea of clothing as the most immediate remnant of a living, behaving person had not yet been developed; élite fashions had only begun to be mass-produced during the 1880s. Rather, costumes were abstracted in display so that they functioned more as shapes occupying space—and capable of distracting the passerby by their very violation of the values of balance and symmetry—than as vestiges of an active human body.

Fashion photography at the turn of the century, closely linked with both formal portraiture and theatre photography, used models who reaffirmed the upper-crust image of three-dimensional display. *Vogue* set and helped maintain the standard:

Throughout its history, ever since its birth as the first illustrated fashion magazine in 1892, . . . *Vogue*'s editors and photographers wanted to portray ladies and gentlemen. Readers were expected to look up to an aristocracy who had all the advantages of position and education and who set the image of what was proper. These early fashion photographs imitated portrait painting. The authority and dignity of the wearer and the quality and style of his or her garments were a message of class difference. The stillness of the pose, the haughtiness of the attitude, and the splendor of the clothes created a distance between the image and the spectator. The woman's expression was hermetic, closed; no emotion was permitted.[9]

By 1910, department stores had through trial and error come upon the floor plan that remains the blueprint for most large stores today: cosmetics, accessories, and impulse items on the first floor, along with men's clothes (on the assumption that men would not be willing to venture farther than absolutely necessary into the store); bargain goods, groceries, and housewares in the basement; and on the upper floors higher-ticket items—furniture, appliances, carpets—whose purchase would ordinarily be planned well in advance. The early stores were cathedrals to the perceived needs of women, not only for goods but for an astounding array of services. By the turn of the century, the Emporium in San Francisco, for example, included "a parlor with papers, periodicals, and writing materials; a children's nursery; an emergency hospital, with a trained nurse in attendance; a Post Office station; a Western Union telegraph office; a theater-ticket office; a manicuring and hair-dressing parlor and a barber shop; public telephones; a lunch room; an information bureau; [and] almost always some free exhibition in the art rooms—all of these under one roof and most of them free."[10]

Ideas about personifying or dramatizing the merchandise entered into the common parlance only in the 1910s, when goods in windows were first glamorized through isolation or presented in elaborate accessorized settings that evoked the moment of use. It was during this decade that Adolf de Meyer introduced to *Vogue* an "artistic" fashion photography, which privileged the mood and aura of a garment over a close depiction of its details. A 1920 photograph of Helen Lee Worthing showed a coy, baroque bride checking her beauty mark in the mirror, as light shone through the high, misty tufts of her veil. De Meyer's idea of selling a garment through a vision of its dream value became practically synonymous with the large-scale fantasies of twentieth-century display.[11] It was also consistent with the association, established during the 1880s and 1890s, between consumer products and dreaming, when mail-order catalogues—"wish-books"—were marketed as the inspiration for extended consumer daydreams.

In the 1920s capitalism, abetted immeasurably by print advertising and by display, propelled both the economy and new cultural identities. The membership of the International Association of Display Men, founded in 1898, had grown to more than one thousand by the end of World War I.[12] According to anthropologist Stephen J. Fjellman, industrial capitalists such as Henry Ford and Edward Filene, needing to stimulate consumption to a rate ever faster than that of production, "did not just want to sell large quantities of particular items: They wanted to invent a new ontological category of human being. Their interest was partly economic, but it was also philanthropic. As did many others, they believed this new kind of person—the consumer—would be capable of living a rich human life beyond the capabilities of his or her forbears."[13] Advertising was to be the "ignition system of the economy" and would jump-start individuals with buying power into thinking not of "marketing" but of "shopping"; the advertising strategist Earnest Elmo Calkins predicted a resulting "increased focus on the act of consumption" as being pleasurable in itself.[14] The distinction was predicated on a fundamental change in the mode of perception and in the values associated with consumption: "'Marketing' means simply buying items in the marketplace, 'stocking up.' 'Shopping,' on the other hand, is a more leisurely examination of the goods; its behaviors are more directly determined by desire than need. To shop: as a verb, it implies choice, empowerment in the relation between looking and having, the act of buying as a willful choice. To shop is to muse in the contemplative mode, an activity that combines diversion, self-gratification, expertise, and physical activity."[15]

As the focus of consumers shifted during the twenties from marketing for specific objects to shopping as an experience in itself, fashion began in certain critical ways to dematerialize: fashion began to emphasize line over mass, and the design was planned to become stylistically obsolete long before the clothing wore out. During this invigorated period of consumption personality began to be viewed as separable from the person. And personality, not coincidentally, became *salable* in the various social and economic markets: "Personal traits, once the facets of a person's character, were . . . being mass produced as instruments of persuasion, masks to cover those aspects of character that might get in the way of sales."[16] Emotions were appropriated as adaptable and evocative selling tools; in some theories of advertising taking hold during this period, emotional needs underlay the most basic appeals for the potential buyer, employer, or mate.

De Meyer's dream style of advertising photography was related to a popular style of advertising copy known in the 1920s as "impressionistic copy" or "atmosphere advertising," which competed with the harder-core, "salesmanship-on-paper" style of copy. Each approach had its cycles of popularity and its counterpart in the ethos of window display. Rather than giving cold, hard facts about the value of a product, suggestive or associative advertising seemed more spiritual—or at least above crass materialism; copy that appeared to transcribe the rational persuasion a live salesperson would provide seemed "less like advertising" and so more trustworthy.[17] Similarly, atmospheric window displays appeared generously willing to sacrifice limited window space purely to the visual pleasure of the spectator, whereas, like much of nineteenth-century advertising, straightforward displays reassured buyers that they were getting what Orvell calls the "real thing," not just a fraudulent image.

The 1925 Exposition des Arts Décoratifs, which origi-

nated in Paris but the next year traveled to New York, Chicago, and Boston, marked an important change in display aesthetics, the end of the let's-show-them-everything-we've-got "clutter" window. So striking was the difference between pre- and post-1925 display that in 1937 a writer for *Fortune* magazine observed, "Twenty-five years ago, had anyone thought of discussing the art of window display, he must have recalled that old natural-history book with its famous chapter on 'Snakes in Iceland,' which began and ended: *There are no snakes in Iceland.* For as recently as before the War there was no art of window display." Many of the ideas circulating within the avant-garde visual arts were passed on to the design community with the 1925 Exposition. *Vogue* proclaimed, after viewing the first "modern art" mannequins exhibited by Siégel and Stockman at the Exposition, that "the art of the mannequin, which did not previously exist, has now been perfected." One writer for *Time* noted in 1938 that it was the Exposition that popularized the notion that fine art should be placed in service as the "handmaiden of Industry."[18]

The explosive growth of the display industry during this period was reflected in the abundance of plaster objects displayed for the first time at the Exposition, objects that had been designed and produced exclusively for display purposes. As Lester Gaba, forever a critic of the "Arty—with a capital A" style, put it, they "could not conceivably be used anywhere else."[19]

That the Exposition was held in Paris is also significant, for other innovations that influenced design in the United States had originated there and would have been visible to American visitors during the twenties. In 1923 show-window stylist H. Glévéo wrote about a new Parisian display style to which he had contributed in which a single object or a set of identical objects was showcased and highlighted, arranged so as to create a mood of mystery and visual seduction through repetition. America had also never seen anything like the new Pierre Imans mannequins, whose astonishingly realistic wax faces and body attitudes evoked discernible emo-

Siégel and Stockman abstract figures, ca. 1929. Courtesy of the Mannequin Museum archive.

tinues today: were mannequin design innovations self-satisfying tricks performed by artists and the display industry, gimmicks whose effect on consumers (and hence on sales) would be sure to be detrimental? Gaba blamed the 1925 Exposition for providing "no standard except a bad one" to the hungry and undiscerning display man.[20]

The art movements that were particularly critical for mannequin and display design—cubism and surrealism—first reached a wide audience in fashion magazines, which disseminated new aesthetic trends and tastes.[21] Surrealism may well have been the ideal style for advertising, since it permitted the interdependence and interaction of the dream world and the real. Richard Martin holds that "it was precisely Surrealism's ability to juxtapose the real and the unreal that made it a primary form for advertising and media expression. Merchandise, in its crassest form, could be seen; the dream of the consumer product, whether fashion or otherwise, could also be envisioned. The simultaneity of an optical truth and its dreamed doppelgänger could render the product enticing."[22] Many surrealist artists played with the man-mannequin boundary; several also worked enthusiastically as display artists. Surrealism remains the hallmark style of displays that depart even slightly from realism.

The peculiar tie between mannequin stagings and surrealism, as opposed to other avant-garde movements of the early years of the century, may derive in part from the surrealists' interest in anthropomorphic art. Although earlier artists, most influentially Giorgio de Chirico, had painted mannequins and dress forms as if they were human subjects, surrealism amplified the interest in the relation between animate and inanimate female figures. Man Ray's well-known surrealist work for *Harper's Bazaar* featured motifs that would later become hallmarks of display style: individual body parts wrought out of proportion; the use of the model's body as mannequinlike potential fake; the merging of body decoration and clothing, as in the portrait of a woman's hands whose gloves Picasso had *painted* on; the juxta-

tions. Animation of mannequins began to be exploited in display windows: the department store Printemps displayed "carefully staged clichés," in which each mannequin played a part in the re-creation of a scene. The Red Cross, a children's party, a baby's nursery, a cruise—any theme might inspire a scene staged with mannequins of all sizes and with meticulous attention to detail.

While some eagerly flocked to the influential expositions of 1851, 1925, and 1937, others decried the destructive effects these expositions had on popular taste. Manufacturer Lester Gaba—and other critics less tied to the fate of the mannequin industry—questioned the taste of the presenters, opening an argument that con-position of live models with surrealistic paintings, such as *A l'heure de l'observatoire—Les amoureux;* and the displacement of the body onto inanimate objects, as in the portrait of a nude, her back made up with the delicate swirls characteristic of a violin body.

William Leach argues that all display and decoration after 1890 was surrealist on some level because it "tried to invest artificial and material things, whole urban spaces, with plasticity and life, breaking down the barriers between the animate and the inanimate." Surrealists treated the object as "the surrogate of the figure." Garments were viewed not only as vestiges of living persons but as substitutes for them, as in Magritte's 1934 painting *Homage to Mack Sennett,* in which a long gown hangs in the closet in the veritable form of woman; the nipples of full breasts push out against the fabric. Martin writes that "the interpretation of the body became an abiding Surrealist premise. . . . The partial figure, the dislocation of body parts, and the placement of the figure and/or its parts in unanticipated settings were adopted for promotional imagery and for the new imagery of fashion in the 1930s."[23]

The surrealist decontextualization of familiar objects—particularly parts of the body—is a precursor of the abstract mannequin and the mannequin alternative, as well as of display's penchant for suggesting entire figures or personalities through the use of individual body parts. Surrealists typically juxtaposed two objects that had only a glancing association in order to make the viewer see unexpected relations and imagine new contexts that could embrace both objects and still permit them to jar. The objects—or ideas, or words—were lifted out of former contexts and presented in cut-out form, and the viewer who tried to reconcile the juxtaposition had simultaneously to excise and to call upon the usual contexts of the objects. Surrealists extended this technique to the body, substituting one body part for another or small, inanimate objects for particular body parts, sometimes removing body parts from the context of the body altogether. Although Rodin had been an innovator in sculpting partial figures, the sur-

realists brought to a new and popular level the presentation of disembodied body parts, especially eyes, lips, hands, and feet.

In Paris in the 1930s, surrealism dominated fashion as well as portraiture. Fashion designer Elsa Schiaparelli was well known for her hats in the forms of shoes: clothing normally reserved for one part of the body suddenly appeared on another, a trend revived for the 1985–86 season, when Karl Lagerfeld introduced a corset hat. (The hat was the favorite surrealist fashion garment, a vehicle for mannequin abstractions relying on deformations or severings of—or substitutions for—the head.) Fashion may be the central surrealist metaphor for, in Martin's words, "the traffic between the interior and the exterior worlds."[24]

As art movements influenced the creators of display, many artists working in the fine-art avant-garde were being drawn to the windows. Before World War I, such artists as Picasso and Seurat had imported advertising, newspaper, and packaging images into their work, and dadaists and surrealists were drawn to the form. Painter Fernand Léger saw window display as capable of realizing "his dream of a new kind of realism in painting, in which the most mundane objects could be shown with a gravity and a weight previously denied them." Francis Picabia perceived display as a means of "making mundane commercial artifacts into mythical personages."[25] Both artists were concerned with heightening the appeal, power, and personality of the object.

Gaba was perhaps correct to fear the importation of surrealist, cubist, and other avant-garde styles into his medium, as the attraction of these styles for display men undermined their commitment to realism. "Modern" was an adjective of approbation. Frederick Kiesler proudly claimed that his series of fourteen windows for Saks in 1928 was the first "extensive presentation of modern show windows" in America, following the "first representative exposition of modern interior decoration" seen in America the previous year at Macy's. A third event, a 1928 exhibition of French decorative art by Lord & Taylor, "brought the contemporary industrial

art of Europe to the knowledge of the general public. . . . Wherever a newspaper was opened, in the remotest villages, the syndicated reports of the sensational novelty brought a knowledge of the coming revolution in taste."[26] By the 1920s, display had become newsworthy. It had also been identified as an "American" art form.

For Frederick Kiesler, display was a quintessentially American form, capable of serving "as the interpreter for the populace of a new spirit in art." As an expression of American progress and mass production, the machine would play a central role in developing this form. Kiesler exulted, "We are gradually approaching the solution of a nation's most profound cultural problem, an art of its own." For Kiesler, display's increasing professional stature both solved a peculiarly American problem—the lack of a secure and independent artistic identity—and made use of the "American" gift for mass media. "Americanism" was also closely associated with industry, as industrial philanthropists such as Henry Ford funded museums as monuments both to national pride and to their own ingenuity as capitalists. Michael Wallace maintains that an "older patrician élite" had since the nineteenth century viewed museums as a tool to "Americanize the immigrant working class." As such, museums marketed a sense of culture to the working class that "supported their sponsors' privileged positions."[27] Museums and retailing thus had a linked history beyond the style of display: both appeared to offer to a wide range of Americans the chance to better their position by selling them culture.

During the modern period the *applied* artist—photographer, engineer, industrial designer, and graphic artist—created the sense of national identity in the United States for which European romantic artists had strived throughout the nineteenth century. The advertising industry, too, benefited during the twenties from an unparalleled confluence of felicitous factors: the industry had earned the public's favor with its work on behalf of the war effort; the economy was booming; the government offered its endorsement—and advertising

became a major industry. Glowed Calvin Coolidge, "Advertising ministers to the spiritual side of trade."[28] In this climate, the dream images of advertising converted luxury products into apparent necessities. Fashion was one of these new necessities.

Live fashion models were an important part of the education of the fashion consumer in the succeeding decades, particularly in "contact" modeling, in which the model performed live. A model needed to learn not only how to walk and to wear makeup, but also what to say. "A good fashion show," wrote Helen Ignatius, "is or certainly should be presented not to glorify the models but to instruct the women in the audience." Clyde Matthews admonished his would-be-model readers that they must be ready if asked to quote the garment's price to a prospective buyer. In addition, the model must serve as a vehicle or missive for the corporate identity of the designer. Marie P. Anderson instructed potential models on the techniques and benefits of private, or retail, modeling: "Becoming a designer's private model can earn you prestige as well as money. Models who move in a couture designer's circle are known as his or her 'cabine.' The designer teaches the models exactly how to behave, regardless of the environment, which ensures that the designer's public image is always consistent."[29]

Demonstration was one method of public education. One writer suggested that a scene be staged for a fashion show in which the model "accidentally" spilled something on her dress. She would slip behind a screen to take off the soiled garment, wash it in front of the audience, hang it up to dry during the rest of the show, and put it on again at the end, thus proving triumphantly that wash 'n' wear fabric is for real.[30]

The style that a model adopts should, according to Matthews, be geared to showing off the unique features of the garment on display, using movement to teach the audience how it should be worn, how it should be accessorized, how it should be "played" or animated through simple characterization, and what its unique points of interest are: "Street dresses . . . should be modeled with an air of casualness and freedom. If there are pockets, they are usually an important part of the design and may be brought to the attention of the buyer merely by slipping the finger tips into the pockets, and if they are false pockets, run your fingers over the false openings to indicate their nature. . . . Attention can be directed to any . . . feature or details of the dress by simple graphic motions indicating their presence and use."[31]

Product education indoctrinated consumers "into the world of facts of the marketplace"—the facts, that is, of the producers' culture—in order to intensify the consumers' financial commitment to that world. Luxury consumer goods were presented to consumers of all economic levels, not only to those with the highest incomes, as a diversion from "the ills of industrial life." During the 1920s advertisers specifically targeted immigrants to teach them the American way of shopping: a lot more trusting and not so much handling and questioning before buying.[32] The term *desire* has been a part of the vernacular of trade from at least as far back as the 1880s; Lester Ward, "the founder of American sociology" defined consumption in 1902 as "the satisfaction of desire."[33]

Consumers also "bought" the patina of high status and could partly satisfy their fantasy of shimmering superiority to others by gazing at the early fine-art windows. The first recorded instance of a collaboration for a window display between a display man and a fine artist took place in 1929, and a similar collaboration ten years later produced the most famous window in American display history: the 1939 "Narcissus White" window at Bonwit Teller, for which Salvador Dalí is credited. From a technical standpoint, "Narcissus White" made news for several reasons that are pertinent here: It made literal the breaking of the fourth wall, a motif in both display windows and artists' windows. At the same time, it magnified the association of window display and fine-art celebrity. And, above all, the window's gossip mileage demonstrated the power of a live, apparently quite spontaneous, performance in this public—and usually static—space. According to Sarah Lee, the widow of the surrealist artist Tom Lee, who directed

display at the store, the window represented a partnership between Lee and his friend Dalí. Lee congratulated himself on the window's preparation, "You, Tom Lee, have contributed a third dimension to Surrealism."

The display featured a claw-foot bathtub covered in white fur. More than one hundred mannequin hands rose out of the tub holding mirrors up to the face of a glamorous old mannequin with a bisque face, tears of blood, and long, blonde hair crawling with beetles. She wore only a negligée of coq feathers. The bathtub was filled with water that was "dirty and grimy, like a swamp"; it offended passersby and frightened store management.[34] More renowned than the window's disputable content is the commotion after Dalí learned that "Narcissus White" would not stay in as planned. According to some reports, Dalí, ordered to empty the filthy water from the tub, furiously drove the tub through the glass pane onto the street. Noticing police on the street, he dove out of the window, hoping to make his career with a publicity stunt.

But according to Mrs. Lee, who was a Bonwit Teller advertising copywriter at the time, the window was altered without either Tom Lee's or Dalí's permission or knowledge, and the nude mannequin was garbed in a prim suit. Bringing an entourage of comrades from the art world to see the window, Dalí saw the alterations for the first time from the street and was infuriated. Given the artist's broken English and passionate temper, no one could communicate to him the controversies the window had spurred or the kinds of changes that would be required. The dishonored artist entered the window from the store and tried to destroy the display, upsetting the heavy tub and accidentally breaking through the glass. The police arrested Dalí, taking him first to the store's handbag stockroom and then to jail to await his hearing at night court. The Lees went to bail him out—filling his eccentric request for "tinned pears." The court fined the artist for "malicious mischief": $500, the exact amount of his commission.

Less scandalous collaborations between artists and display people suggest that display had developed at least a conversational relation with fine art. For Kiesler, window display was not a mere extension of painting into a three-dimensional format, but the paradigmatically modern link between everyday life and the fine arts. Display in the thirties attempted to retain the flattering bonds with high art that the twenties had forged, despite drastically altered circumstances. Depression budgets produced surprisingly rich work during what Barry James Wood called the "golden age of window display." The techniques that emerged from the period's hardships continue strong sixty years later, and were particularly popular in design resurrections of the 1970s. Most long-lasting, perhaps, is the lesson it taught display people about the value and the necessity of ingenuity, of getting the most mileage possible out of the cheapest available materials. This ingenuity, and the development of the ability to make inexpensive materials look costly, may have been a precursor to the techniques of camp. When Richard Currier received his first training in display at Saks at the hands of the then-reigning master, Henry Callahan, he put Callahan's thrift down to "Yankee ingenuity." According to Currier, Callahan insisted, "You've got to make magic, and you've got to create it with nothing."

During the Depression such cheap materials as cellophane and corrugated cardboard were substituted for the more expensive woods and metals that had characterized the luxurious twenties. Lester Gaba preached the need to save and use wisely. In his 1939 book, he advised those who wanted to use soap sculptures in display (as he sometimes did) to dress and decorate the figures with everyday household materials: sponge, felt, cords, fringe, feathers, artificial flowers, rope, seashells, cork, and inexpensive jewelry. For Frederick Kiesler, a De Stijl artist, the fewer the materials, the better, because materials recycled from other uses represented "the idea of efficiency raised to a higher sense."[35]

As merchandise became more conservative and less eye-catching in the 1930s, goodwill or "image" windows were more common, in keeping with the Depression axiom, "Sell the store as well as the merchandise."

A 1937 article advised, "If the first law of display is to be functional in terms of the merchandise, the second is to be expressive in terms of the store." In the same year Dana O'Clare called for "a staff of experts" to handle the increasingly sophisticated job of display. The consumer movement blossomed in the decade, and image-based advertising may have seemed less materialistic during a period when people had little money to spend. Appeals to consumers' unconscious needs and desires (as advertisers saw them) were common, and ads of the period offered women "daintiness, beauty, romance, grace, security and husbands through the use of certain products."[36] Windows that promote a store's image and encourage customer loyalty remain an important category of display, representing a clear departure from the notion of windows as direct advertisements for specific merchandise.

Theatrical lighting was also adapted for the purposes of display during the 1930s. Irving Eldredge, the display director at Macy's, commissioned Stanley McCandless, a theatrical lighting designer, to rewire Macy's windows for increased wattage. McCandless also put adjustable spotlights in the windows and introduced the use of filters. These innovations helped focus the viewer's attention on what lay behind the glass rather than on his or her own distracting reflection. Gene Moore, always emphasizing the importance of lighting, kept track of trends in theatrical lighting: "Although . . . I don't believe I was the first display director to install baby spotlights in windows . . . I certainly used them, along with track lighting, but my contribution was trough lighting, running fluorescent lights along the back of the window. I knew that sending light up the back wall would create the illusion of depth."[37]

In 1930 Kiesler wrote extensively about the display window as a form of "static theatre," drawing elaborate parallels in what he termed "a comparative study of the evolution of stage and the dramatization of merchandise in the store." Kiesler divided the evolution of the stage into three periods. The first was characterized by the use of the painted backdrop, which he likened to the temporary background in the show window. Next came an architectural period, with the development of plastic forms and the use of three-dimensional scenery on the stage, corresponding to semipermanent backgrounds in the show window. The final period was defined by theatrical and display stages that were influenced by the motion picture and that produced work in a "mechanical or constructivist" style.

Kiesler predicted that further theatrical evolutions would eventually filter down, and that in its fourth period the show window would reflect the influence of "talkies," as it began to deal with sensory phenomena beyond the visual. Kiesler's farsightedness and the futurist idiom in which he spoke are evident in his projection of a further state of theatrical/show window development. Here, the show window would at last lead the theatre: "This era will ripen into a fifth state with the perfection of television, whose functionings will embrace and fuse all the dramatic arts through mechanical means. Real actors and stage volumes are eliminated. . . . Here the commercial world, always alert for new media of exploitation, will speed its acceptance far more rapidly than the theatrical world, which is weighed down and ossified beneath a mass of tradition. For the first time, the roles will be reversed, and industry will take the lead in perfecting a new means of decoration."[38] By the late 1930s, it had become an accepted cliché for a display man to speak of "dramatizing the merchandise," a theatrical metaphor that remains dominant in the field.

That Kiesler should have been able to suggest that technology could help erase the human element or diminish its influence in display is evidence of the growing comfort with abstraction in the show windows of the thirties. It is also a sign of the influence of abstraction in the theatre. Antirealist director Gordon Craig saw the actor as a tool in the director's hands and threatened at times to replace actors with marionettes. In 1930, Kiesler urged display people to abandon the prescript that human height be used as a yardstick for the placement of merchandise. According to that guide, hats, for

example, had to be placed at the height on which they would fit the head of the passerby. Kiesler urged display people to place any article of clothing at any level, so long as they made sure to guide the observer's attention properly to the focal point of the window.

Kiesler's analysis, though typical of the grandiose evolutionary systems of the period, prophesied many of the concerns that were to occupy display people later in the century. The ideas of Freud, Jung, and Pavlov filtered through to advertising consciousness—perhaps first with the publication in 1932 of Roy Sheldon and Egmont Arens's *Consumer Engineering*—and encouraged advertisers to appeal to the sense of touch that civilization had demanded that individuals repress. The synesthesia characteristic of many of the early avant-garde art movements also influenced workers in the consumption industry. Media that had relied primarily on the visual began to tap the power of print advertising and window display to evoke potentially more powerful sense impressions.

Dana O'Clare pioneered olfactory display in the 1930s, when he pumped out to the sidewalk a diluted version of a perfume that was featured in a window. Later display artists concerned themselves with increasing the sound dimension of display. And the image of the television—usually smashed or in place of the head on a mannequin—was a prevalent motif of 1970s and 1980s display. Japanese visual merchandiser Toshi complains that the entire English-language concept of display implies that merchandise presentation is "something done merely for the eye." In his work he tries "to involve all the senses in my visual merchandising designs, even taste and smell if appropriate."

The suggestion of movement would also eventually become a value in the static form. The Hungarian sports photographer Martin Munkacsi brought suggested motion to fashion photography in the 1930s. He began to take photographs out of doors, and encouraged a model to run as he snapped her picture. The model jumping over a puddle, her legs crossed away from the viewer, her body twisted welcomingly toward the camera, is a now a staple motif of fashion photography. Munkacsi brought a new dimension to the still, reserved, dreamlike fashion photography that surrounded him; he "shot fashion as if it were news or sports photography, that is, spontaneously."[39] This and other changes in fashion photography not only affected the forms of window display, but helped create its audience.

During the same decade, the museum world became aware of the impact that the visitor's own movement within a display has on the construction of an orderly narrative. Walter Gropius and Herbert Bayer, members of the Bauhaus, "placed exhibits in a definite sequence to express an organic flow" in their 1930 *Deutscher Werkbund* exhibition. They also introduced changes of level in the exhibition as a means of punctuation. In 1938 Bayer curated a Museum of Modern Art exhibit on the Bauhaus, for which he painted shapes and footprints on the floor to show visitors the path they were to take.[40] The same principles led viewers to perceive isolated window frames as scenes from a narrative.

The World War II years and the 1960s are universally considered the "dry seasons" of display. After the war display directors received high budgets once again, and the era of doilies and paper hearts was born. Nevertheless, advances in and the popularity of fashion photography and live fashion modeling would have impact on display that would become visible during the late 1960s and the 1970s.

One such development was the mannequin taken from life. "I have always used real people as the models for mannequins I have designed," wrote Gene Moore in 1951, "and these people are chosen for something more than just beauty of face. They must look intelligent, be able to wear clothes well, and be adaptable to everything from bathing suits to evening clothes."[41] Although Moore seems to imply that he scouted the streets for the woman of character, in fact he chose the most celebrated stars of his day: Audrey Hepburn, Vivien Leigh, Mary Sinclair, Rosalind Russell. Since the 1920s and 1930s American women had been encouraged, through fan magazines, to dress like and to model their wardrobes and their lives after their favorite movie stars. Moore chose his stars for their "subtle modeling and bone structure" or for their versatility in displaying different types of garments. (Mannequins before the sixties were not differentiated as to use in particular kinds of garment merchandising beyond women's and junior's sizes—essentially an age division at that time.) Lillian Greneker went so far as to include "good character" among her requisites for a mannequin model, so as to convey an appropriately ladylike image in an industry that continually had to contend with imputations of bad taste and a theatrical immorality.

In the early 1960s mannequin designers suffered a sudden shortage of film stars who were considered good inspirations. When only the two Hepburns remained, the display industry turned to other sources. A few display directors, Saks' Henry Callahan among them, began to employ well-heeled socialites, known for their expensive wardrobes, as models. Others started to use fashion models—in this pre-supermodel era—rather than celebrities.

After the dark period that World War II represented for the industry, fashion photography began to take itself seriously and broke out, away from the "reality" of the model. Lightweight, high-speed photographic equipment that was developed in the early 1960s enhanced both the ability and the inclination to have models and photographers move freely during photographic sessions. Richard Avedon experimented with the "locationless shot," a technique he resurrected from fashion photography of the thirties. He shot his models in Munkacsi-influenced active poses in the studio, isolated from their environment by plain white backgrounds.

For many within the display industry, advertising and fashion photography provided an idiom for the styling and stagings of mannequins. In the 1950s, Gene Moore worked directly from his friend Avedon's photographs—and sometimes expressly sought models that Avedon had used. Moore's sense of narrative or progression from one of his five windows at Tiffany's to the next may have been influenced by Avedon's photoromans, in which the photographer tried to control how the reader would proceed from one photograph to the next in a layout.

Deborah Turbeville, well known for her moody groupings of women in suggestive real-life settings, was a clear influence on the mid-1970s display powerhouse Candy Pratts. Nancy Hall-Duncan remarked that "the directions Turbeville indicates for fashion photography have implications for areas outside fashion publishing. For instance, aspects of her fashion photography—the off-center composition, the dissociated sense of isolation, and the evocation rather than the statement of fashion—have become the main features of a new style of window design."[42] Turbeville's portrayal of her female figures became a clear model for the more lyrical of Pratts's stagings. Turbeville has said her women are often "a little out of balance with their surroundings, waiting anxiously for the right person to find them, and thinking that perhaps they are out of their time. They move forward clutching their past about them, as if the ground of the present may fall away."[43]

The connection between contemporary fashion photography and the display industry is well entrenched. Today's mannequin manufacturer maintains a clippings file of poses torn from American and European fashion magazines and draws from this file when designing a new collection. Live models that George Martin of Patina-V brings into the studio take on poses that he has collected from home furnishings, art, and fashion magazines. And to Michael Southgate, a mannequin is more like a fashion photograph than a real person; with both one glosses over even the perfectly natural flaws, such as the fine lines around the eyes.

By the 1960s, fashion photography had begun to impinge on display style in two ways. One, as we have seen, was to portray "real people" rather than models, Moore's women of character. The other was to incorporate image advertising, made famous in its most recent incarnation by David Ogilvy. Image advertising dealt suavely with the psychological world a product could evoke and associated products with identifiable characters. One overwhelmingly successful example in the 1950s was the eye patch–wearing model for Hathaway shirts, who presented an image of the man who would identify with the product. Image advertising was an extension of the personalized advertising that became popular in the 1920s: personable and fictional characters who as company representatives attracted thousands of phone calls and letters from consumers seeking advice about cooking, romance, and other "female" subjects.

During the 1970s, models began to clamor for recognition of their creative contribution to the presentation of fashion. Debate raged about the now-common practice of listing models' names in fashion magazines alongside the credits for design and photography. Kennedy Fraser was shocked when, at a 1977 fashion show, the models seemed to present themselves self-consciously as performers:

> As one experiences the motley events that are the new fashion shows, one aspect of the whole does seem to present itself as a valid object of critical scrutiny—the performance of the models. This is a surprising development, because no spectator at a traditional fashion show was ever particularly tempted to think of these young women as performers, let alone as people bent on expressing themselves. Their emanations, when not completely neutral, used to be vaguely animal-like. They were gazelles and, in some cases, jungle tigresses at first; when, five years or so back, they started dancing down the aisles in youthful-looking fashions instead of gliding by in mature ones, they became more like puppies. But now models seem anxious to be seen as human beings, in some direct and equal relationship with the human beings who come to gawk at them, and they are encouraged—in varying degrees, according to the designer's taste—to project their personalities. Fashion shows have become more elaborate in part because the job of modelling, within its own peculiarly circumscribed range, has started to evolve.[44]

Fraser remarked how these models varied their performance style from one designer's show to the next and how they appeared to look down at the old way in which models presented themselves: "In smaller, more traditional shows, when they are simply walking down the runway in new clothes, their expressions betray the prickly defensiveness characteristic of people who feel overqualified for their jobs."

Fashion photography tried to expose the reality of living action. Guy Bourdin's photography in the 1960s dealt with violent subject matter and with the fragmentation of time, showing viewers only a slice from a sequence of action or development. In Bourdin's work, "we are only aware that we are dealing with a specific moment: something has happened or is about to happen." Bourdin influenced photography of the 1960s and 1970s, and street theatre display of the mid-1970s, by creating images that attracted the eye and the attention by their gore, photographing, for example, "a model in a high fashion outfit in front of a butcher shop storefront, its bloody carcasses swinging just above the model's impeccably-turned head."[45] The scenes of simultaneous attraction and repulsion did not always have apparent human protagonists: one of Bourdin's ads for a Charles Jourdan shoe pictured the merchandise amid the wreckage of a car accident.

In displays created by Bob Currie, Candy Pratts, and others working in street theatre, mannequins were pressed into service as characters in suicides, bomb threats, drug overdoses, murders, and other stark scenes of photojournalistic "reality." These graphic scenes showed a series of clues to what had just preceded the scene before the viewer. Yet because the mannequins seemed to "stand in as"—or in a Brechtian sense, to *demonstrate*—characters more than *be* characters, the scenes implied the creation of a fictional world around the mannequins; people tended to look at the street theatre displays for their "stories," not for the realities they conveyed.

Helmut Newton's photographs and the contemporaneous street theatre windows dealt with what Edward Behr terms "what the butler saw" visions. Newton combined live models and mannequins, in the tradition of the surrealists, and photographed them in lurid and disorienting scenes of sadism-edged romance. By blurring the distinction between flesh and fiberglass, Newton attempted to force the viewer to become a participant in the scene. Bourdin had cast the spectator as a detective reassembling the clues in a mystery; Newton made him a voyeur for whom the action must play itself out. Street theatre capitalized—aesthetically and financially— on the capture of the viewer.

Although display's hold on the public has come and gone in cycles, the mid-1970s constituted one of two major periods of deliberate looking at window displays in America.[46] One reason was that "looking" had assumed an enhanced value in both commercial and artistic arenas. Museums during the period began to mount "blockbuster" exhibitions, which required far more money than had ever been budgeted. For many exhibitions, separate admission fees were charged. Exhibits traveled nationally and internationally, heralded by carefully plotted advertising campaigns. Few major exhibitions were mounted without the simultaneous publication of books or exhibition catalogs that brought in additional revenue, much like modern movie production is tied to the marketing of source novels and audio-cassettes of the film's score. The rising self-promotion and commercialization of museum exhibitions may have contributed to the sense that looking at highlighted objects was in itself an activity worthy of attention, not merely something done hurriedly in passing.

Display's focus was redirected into the window in the seventies—perhaps a relief from the fifties, when television had kept people home not only from movies but also from shopping, and from the sixties, when anti-mannequin sentiment and the proliferation of mostly windowless malls caused interior displays to claim more of display men's attention.

A period of "stars" in display began in the 1970s, although many of those stars would leave display altogether in the next decade, some of them felled by AIDS.

The financial troubles besetting retailing also contributed to the congealed quality of much of eighties display and to the nostalgia for the richness of the seventies, a decade whose windows were characterized by resistance to the givens of display and a desire to challenge viewers' expectations of what was proper treatment of the window space.

Before this period, display directors had—with few exceptions—passively accepted the architecture of their stores, and had uniformly treated each window as a separate entity. But Colin Birch and Candy Pratts ripped out architectural dividers between windows—at Bonwit Teller and Bloomingdale's, respectively—to create windows that better suited their visions. The ironic treatments of the window frame that became prevalent in the 1970s depended on displays that extended beyond a single window. One writer noted that "the window is not now being looked at as a window, but rather a bank of windows, if you have more than one, and the presentation of merchandise is being treated as a complete story coordinated within all windows in the bank. That bank is treated for what it really is—a piece of space, a piece of architecture."[47] The reassessment of the conventions of display could only have come from a simultaneously stronger and more fluid sense of what display design—and the display designer—could be.

The conditions under which display directors work vary a good deal, of course, and the style of work that emerges is only what the culture of the individual store permits to emerge. Some store presidents set strict limits on what can be portrayed or used as materials in the windows. Richard Currier recalls that when he joined the Visual department in the early 1980s, Bergdorf Goodman had had long-standing taboos against the use of broken glass or unpolished or high-tech materials. The store wanted both to project an image of untouched refinement and to avoid associations these materials had accrued by their use in other stores. Currier found that he could bypass these strictures simply by abstract-ing the use of rough, inelegant materials, forming, for example, a Corinthian column out of rubber bands.

More permissive attitudes at other stores made possible some of the most inspired work in the history of display. Walter Hoving, president of Bonwit Teller and of Tiffany, gave Gene Moore a long leash for thirty-nine years. Moore records that when Hoving offered him the Tiffany position, he set down what would be his continuing policy: "'I want three things,' he said. 'In the first place, don't ever tell me what you're going to do. Just surprise me. Secondly, don't ever try to sell anything. That's my job. And lastly, make the windows beautiful from your point of view, because I know your point of view is going to be, generally speaking, my point of view.'" Many within the industry attribute Moore's blossoming and his longevity to just such a liberal partnership, though Moore, in part, trained Hoving. Moore was already the interior display director at Bonwit's when Hoving bought the store in 1946. Early in their partnership, Hoving walked into the artist's office and said that he didn't like the new windows. Moore recalls that he stated his position clearly and quickly: "'Listen, Mr. Hoving,' I said. 'Firstly, I must please me; secondly, the public; and thirdly, I hope you like them. If you don't, too bad.' He left my office, and I began another day at Bonwit's."[48]

What caused display to flower in New York first during the late 1960s and the 1970s? At the turn of the century Chicago was the retailing and display center of the country, but by the 1930s New York was considered the leader in display techniques nationally. *Fortune* magazine reported in 1937 that the display industry "now regularly buys reports on New York window activities and even photographs of the actual windows, and it studies both for suggestions and ideas and sometimes unblushingly copies them."[49]

Almost half a century later, the situation held fast. At the height of street theatre, a subscription notice was sent out by the publisher of *Views & Reviews*, an industry reference source that periodically issues photographs and descriptions of displays in New York and other major cities to display directors around the country:

It's time for you to
- shock and rock the boat a little
- entice and excite
- seduce and startle
- be sensational or surrealistic, sinister or silly, suggestive or spaced out
- have fun with fantasies
- Be a dynamite director who is noticed, admired and imitated.

That's what the new breed of brilliant window designers have been doing with spectacular results. Display directors such as Bloomingdale's Candy Pratts, Bendel's Bob Currie, and other daring pace-setters have thrown away the book and come up with windows that are sensational, compelling, talked about and looked at. Not only by customers and store brass, but by the media throughout the country, from TV to daily press, magazines, news reviews and trade papers. They've created a climate of excitement that works: for them, for the customer, and above all, for the store. They've added a whole new dimension to merchandising. One that can rev-up your own operation.[50]

Barry James Wood prefaced his examination of the work of prominent display artists, *Show Windows: 75 Years of the Art of Display*, with an explanation of why New York photographs dominate his study. Although his analysis is perhaps overglowing, it illustrates why New York display was regarded as not only the best but as most cutting edge. For Wood, that there are so many more photographs of New York displays than of others "does not mean that creative work is not done elsewhere; it is just that New York has always been the acknowledged capital of display, the place where rebellions and innovative ideas have had the best chance of succeeding. New York is also the last major city to give prominence to windows; in many other cities, more energy is devoted to store interiors."[51] The display industry credits New York audiences with greater sophis-

tication, a deeper appreciation of the theatrical aspects of presentation, than other audiences.

One reason for New York's leadership in display is the centralization of the American fashion industry. Less obvious reasons, however, have to do with a way of life that exists in New York as in few other places. Nory Miller points out that the major visual merchandising trade shows are held twice a year in New York and once a year in San Francisco, "the two most 'walked' big cities in the country."[52] A related factor may be the special significance and attraction that space holds for cramped New Yorkers, for whom an expansive lobby—or even a department store floor—is always a jolt, an opportunity to speculate, "How many apartments could *this* make?" Richard Currier called the main task of display the conceptualization of space. After removing the walls dividing three Bloomingdale's windows, Candy Pratts commented: "We're all so crowded in our environment that to have space is marvelous. There never seems to be enough of it. But, to have space does not necessarily mean it has to be used. One expansive window with, say, just one mannequin in it, I feel, has a tremendous impact."[53]

On the international scene, New York's display still looks daring. Currier found European windows to be "time capsules," running years behind American display.[54] In a speech to the National Retail Merchants Association, manufacturing executive Leslie Bott summed up her observations about the differences between the U.S. and European markets:

Tradition has it that European visual merchandisers are more business oriented and Americans put more emphasis on the creative aspects. Europeans apprentice in the field for years, where, by comparison, Americans jump right in. Not too long ago, a European firm ordered 500 mannequins with no specifics for body color, hair color or position needs. They only needed 500 bodies. This would never happen in the U.S.A. . . . Europeans tend to stretch definitions and traditions, while Americans allow themselves more frivolity. . . . Americans go all out for theatrics, while Europeans lean more toward the literal. Americans don't mind ruining a pair of shoes for a baseplate, but Europeans, for years, have simply laid the shoes on the floor.[55]

In the early 1980s, Colin Birch, then the vice president of visual presentation for Bloomingdale's, was asked to contrast his experiences working in England and in the United States. Birch's comparison of the two countries' approaches to display suggests the difference between a variety house and a repertory theatre. Whereas British display changes as little as possible when new merchandise is showcased, New York regards the backgrounds and propping as a central part of the presentation of the "starring" merchandise: "In the UK they'll change the merchandise but leave in backgrounds for months on end. In New York we may change every week, strip out everything, change the backgrounds—the lot." The underlying reason behind the difference, Birch hypothesized, is that Americans perceive a cause-and-effect relationship between sales and display techniques, whereas the British think of display as something "purely decorative," with no practical value. In the United Kingdom, Birch would have been able to put the only garment of its kind in stock on a mannequin without problem; in the States, no window space would be allotted to show a garment that was not also well stocked for sale.[56] Michael Southgate commented that in England, where Adel Rootstein is based, display is marked by "excellent inspiration, bad execution."

According to Richard Currier, Paris display uses mannequins "sloppily." Milan, by contrast, is far ahead of the rest of the world in display ideas but shuns mannequins altogether, laying the merchandise out flat for display. Michael Southgate reported that in both Paris and Milan, display people work in the boutique style—without mannequins, laying the fashions out on the floor.[57]

Hence New York combines the strengths of the European fashion capitals: its conceptual innovations in staging and its technical skill in rendering (particularly realistic) scenes bring the entire realistic-abstract continuum within reach, making display a form of theatrical play. The personae of the protagonists—and of the passersby—are deconstructed successfully in New York windows; the personae of the devisers of these windows are just as carefully constructed.

As the Field Defines Itself

The visual merchandising industry defines its members by a series of titles that reflect the changing roles and images of the display artist. From the turn of the century until the 1920s, display artists were referred to as *window trimmers*, men who simply decorated the windows to show off merchandise. The more suave *display men* were the counterparts to the *ad men* of the twenties, their title reflecting the field's growing sense of its alliance with—and occasional improvement upon—the print medium; the term also conveyed the ongoing post-Victorian association of men with production and women with consumption.[58] Although the current and more gender-neutral term, *visual merchandiser*, appeared as early as the late 1940s, it came into general usage in the industry only in the 1970s.

The gender specificity of *display man* was fairly representative of the gender base of the field, for women were long discouraged from entering a profession with little geographic stability and one in which the lifting and manipulation of two-hundred–pound mannequins was a daily task. The "hauling" aspect of the job was partly responsible for ensuring that display remained a field for men; display for years was a theatre in which not only the lights, fixtures, and props, but even the performers were heavy and unyielding. Gene Moore also notes that for years in New York, women were prohibited from working past 10 P.M., which effectively barred them from display, where windows are changed at night. When Candy Pratts came to power at Bloomingdale's in 1974, the fact that she was a woman—and a relatively slight one—may have accounted as much as her shock tactics in the windows for the amount of publicity she received. Any tendency in this book toward referring to the display worker as "he" and the customer as "she" reflects the actual gender bias of the profession and the marketplace.

The industry defined itself as a group of men who catered to the otherwise unfulfilled needs of female consumers—and who at the same time created those hungers. This self-definition is borne out by the early staffing of department stores and by the socialization of

Gene Moore partnering one of his mannequins. Courtesy of the artist.

women as the prime decision makers for family consumption in Victorian culture. Department store managers, overwhelmingly male, tended to hire female clerks, at least partly on the belief that women would be more intimidated into buying from other women through the competition thought to be natural to the sex. In addition, the new department stores, largely because of their association with the female-associated act of consumption, provided a newly acceptable forum for the "public appearance of women."[59]

The changing title of the primary journal of the field—currently called *VM +SD*, or *Visual Merchandising & Store Design*—parallels the evolution of the job description and perception of the display artist. Before 1983 the title of the magazine was simply *Visual Merchandising*; its more primitive title, until 1975, was *Display World*. And yet the terms didn't change easily. A humorous editorial on nomenclature dealt with the profession's ambivalence circa 1976 about its identity: "When talking about the showing of merchandise, which is it? Merchandising presentation? Visual presentation? Display? Or my favorite, visual merchandising? Are you a merchandising presentator? a visual presentator (some people have been arrested for that)? a displayman? or a visual merchandiser?"[60] Visual merchandisers, the author noted, are involved with much more than "mannequins and trims." They make decisions dealing with fixtures, lighting, new store construction and design, wall and floor treatments, and store layout. Typical of the new, compound role of the visual merchandiser was Robert Ruffino's assessment of his job in the early 1980s. His task was not so much to create original and riveting presentations of merchandise himself, but to train salespeople in the presentation of merchandise, to infuse display knowledge throughout the store. A visual merchandiser no longer comes into the store once a week to strike and reset the window. Rather, he and his talents for visual presentation become central to policy setting and image creation throughout the store.

The eighties added executive titles to the baseline terminology. At Gucci, Guy Scarangello was corporate director of visual presentation. For some old-timers within the industry, it is a matter of pride to insist on a dated title. Gene Moore, the grandfather of American window display, who reigned as display director at Tiffany into his eighties, scoffed at his interviewers' attempts to label him a "genius" or even a masterful visual merchandiser. "I'm just a trimmer" was his inevitable response—choosing, perhaps, an antiheroic means of pulling rank, a cherished title that predated even him.

In spite of his authority as a beauty expert for both the merchandise and the woman who craves it, the display man lives a double life. Increasingly in the 1970s and 1980s, he was strung between roles of artist and businessman. Retail management began to view display as a corporate and merchandising function of the store, not just literal window dressing, and many people who worked freelance or on a part-time basis in small stores were suddenly hired into demanding executive positions that put them in charge not only of windows but also of interior displays, merchandising strategies and promotions, and design direction for branch stores. Dana O'Clare once urged the display man to remember that he must be "a businessman as well as an artist," whose reward for his work would be "the triumphal march" to the music of the "cold, clear ring of the cash register."[61] Nevertheless, some display people hold dearly to their status as artists, leaving to others the mercantile role as much as possible. Victor Hugo, who in the mid-1970s created provocative and magnetic street-theatre windows for the designer Halston's boutique, stressed that he is "an artist, not a merchant."

Few display people have a background in business. More often, they are visual artists: Andy Warhol, James Rosenquist, and Robert Rauschenberg all worked as freelancers under Gene Moore at Tiffany. Manufacturer Robert Filoso's touting itself as "the only sculptor/ designer-owned mannequin business in the world" exemplified the typical polarity. Even many display people who work full time and hold executive positions began in display as a means of supporting their own artmak-

ing. When he entered the field in the early 1970s, Jim Mansour of The Limited saw display "as a nice way to spend your time and not feel particularly compromised." Indeed, Mansour's move into display was motivated in part by a desire to see how people who used art for profit did it. At the time Mansour was running an experimental theatre company that was having difficulty making ends meet, and he hoped to return to the company with fresh ideas about how to raise and manage funds.

By contrast with the majority of modern display executives, Richard Currier had a business identity before his artistic one. The director of visual presentation at Bergdorf Goodman, Currier completed a bachelor's degree in economics at Brown University and worked for several years in a bank before going into display. Currier maintains that he is better suited to display than he ever would have been to fine art; his ability to satisfy the continual demand for "cleverness" and the incessant need to generate fresh ideas, he suspects, might be evidence of an attention span too short for a painter.

In their descriptions of the qualities required of the true display artist, writers wax extravagant, and technical and professional skills are only the beginning. Dana O'Clare maintained that the ideal display person "must have the curiosity of a cat and the tenacity of a bulldog, the friendliness of a child and the patience of a self-sacrificing spouse, the diplomacy of a wayward mate, the enthusiasm of a movie fan, the assurance of a Harvard grad, the humor of a comedian, and the tiresome energy of a bill collector."[62] If O'Clare was attempting to be witty, a description of the role of the visual merchandiser from a catalog of the Fashion Institute of Technology seems no less expansive: "Display and exhibit design is a field that combines the creativity of a designer, the technique of an architect, the eye of a stylist, the hand of an artist, the instincts of a trendsetter, and the dramatic flair of a Broadway producer." Even the occasionally self-mocking grandiosity of the industry's words about its work reveals just how far-reaching its inspiration and sources are.

The theatrical metaphor has appeared in the language of display artists almost since American display began to take pride in its distinct identity in the mid-1920s. In the FIT description, the "Broadway producer" is given a precious final billing, but in one source Dana O'Clare described the job entirely in theatrical terms; the display manager must be "stage manager, director, artist and playwright, rolled into one." Colin Birch, display director at Bloomingdale's from 1982 until his death in 1988, saw as his role "to design and direct." Expressing identities both as an artist separate from his role as a display executive (at Saks) and as a theatre person working for the present on a more contained scale, Robert Benzio was once quoted as aspiring "ideally . . . to tackle the biggest window display of them all—the theater."[63]

Like theatre, display is a fugitive time art. Window trimmers must accept that even their best work can stay up for no more than two weeks; often it comes down after less than a week, sometimes without a single slide or memo to document that it was there at all. Display people rely on the memories of co-workers and audience. Robin Lauritano, the operating vice president of visual presentation at Bloomingdale's, acknowledged that the dependence on constant change makes "display . . . a burnout job." For her, it was hard at first to let her display work be "struck": "The hard thing is getting used to taking it down after a week . . . but once you get used to it, and work *with* that, it's sort of fun. Now when we do Christmas windows or a country promotion and the windows stay in longer, I do find myself getting bored looking at them. I'm used to that fast pace." For others, such as Simon Doonan, the transience of display is appealing: "You put it in, then rip it out the next week. It's very dynamic, like the fashion business."[64]

With a willingness to let one's creations be almost immediately struck must come the ability to readily replace them. Richard Currier called this faculty to generate new ideas without repeating oneself the most important for a visual merchandiser. When visual departments of stores keep archives of window and in-

terior designs, they are guarding against repetition. Display man Bob Currie maintained that windows must be right for their time, and the display artist has a peculiar obligation, particularly with gift windows—such as Christmas windows, which spread good cheer more than they promote specific merchandise—to "reflect" the times to the passing audience.

L. Frank Baum, the first American window trimmer of renown, wrote in one of his "Talks to Beginners" that the display man must "arrest the gaze" of the passerby. The job of selling the goods is "half done" once the display man has transformed a passerby into a lingerer. This task of halting the forward motion of the scurrying pedestrian echoes throughout display history. In 1950, Robert J. Leydenfrost wrote, "If we stop, the window display has accomplished its primary purpose." One of the means of relating to the passerby that Baum recommends has to do both with the beauty of the window and with that of the woman who stops before it. Although Frederick Kiesler would later take the view that the display manager must be a "beauty specialist in merchandise," Baum concerned himself with the display man's ability to cater to the beauty of his customer through the merchandise. The window trimmer who is trusted by his audience will be the first one she consults in order to learn which colors flatter her complexion.[65]

The power of the window display to attract the passerby by means that depend on but also extend beyond the visual became evident in the 1930s. By then, display had recognized itself as an applied art in its own right, not as a hopeless aspirant to high art. Paul Hollister, Macy's publicity director in 1937, proclaimed window display to be "a combination of a poster, a newspaper advertisement, a stage set, a speech, and a scarf dance."[66] Hollister's sentiment reflected the notion that a window display was an improvement upon the newspaper advertisement because it presented the goods at the very moment the customer was in the place for buying, and in three dimensions—making them available to touch.

In the 1930s, display manuals began to deal in greater depth with the desired psychological effect on the spectator. O'Clare wanted his windows "to awaken a memory, a wish, a desire, dream or need." Display men acknowledged effects that break through the windowpane and penetrate beyond the mere vision of the spectator. Frederick Kiesler, architect, window dresser, designer for Erwin Piscator, and compatriot of the De Stijl artists, demanded that the display manager "create an atmosphere of tension between several pieces of merchandise exposed with the frame of the show window."[67] Given the psychological idiom of the period, Kiesler's "tension" might refer not simply to the formal compositional qualities of the window, but also to tensions of use among the featured items, tensions that depend upon the spectator's apprehension of how these objects relate to each other in use and how the spectator, though physically outside the picture frame, may fit within it.

Even writing about the specifically visual effects of the windows took on a psychological dimension and a greater sophistication as American display came into its own in the 1930s. One journalist referred to window display as a "rather frightening hypnotism of the public." According to this view, "most display . . . has no choice but to leap out at you . . . [but] in the very act of leaping it must create the impression that it is drawing you to it." Deception of the consciousness plays tricks on the eyes themselves, substituting windows for doors: "Before the spectator leaves the window, he must be looking for the door" to enter the store.[68] Kiesler urged display people as much as possible to "make the window look like an entrance and the entrance like a window," as if to give the spectator at the window the sensation of entering the store.

Writers have referred to a gap between what the customers are and what the display (and the merchandise it features) can provide for them psychologically. Raymond Loewy, a celebrated and versatile industrial designer as well as a Macy's display man, said in 1937 that "people's eyes should goggle less, their mouths should water more. The point is to make them feel they are missing something." Kiesler pointed out that the

display man must create demand: "Don't forget that when a customer is in definite need of something, she just goes into the store. The windows do not interest her. She walks right in."

The gap between what the customer has and what the window can fulfill remained a theme in the 1980s, and that projected customer continued to be female: a 1986 survey by Retail Reporting found that 85 percent of mall shoppers were women.[69] A new emphasis, however, has begun to fall on filling intellectual aspirations as much as unvoiced emotional needs. Esprit's "comprehensive design principle" emphasized that visual display is in essence a "magnet for curiosity." In creating its displays, Esprit hoped to "engage our customers in a . . . game and to have them see Esprit as a company of ideas and cleverness that goes way beyond product."[70]

The informational purpose of display is a language that was amplified in the antisentimental mass-marketing of the eighties. This language treats display as a complex retail function that impinges upon marketing, merchandising, advertising, and sales promotion, and is concurrent with visual merchandisers' shift within the retail setting from being window people to being executives reporting directly to store presidents. Displayers have responsibility for store planning and other functions that were previously considered outside their domain. In line with this focus on the cognitive function of display, Toshi maintained that the visual merchandiser must make the merchandise not only beautiful but also easy to understand; a stunning composition that cannot be read in an instant cannot make a successful display. Esprit sees visual display as a form of customer service that provides "a stimulus, a suggestion, a direction"; it has the power to point customers toward what they might need (or find they want) and to demonstrate how they might put it to use.

Some display artists have spoken of emphasizing or performing the psychological relationship between the artist and the merchandise as a means of attracting the customer. Visual merchandiser Thomas Natalini defined display as the "romancing of the merchandise." Dan

Robert Benzio window series built around an art deco train set, 1978. Photos by Fifth Avenue Display Photographers. Courtesy of Saks Fifth Avenue.

The history of educated men advertising to needy women takes an interesting turn in the contemporary display scene. New York display people are disproportionately gay men; a lesser but still striking number of gay men figure importantly in manufacturing. So in many ways there may be two audiences for display mannequins in New York: the straight female population, generally assumed—whether or not correctly—to be in need of fashion education, and a design-conscious gay male population both within the industry and outside it.

Indeed, a good number of the display artists represented in these pages and a large number of artists working in manufacture are gay men, many of whom were involved in a highly fashionable, high-profile New York lifestyle during the 1970s. Is there a connection between the styling of the mannequins and their staging in show windows and the personal lives of these men?

It may be tantamount to ghettoizing a group to insist that their work can be reduced, even in part, to a reflection of their lives. For many artists, the imagination may have a life quite independent of the biography of the artist, and it would be presumptuous to state definitively that a lively gay man's sexual and social experience was reflected in his display work. Still, there is enough circumstantial resemblance between display work and certain aesthetic styles that have been identified with gay culture to make such an exploration worthwhile. In addition, some display artists—most openly Victor Hugo, exuberantly involved in gay life—have themselves drawn the connections between their sexual and social lives and aspects of their display work, ranging from replications of scenes from their lives to the ways in which figures are sculpted and posed to reflect gay theatrical posturings.

Camp has been identified by a number of writers as a particularly "gay" aesthetic; it is a style of objects and of the presentation of self that, in Susan Sontag's formulation, delights in unabashed artifice, in a "love of the unnatural." Jack Babuscio names four features, also central to display window aesthetics, as being central to

Arjé, for years on the display staff at Bonwit Teller, spoke of the need "to display, explain, romance, present" the merchandise. For these display artists, "romancing the merchandise" means showering it with the candlelight, the champagne in crystal bulbs, and the flattering lighting that signal to the passerby that the artist has regarded this merchandise as something special, an object of desire. The feminization of the merchandise that is implied by "romancing" suggests that the merchandise is presented to the female consumer as a substitute for human companionship and nurturing: by purchasing an item that has been displayed with such care, the shopper purchases as well a feeling that she is being cared for. Robert Currie, though he did not speak of romance per se, believed that it was necessary to see "the hand of the artist" in the window in order to involve the spectator: "As long as the viewer can see the sentiment involved, or the sentiment that went behind creating it, that's all that matters to me."

camp: irony, aestheticism, theatricality, and humor. Susan Sontag also notes that camp has a special affinity for the decorative arts, for it emphasizes "texture, sensuous surface, and style at the expense of content." She also makes the point that camp "is the glorification of 'character'"; it treats the human persona as the privileged site of the unnatural. As such, the persona-creation of display may even be more pivotal within the camp aesthetic than are certain types of role playing, such as impersonations and caricatures: a mannequin, no matter how realistic it may look, may be determined upon prolonged staring to be a "dummy," a fake, a stand-in for reality. Indeed, the realistic mannequin is an attempt to create a "virtual reality" of the human that is on some level consciously doomed and deemed to fail, whereas the attempt to create a human simulacrum remains the most potent modeling possible.

The perception of some industry observers that certain mannequins—Rootsteins are named most often—appear more like drag queens than like women is also borne out by Sontag's theory of camp: "As a taste in persons, Camp responds particularly to the markedly attenuated and to the strongly exaggerated. The androgyne is certainly one of the great images of Camp sensibility. . . . Here Camp taste draws on a mostly unacknowledged truth of taste: the most refined form of sexual attractiveness (as well as the most refined form of sexual pleasure) consists in going against the grain of one's sex. What is most beautiful in virile men is something feminine; what is most beautiful in feminine women is something masculine."[71]

Candy Pratts remarked that her best assistants were all gay men, who grabbed her ideas for treating the mannequins as characters in a situation and ran with them: in her estimation, "the guys [her assistants] *were* the girls" [mannequin-characters]. They would execute her instruction, often quite visual as opposed to strictly character-centered, and play around on the "set," speaking for the characters' point of view, motivations, and emotions.

Sontag acknowledges a connection between camp and "homosexuals, by and large . . . [its] vanguard—and . . . most articulate audience," but doubts that the relation is essential; if gays had not invented camp, she believes, some other group would have. Babuscio, on the other hand, posits an essential connection between camp and "gay sensibility." He writes that gays have a highly developed faculty for theatricality, drawn from lifelong experience of passing for straight: "The act of passing is an acting art: to pass is to be 'on stage,' to impersonate heterosexual citizenry, to pretend to be a 'real' (*i.e.*, straight) man or woman. Such a practice of passing means, in effect, that one must be always on one's guard lest one be seen to 'deviate' from those culturally standardised canons of taste, behaviour, speech, etc. that are generally associated with the male and female roles as defined by the society in which we live."[72] For Babuscio, passing is not just a reflection of gay life, but may be "productive of a gay sensibility," for "it can, and often does, lead to a heightened awareness and appreciation for disguise, impersonation, the projection of personality, and the distinctions to be made between instinctive and theatrical behaviour."

Michael Bronski holds that mass advertising since the mid-1970s has made a special point of appropriating gay themes and images and of presenting them in a tacit form: "A trend developed of using homoerotic images in mass advertising. The products thus advertised ranged from cigarettes to western gear, from liquor to expensive clothes. The ads presented a male image considerably different from the standard ad images. Images of men in ads had previously been calculated to make the buyer feel he needed this product in order to fit in. In contrast, the new male image was focused on being different."[73] Bronski identifies two major strains, the isolated, virile Marlboro man figure and the slender, graceful European model figure, each of which had "firm roots in the traditions of gay sensibility." He also notes that disco was originally a function of gay and black culture and only later became embedded in both men's and women's mainstream fashions. Willo Font contends that the dance style called voguing is visible in contemporary mannequin poses.[74] Display directors are certainly familiar with the style; Simon Doonan at Barneys, for example, has been in charge of staging Barneys' voguing entry in the competition at the Love Ball, an occasional fund-raising event for the Design Industries Foundations for AIDS.

The other aesthetic that seems particularly allied with both gay and display sensibilities is kitsch, a fundamentally bourgeois form defined by Gillo Dorfles as a "good taste in bad taste." Dorfles finds a historical source for kitsch in the middle-class quest for the appearance of upper-crust taste. Linked by Dorfles to the style of certain nineteenth-century brothels, kitsch has associated "vice and pleasure," much the way windows today seem to laugh off spending as self-indulgence.[75]

Are mannequins and windows created by gay artists the result of the artists' direct familiarity with camp or kitsch, taken as a "gay aesthetic"? Or has display itself been so long linked with these styles that artists merely respond to earlier influences within the history of display? The foregoing discussion of aesthetics tells us more about what links many of the windows than about how and why those windows were created. Candy Pratts, as we shall see, has demonstrated that a straight woman could play out the "gay" aesthetic of camp as capably as a man.

And here we turn from the connection between the artist's personal biography and his or her work's style to the relationship between two competing—and sometimes cooperating—values inherent in that work: the commercial and the aesthetic.

2 Performance/Art

In a provocative article about the convergences and divergences of art and commercial window display, John Perreault warns us not to repress what he sees as the essential connection between art and commerce—neither of which can exist outside its relation with the other. Should we pretend that no such connection exists, Perreault warns, we risk turning art into nothing more than display, which Perreault defines as "the creation of desire," or an excessive attentiveness to holding the attention of the audience.[1]

Display directors have made a tradition of confusing such boundaries, however, and store windows are a good example of the commercial aesthetic either masquerading as art or appropriating it, as if art costs nothing yet can confer all good. Display directors have long shown the work of aspiring visual artists, using the windows as a kind of gallery space, during periods when their own display budgets were low. Artists were more than willing to lend their work—which was often sold straight out of the window—in exchange for a window credit. Gene Moore asserts, "I've always paid a rental fee for any art used in my windows, and when a piece is sold out of a window, as has often happened, I don't ask for a commission. But money isn't the reason artists come to see me. From my first windows at Delman's through the sixteen years at Bonwit Teller and now thirty-five at Tiffany's I've always given artists credit. I

was the first display director to do so regularly, and the knowledge that their name would appear on a credit card—a slip of paper—in the window has drawn the artists to me."[2]

Display directors such as Richard Currier and Gene Moore affirm their commitment to helping younger artists get started. Moore takes credit for helping to launch the careers of Andy Warhol, Jasper Johns, Robert Rauschenberg, and James Rosenquist. Rauschenberg and Johns, Moore remembers, served "as a kind of display house" for Tiffany's: "I'd tell them what I wanted, and they'd go off and make it. I never knew which of them did what, they worked so closely together, even sharing the same joint pseudonym, Matson Jones, which I think they made up from their mothers' maiden names. They started using that name when they began to get recognition as artists—they didn't want their commercial work confused with what they considered their real art."[3] By contrast, Andy Warhol made no distinction between his own art and his work for Tiffany and Bonwit Teller and had no compunctions about being recognized as a commercial artist. "Raggedy Andy," as Moore calls him, had "had success with book-jacket designs . . . and with his drawings and paintings for . . . shoe ads . . . but stories about his mishaps were making the rounds. When he'd zipped open his portfolio to show his work to the art director at *Harper's Bazaar*, a cockroach had crawled out. Poor boy, that Raggedy Andy. But *Harper's* had given him assignments. He won awards for his work, for his 'commercial' art, and he never pretended a difference between what he did to survive and what he called his art. To his credit, I think it was all the same to him."[4]

An artist may have business sense enough to take on commercial work, but a display director needs sufficient commercial acumen to satisfy the store owner. Artists supply the work, but it is the display director's job to use that work to sell merchandise. The artwork must serve the needs of the merchandise in the windows, even if that means being totally blocked by it. In 1961, Bonwit Teller gave Andy Warhol his "first major exhibition as a capital-A artist."[5] The window featured five mannequins, placed directly in front of five of the artist's paintings, including a collage of advertisements and a before-and-after nose job.

Simon Doonan at Barneys may have gotten the last laugh on Warhol and his artistic double identity when he made a controversial Andy Warhol mannequin for a 1989 window. Jeff Weinstein mused, "Why is it startling to see Andy Warhol as a window dummy? Not only was he in real life everywhere to be seen, floating through flea markets and shops, trailed by an entourage of shopping bags, but representations of the artist—not by the artist, *of* the artist—have shown their faces everywhere as well. Did Warhol, short-circuiting and reversing the myth, pygmalion himself?"[6] But Doonan is typically iconoclastic about boundaries between art and commerce and between art and design. In 1988, he made an entire series of "appropriated" artworks for his window displays; each one imitated and altered a prominent contemporary artist's work and was signed with a prominent "With Apologies To . . ." attribution. Doonan remarked, "A friend suggested that I add the line as a polite way of eluding charges of plagiarism. People went from one window to another, eager to see which artist would be appropriated next. These artists invented a style that I didn't besmirch but, rather, paid homage to." Responded artist Barbara Kruger, one of the artists

appropriated: "How can I, an appropriation artist, worry about somebody else appropriating my work? I'll be using a picture of 'my' window in an upcoming lecture. In fact, I think it's very pretty."[7]

The quotation or borrowing of artworks adds to the public prestige of the display directors. By using art to show off—or, as they would have it, to elevate—the merchandise, these directors may themselves earn the status of fine artists. Richard Currier received attention from the fine arts press during the 1980s, when he frequently used paintings and other works of outside artists to enhance the merchandise in his Bergdorf Goodman windows. Using existing artworks without paying for them was a ready way of making a window exciting during a period of low display budgets. In addition, the publicity that the street theatre movement of the previous decade had generated helped make window display-as-art a fashionable medium for the art crowd.

Moore proudly remembers the 1965 article written on him by Aline Saarinen as the knighting of window display by the fine-arts press. In Moore's windows the selection of artwork usually dominates all other considerations. It has been widely and approvingly noted that when Moore prepared a Tiffany window, he simply walked through the store and selected a jewel, goblet, or other trinket that would best show off the artwork he was husbanding through the window. Few display directors are given the latitude to select their own merchandise; fewer still allow the artwork to *determine* the merchandise.

Besides treating the window as alternative gallery space, Moore recognizes the status that windows can acquire by associating themselves with the official art-circulation worlds, the museums and galleries. In the spring of 1962, Moore created a series of windows to commemorate a citywide showing of Picasso's work. The windows were three-dimensional representations of paintings by Picasso, done with cut-out forms. On the opening night of the nine-gallery exhibit, busloads of art lovers stopped at Tiffany to view the windows. A critical biographer noted that in Moore's work "the dis-

You look like a million

OTH... BY ...S B.
...H AP...ES TO BARBARA KRUGER

One of a series of
appropriation-art windows
for Barneys, each offering
"Apologies to ———."
Courtesy of Simon Doonan.

tinction between fine and commercial art grows hard to make. Art has become a magic merchandising word. . . . More and more, today's museums function like merchandising marts, and department store interiors have been broken up into a series of boutiques that simulate the special atmosphere once characteristic of galleries."[8]

Windows may also refer to art without serving even in part as a gallery space for the work of living artists. Fiorucci and other stores have sometimes suspended garments between sheets of plexiglass or within a painting frame on a window's wall. The Gallery of Wearable Art, a Soho boutique, sold one-of-a-kind art garments. The owner, Bonnie Kupris, made it the "fundamental premise" of the store that clothing is art.

The desire to appropriate the status of the art world appears even at the level of mannequin manufacture, and nowhere more prominently than at Pucci Manikins, the sole manufacturer that has not only showroom but also factory in Manhattan. Pucci strives to be considered an "artsy"—or perhaps "artisty"—design firm in its Soho location. At the showroom, all of the creative contributors are credited on the walls: mannequin designers, wig and makeup artists, and the painters, photographers, and furniture designers whose work appears in the self-consciously gallerylike setting.[9] Classical music is transmitted over a state-of-the-art sound system.

Ralph Pucci boasted that his was the company that started the trend of having outside artists and designers contribute to the display supply industry. In 1986 he commissioned Andrée Putman, then well known as an architect and interior designer, to design her first mannequin for the company, rousing both the visual-merchandising industry and the art world. Pucci says that at the debut party for the mannequin at the Pucci showroom—to which Putman brought Andy Warhol and Keith Haring—he realized that the art world and the commercial design world were really one industry. And, he says, artists were as eager to work with him as he was to work with them. For collectors who were attracted to the display work, the artist Lowell Nesbitt designed a signed, limited edition of ten of each of the four poses of his "Man of the '90s" hulk mannequin for Pucci, each cast whole, unlike regular mannequins.

The conjunction of fine and commercial display aesthetics reflects the symbiosis of art and commerce in the twentieth century. Orvell noted that "the contemporary museum has a hard time drawing the line between art and advertising in the photography from the 1920s and 1930s; without the social context and purpose, the differences may be few."[10] Margaret Hall's 1987 description of the aesthetics of museum display reflects just how similar these have grown to visual-merchandising strategies in the commercial setting. Many display men speak of the need to develop design ideas, even more abstract ones, out of the aesthetics of the merchandise itself. Now that the promotion of museum exhibits has become an international industry, replete with expensive exhibition catalogs, reprints, and television documentaries, marketing of exhibitions is also developed from "the merchandise"—usually a pivotal object in the exhibit. The curator becomes marketing expert: "In many exhibitions a single unique exhibit is selected to be featured as a 'logo,' for use graphically on printed publicity material and repeated on boardings and banners at the entrance. Ideally, the symbol must arise from the material."[11]

Christopher Knight, the art critic for the *Los Angeles Herald Examiner*, wrote caustically about a 1982 exhibition at the La Jolla Museum of Contemporary Art on Italian design, which presented hundreds of objects in an order that reflected their use during a typical Italian day. According to the curator, Piero Sartogo, the purpose of the exhibition was to explore neither "the Italian way of life" nor objects for their own sake, but "the object-user relationship." Knight complained that the exhibition, by preventing museum visitors from handling the design objects themselves and developing their own "object-user" relationship, only served to stimulate desire on the part of the viewer, "a desire whose fulfillment can only be approached if we go out and purchase the product. . . . The wholesale conversion of an accompanying catalog culminates in a four-page list of firms that participated in the exhibition—complete with addresses and telephone numbers, should the thought of mail order creep into your head."[12]

For Perreault, the desire to buy is commonly stimulated by contemporary museum design, and this stimulation is by now premeditated: "Even though the viewer cannot purchase the particular artworks on display in a museum exhibition, he or she is often aroused enough by the display of information, pleasure, and implied wealth to be stimulated to buy something else—anything else. Hence the proliferation of museum gift shops, and outside the premises, the lineup of boutiques, high-fashion emporiums, poster shops, home and design stores, and expensive restaurants." Taking the metaphor of possession a precipitous step further, Perreault writes that such desire can be consummated only "at the cash register or as a pale but related substitute, in bed, which may also explain why museums and galleries are well-known as places for romantic or sexual pickups."[13] Perreault's unabashed sexualization of the moment of purchase makes explicit what Marcel Duchamp called "the coition through the glass pane" of the display window—that the combination of looking and desiring created a kind of voyeur's sexual concourse. The moment of purchase is the climactic moment in the dance between a human being and a desired object. Contemporary display and advertising consciously position purchase as the consummation of the experiences of looking and visiting. Disney World designers ensured that commodity purchase felt like an inevitable completion to segments of the visit to the theme park:

> You're in the middle of one of the most famous amusement resorts in the world. Everything around you is full of fun and fantasy. A castle straight out of a fairy tale beckons you onward. Characters you've known since childhood's cartoon-filled Saturday afternoons at the movies suddenly come to life and mingle with the hordes of visitors wandering from shop to show. You join them in a stroll down a street that would fit right into turn-of-the-century America and stop in at an old-fashioned confectionary shop for a snack . . .

but what you buy is more than just another candy bar. You purchase a piece of the scenery, and become in the process an integral part of the production at Walt Disney World's Magic Kingdom in Orlando, Florida.[14]

Many of the audiences or buyers for display are the same as those for museum exhibitions—and the biggest patrons of retailing's more "artistic" events are likely also to be art patrons. When in 1986 Colin Birch staged an India promotion for Bloomingdale's, he wrote to Marvin Traub, the chairman of the company, to suggest that a set of jewelry and shawls be introduced and offered for sale at an invitation-only event after their use in the promotion: "May I suggest," Birch wrote after viewing the decorative pieces on location, "that a cocktail party be arranged for customers, connoisseur/ collectors of this type of art. Since it is of museum quality rarely offered at retail in the United States, I feel sales are only possible to educated collectors or connoisseurs. Maybe a press release."[15]

For the 1986 Christmas promotion Birch designed a "Bloomingbear" as a corporate mascot. Unlike a mannequin, the Bloomingbear invited touching, holding, and possession (through sales, of course). Birch proposed various merchandising strategies to Traub, including anthropomorphic scenes of "giant Bears decorating *their* home," show windows featuring "giant life-size bears dressed to co-ordinate with gift merchandise presented differently in each window," and "Giant Bear Heads worn by 'direction/information' assistants on each floor/store (as Mickey at Disney World)." Yet the cultural aspect of the promotion could not be overlooked, for it was an essential part of creating the perception that Bloomingdale's was a company with Ideas. Birch suggested exhibits in the store on the history of the teddy bear and on the bears of famous people or designers, as well as "a salute to the *real* bears," with information furnished by the National Wildlife Society on the worldwide outlook for bears. For a promotion entitled "100 Years of Bloomingdale's," Birch planned a combination of historical inquiry and self-congratulation, fur-

thering the image of the store as being about "Progress—Innovation—International Retail Leadership."[16]

Art references—often in the form of copies of well-known paintings or the iconography of high art—suggest to the consumer, as Nory Miller puts it, that "you are not buying fine things because you are a coarse, ostentatious acquirer of new money, but because you are a patron."[17] During both the 1930s and the 1970s, fashion designers, seeing how art and desirability begot money, created clothes that made explicit reference to art. The narration at fashion shows in the seventies, perhaps as a response to lifestyle merchandising, became "more fanciful than ever in an attempt to conjure up symbolic images and correspondences between clothes and the arts."[18] Saks Fifth Avenue's Bill Lorenzen regarded this trend toward facile quotation as a function of the ready availability of international travel, which meant that ethnic fashions could be picked up and quoted as readily as art.

The references in the windows need not even be to high art to have the intended effects on their viewers. According to Philip Monaghan, the art director at the Fiorucci boutique in the 1970s, windows often played upon or satirized street art of the period, which captured one of the two audiences that the boutique played to: an artsy, Mudd Club-type crowd that frequented the store particularly for its wild live windows and for such themed interiors as "Cow Family," "Industrial Choice," and "Summer in the City." That crowd helped give the store its patina of fashionability for the much more conservative people who actually bought the jeans and other midprice items the store sold.

Claes Oldenburg, articulating the sentiments of a sixties and seventies art world that treasured disposability and ephemerality, wrote, "I am for art that is put on and taken off, like pants, which develops holes, like socks, which is eaten, like a piece of pie, or abandoned with great contempt, like a piece of shit." In such a view, links both with theatre and with merchandising made a lot of sense. Oldenburg opened a store in the East Village whose career he documented in a 1967 book entitled *Store Days*. The store, open Friday through Sunday afternoons and by appointment, sold clothes, made objects, signs, billboards, and other miscellanea. Oldenburg and friends performed silent plays or scenarios in the windows, sometimes to musical accompaniment. Eventually, the store became known as the Ray Gun Theater and produced short performances indoors. Oldenburg wrote, "Theater is the most powerful art form there is because it is the most involving . . . but it is forever becoming lost in trivialities. . . . I no longer see the distinction between theater and visual arts very clearly."[19]

Artists' Windows

Visual artists in many media have employed the window as a special means of getting their work across to a wide audience. Perreault notes that window display has become "something of a validated art genre in itself," as such downtown New York locations as the Grey Art Gallery, the New Museum, Franklin Furnace, and Printed Matter have all donated window space to artists.[20]

In 1976 San Francisco-based artist Lynn Hershman installed a set of windows not at a sanctioned art space but at Bonwit Teller. According to Hershman, her Bonwit windows "caused quite a bit of notoriety because they were the first that used store windows as public art space."[21] What is remarkable about Hershman's *25 Windows: A Portrait/Project* is the way in which she mediates—not entirely consciously—between the concerns of the art world of the period and the techniques of New York street theatre display artists, with whose windows she was only marginally familiar. Hershman's project demonstrates the close relation between contemporary art world concerns and commercial display work, which some of its prominent artists have treated almost as if it had sprung full-grown from their heads. As with much of display art, it is difficult to determine who originated ideas and who extended them; although few of Hershman's ideas seem either original or unique

within the display world, the vast collection of ideas her windows represent serve as a synopsis of themes that traipsed through windows of the seventies. In Hershman's windows we see, as in the display of the period, mannequins presented as real characters, the intermingling of mannequins and live performers, the concern with at least metaphorically breaking the glass pane to alter the relationship with the spectator, and the need to express a pointed sense of the present moment in history.

The idea for the windows came one day in 1974 when Hershman was visiting New York. Walking down Fifth Avenue, she noticed how the windows seemed very like giant versions of the boxed environments made famous by Joseph Cornell. Rather than design windows in order to sell clothing, she mused, "Why not make windows that showed a portrait of New York?" Hershman was rebuffed by several prominent stores when she came in—literally off the street—to propose doing an art installation in the windows. She liked the windows at Henri Bendel best, but the store management there and at Tiffany and Bergdorf Goodman were protective of store image. But Colin Birch, then display director at Bonwit Teller, was receptive.

According to Walter Blum's account, "to get the job, [Hershman] just walked in the door and asked. 'They said they usually pay their display people $10,000 to do the windows,' she recalls. 'I told them I'd create a work of art for five thousand. So they let me go ahead.'"[22] Although it took two years and the added sponsorship of the Institute for Art and Urban Resources to help complete the installation, Hershman readily got Birch to place his display department resources—staff, print shop, and the store's merchandise—at her disposal. In true site-specific fashion, Hershman was determined to ensure that "all the materials were indigenous to the store."

The artist drew on her own earlier artwork, a series of environmental installations in hotel rooms. For a 1973 installation at San Francisco's Dante Hotel, Hershman rented room 47 and installed "two bewigged mannequins in an unmade bed, surrounded by such paraphernalia as lipstick, rouge, curlers, Tampax, and birth control pills." The amount of symbolic lived detail was overwhelming:

> In the bed, tangled, nearly buried in the sheets and blankets, are two of [Hershman's] "ladies," locked together in penultimate exhaustion. A single eerie green lightbulb burns in the fixture hanging from the center of the cracked, stained ceiling; a similar light leaks out from around the closed closet door accompanied by a woman's voice, recorded, the voice of Siobhan McKenna reciting Molly Bloom's soliloquy from "Ulysses." . . . On a table in front of the window, two goldfish swim in a cloudy bowl, a Photoplay Magazine waits to be read or thrown away, a letter blurs under the influence of vanished liquids. . . .
>
> An AM radio plays from the top of a dresser which is scarred, strewn with cosmetics and Jumbo hair rollers. . . . Clothing spills from the dresser drawers, stiff and garish, mute witnesses to events that have just happened and will shortly happen again, their testimony punctuated by cockroaches scampering in the perpetual almost-dark. The corner sink is dirty, blotched, littered with the flotsam of popular hygiene, burnt-out cigarettes, an empty plastic medicine vial, all the more sinister with its label torn away.

Hershman also created a related installation at New York's Chelsea Hotel, an installation that she reproduced in part in one of the Bonwit windows. Hershman's object in the window installation was to mirror back to New Yorkers the world in which they lived, "to use the windows to develop a portrait of New York."[23] Aside from the placement of mannequins, the techniques of display were not essential to her purpose, though she commented upon consumerism and economically determined notions of beauty and salability. What was essential was the setting: her critique of consumerism depended on its placement in a context that traditionally glorified it.

The *Portrait/Project* windows were organized into treatments of past, present, and future images of New York social life. A blueprint for the work indicates that the windows were intended to be viewed beginning on the 57th Street side of the store, continuing down Fifth Avenue, and ending up with the 56th Street windows. This progression took the viewer from "Illusion" through "Transformation" and to "Reflection." In all the windows, Hershman was exploring what she referred to as "'reality discrepancies,' using existing environments as a sociologist might. . . . 'I try to create portraits,' she says, 'by revealing layers of indigenous elements of a system, in this case, that of a department store.'"[24] *Portrait/Project* dealt with strong political issues: many Americans' dispossession from the consumer-oriented mainstream of American culture; society's equation of women with their exchange value, as determined by their appearances; and the elitism of high art, cordoned off from everyday people as if by a glass pane.

In the windows dealing with the past, Hershman replicated her Chelsea Hotel installation and exhibited a videotape of "speeded-up actual window changes," which were projected directly onto the window pane through the use of mirrors. The "Transformation" windows provided the longest series and dealt most explicitly with the theme of identity transformation through the delights of consumerism. One window showed the twenty-minute transformation, through cosmetics and wigging, that turned Hershman into Roberta Breitmore, a persona she had adopted for San Francisco street performances.

Other "Transformation" windows dealt with aging and the attempts of women to change their identities by altering their exteriors. Two nonprofessional models, portraying women aged twenty and forty, were presented in photographic cutouts that contrasted the appearances of their bodies. In a photographic sequence the twenty-year-old Blaze Simpson was made to appear older the more she undressed, until she looked like the forty-year-old Ruth Stein. As she stripped, the model commented on personal life-cycle changes through the use of dialogue balloons. One window featured two images of the two women, one for the left eye and one for the right, which, when viewed together, were intended to yield a portrait of a thirty-year-old. The real models were present for the exhibition to permit comparison with what Hershman termed their "photographic selves." In this window, Hershman commented directly on the image/reality dichotomy that is so much a part of viewers' experience of realistic mannequins in windows.

One of the "Reflection" windows held representatives from the Committee for the Future, who answered questions about demographic trends from people on the street via two-way microphones. A film on energy rolled in another window, while on the street a dozen poll-takers interviewed passersby on the city government's use of power and on energy use. In three windows, the word "Time" appeared on the glass, "ignited by sunlight," when the viewer stood directly in front.

Other windows related to current events in New York: one used mannequins to reenact a crime that had been recently reported in the city papers, the slaying of one balloon seller by another. In another Hershman covered the heads of the mannequins with cutouts of mirrors so passersby saw their own faces atop bodies dressed in Bonwit Teller's merchandise.

Several of the windows incorporated elements of live performance. In one, Hershman installed a mannequin whom she named "Bonnie," along with a schedule of Bonnie's sightseeing tour of New York that would take place on different days during the week in autumn 1976 that the installation was in place. Escorted by two of Bonwit's display staff, Bonnie visited Central Park, the Metropolitan Museum of Art, the New York subway, Soho, and Times Square, her movements documented by slides which were shown in her window. When in the window, Bonnie answered questions from people on the street in a heavy Bronx accent, her voice provided by Hershman's former sister-in-law. People on the street, Hershman reports, spoke to Bonnie about their lives, while she responded by talking about her image, particularly how wearing Bonwit Teller clothes affected it. For critic David Bourdon, Bonnie was the most exciting part

of the installation and the most effective of all of Hershman's visually enacted critiques of consumerism.

When in the window, Bonnie was presented with one hand rammed through the glass, surrounded by pieces of broken mirror that projected onto the spectators' side. For Hershman, this was "an enactment of a fantasy, of a mannequin being caught inside and finally being able to smash out." In her documentary video on the windows Hershman introduced the mannequin as Bonnie, "who lives inside this window."

Hershman's work shows the common threads connecting avant-garde art with display. Avant-garde art of the period explored the emotional meanings of display, particularly to women, whom the culture had conveniently characterized both as sexualized objects of display and as consumers of fetishized consumer goods. The art world was at the same time enveloped by controversy over the commerciality of the art object—and the marketing of the artist's own persona. Many visual artists had been turning to body art as a way of commenting upon the culture's object orientation, with its needling interest in masterpieces, authenticity, and connoisseurship. Such artists also turned to ephemeral media, such as performance. The inherently throwaway nature of display made it a singularly appropriate showcase for Hershman's socially concerned art. That Hershman's presentation was, by display people's standards, much more successfully conceived than executed was in keeping with her statement about consumerism: appearance counts for only so much.

Artist Colette also brought her concerns from other media into store windows; however, Colette's own body was the focus of her works or performances. A Tunis-born artist who was raised in Nice, Colette has worked extensively both in New York and in Europe. In addition to the many works she has created in other media, Colette's work helped popularize the live window in the early and mid-1970s. Much of it has revolved around the creation and enactment of personas, many of them heroines lifted from literature, art, and mythology who intuitively appealed to her: Camille, Mme. Récamier,

Ophelia, Mata Hari, Olympia, Persephone. Colette's roster of personas and the style of her performances read like a symbolist hornbook. She has a penchant for women who strayed from the norm and ended up in tragic situations or as victims. In many of her live performances she has appeared in the receptive, recumbent position in which nineteenth-century heroines in particular are typically pictured, and she sleeps, perhaps the most convenient action—other than dying—a symbolist heroine can take.

In fact, Colette has not shrunk from "death" in an aesthetic that treasured women as (idle) idols more than as subjects: the artist "killed" herself in a 1978 performance entitled "The Last Stitch" at the Downtown Whitney Museum in New York and was later reincarnated as Justine, executor of Colette's estate and head of the incorporated "Colette Is Dead Co." Inspired by the Sleeping Beauty fairy tale and by the image of the bleeding hand, Colette stapled her own in the Whitney window. When she drew blood, Colette lay down (as in other performances) as if dead. As Jeffrey Deitch put it, "The gap between art and life never existed for Colette, and even now that she's pronounced dead and resurrected herself as Justine, there isn't much of a gap between art and death either." As Colette lies in her window or environment installations, "the walls and ceilings abundantly enveloped by bolts of crushed silk and satin undulating with tactile luxury and luminous resplendence," she appears to be resting, often naked, in a grand coffin.[25] Passersby have wondered aloud, she reports, whether she is alive and just sleeping, or dead, or whether she might be a mannequin. Colette's penchant for victimized, passive characters, as well as for creating deathlike images with her own body, suggests that her art may be not only about the place of the artist in late twentieth-century culture but also about the place of the woman's image. Femininity is disturbingly well represented by stillness, inanimacy, or death. Mannequins—or "vital mummies," in the words Allan Kaprow used to describe the superrealistic sculptures of George Segal—may be viewed as embodiments of the

long-embedded association in Western culture between the female figure and stasis.

Meant to build art in unexpected places, Colette's window pieces at Fiorucci and other New York and German boutiques were extensions of her gallery installations, with the added dimension that people could encounter her there in silken luster without knowing that they were seeing "art" or "artist." The window performances also provided Colette with an enhanced sense of "privacy" behind glass.

For Colette, the opportunity to work in an essentially commercial setting while retaining—at least in her own mind—her identity as an artist allowed her to explore art-life boundaries, as had her "suicide" and subsequent resurrection as a fictional character or persona. Both allowed her, through the medium of her own body, to present questions to a mass audience about the proper role of the artist in seventies culture. She reports that by late in the decade she had become quite well known in international art circles and still found it difficult to finance her lavish and materials-intensive art projects. She found herself caught between two conflicting assumptions: one, that "artists are supposed to be put on a pedestal"—that is, that there should be financial recognition of their influence; and two, that artists "are not supposed to commercialize" or "sell out." For the pre-1980s art world and the cult of the artist-celebrity, the best artist was a dead artist, and Colette decided to try to reap the benefits of death a little early. The character of Justine also gave her the opportunity to bring art into the commercial setting without having herself accused of selling out; "Colette," after all, was dead.

Justine, Colette's resurrection, was an extroverted figure who wrote songs and was the lead singer in a "visual art band which at first performed but did not play." Justine and the Victorian Punks did "conceptual music" and eventually released a single entitled "Beautiful Dreamer," after the Stephen Foster song.[26] Justine had no qualms about seeing art ideas succeed in the commercial arena. A designer bed she created was featured in the 1979 Christmas catalog of an upscale Texas department store for $37,000. During the same year, Justine was the fashion designer behind a limited-edition line of Deadly Feminine (femme fatale) clothes for Fiorucci, based on costumes Colette wore for her window performances.

Colette's interest in commercial enterprises emerged from an almost circular relationship with the design world. The elaborate gathered and fluted costumes that she wore in everyday life, to discos, and in performances were quickly copied by the commercial world. Fiorucci's own designers attempted to copy her clothing style after she began doing performances in the windows there, and the management subsequently invited her to design a line of clothing herself. As Justine, Colette would bring the products to the brink of commercial success, then withdraw them, convert them into art objects, and exhibit them in galleries.

In both the commercial profit that Justine made from Colette's death and in the artistic ideas that she "took" from Colette, Justine "created a whole series of products that were basically ripped off from Colette's image," as Colette later acknowledged. Colette planned to design a

A mannequin that Colette commissioned to be made in her own image, 1990s. Courtesy of the artist.

mannequin after her "own image," an "obvious" choice, she has said, because she was "inspired by my own image to make products." The mannequin was also a medium for her exploration of the art-death boundary.

For the artist, the windows became a means of promoting products that she had created that were not actually for sale. Colette recalls a window she did in Germany as Justine, promoting the "Beautiful Dreamer" album, which at the time was nothing more than a record jacket. People came into the store to buy the nonexistent album; only those who were already familiar with her work knew that she was an artist performing in the persona of a rock star and that there was no record. Colette has termed her infusion of art into the commercial setting Reverse-Pop, after noticing the polarities with the work of pop artists working at the same time: "Instead of placing commercial images and techniques into an art context as my 'Pop Art' predecessors have done, I as Justine had placed products inspired by my personal image into a commercial arena. These would then often be recycled into sculptures and art objects."[27] Jeffrey Deitch speculated in 1981, "After a career of ignoring the gap between art and life, perhaps Justine will now succeed in dissolving the already ill-defined gap between art and commerce."

The term *pop art* has often been applied to Colette's work, particularly because of the work that later prominent pop artists did in window display. Colette maintains, however, that any comparison of her own work in windows with the display work of the pop artists is ill-conceived: "Someone recently said to me, 'Oh, you do windows? Warhol did windows!' And I said, 'No, he didn't. Warhol was a window dresser who became an artist: That's a whole different thing!'"

Colette's investigation of the store window as a simultaneously public space (for her audience) and private space (for herself) afforded her the chance to appropriate the very world of fashion and commercialism, a world to which she aspired through her lively public persona and which in turn aped her, forestalling her longed-for recognition as "a serious artist." The creation of a display mannequin in her own likeness for these performance windows reflects two themes that are of particular relevance here: Colette's career-long emphasis on the residence of meaning in her own body, and the visual and thematic soldering of her body to its environment. In addition to speaking in numerous accounts about the power and alterability of her image, the artist speaks of her presence as *being* the work of art. In 1988 she wrote, "Since 1970, with my first private performance, 'Homage to Delacroix,' I began portraying certain female heroines from mythology, literature and art history. . . . Since 1972 I began performing these works, creating a special environment for my presence where I usually lay still reclining with my eyes closed." And yet her work is to be distinguished from the work—characteristically treated as body art—of Vito Acconci, Chris Burden, and others. For "Colette's concurrent concern," in addition to the use of her own living presence, made manifest through her body as her medium, was with "the body . . . as an armature for the elaborate attire she wore as an extension of her living environment."[28] Her presence and her image at any moment, like a symbolist heroine or a mannequin, are as static and unshaken as possible.

Colette's apartment—or "living environment"— is a performance piece in itself. It is "entirely lined— including floor and ceiling—with dancing waves of a light-colored, silk-like material. The smooth mass of tissues is organized into fatty layers, sheath-like structures, soft and elegant curves. The material is at times spongy and yielding, at times firm and steady."[29] Colette has said that her appearance in her windows and installations is simultaneously an extension of her environment and a projection of her bodily presence onto it: "I created a landscape and then I became part of it." She remains fascinated with the image of a chameleon she had as a childhood pet, a symbol of both physical and psychological adaptation to one's environment. Like the mannequin in a setting that springs from the merchandise, Colette's body—later evidenced in her uniforms, a form of "walking architecture"—is disseminated through her environments. She stages her own persona as display.

The Live Window

Live windows—in which live performers appear, in place of or in concert with mannequins—date to the earliest creakings of American display. From the beginning, live windows have provided a ready hook to attract attention to a store, an animated way to encourage a passerby to become a shopper. In 1935, Albert Edward Hammond noted that, owing to the popularity of "living men mannequins" in windows, several stores had introduced rotating platforms so that their own mannequins could show all the angles of a garment. One retailer used live models in his windows "to demonstrate the ease of installing office partitions" and saw store traffic increase tenfold.[30]

Animated figures of all kinds were long regarded as "automatic window attractions," so much so that the once-powerful Fifth Avenue Association in New York forbade the use of motion in show windows, regarding it as a cheaply theatrical and commercial trick. Less stringent critics urged that movement in windows be evaluated for its sales effectiveness: is it truly "riveting the attention of the passing pedestrian upon the article" for sale, or is it merely drawing attention to the gadgetry involved?[31].

Experiments with moving mannequins in recent years have extended the early interest in automata. Steren Robotics' introduction to the display industry in the late 1980s of "Robbie," a crude robot whose arms, head, and eyes can be made to move from within the frame of an ordinary mannequin, is testimony to the continuing belief that attracting the attention of the passerby is the first step toward augmenting sales of merchandise from the show window. Richard Gilbert, an executive of Steren Robotics, claims that movement in a display can increase attention by 600 percent.

Hess's department store in Allentown, Pennsylvania, even developed a "talking" mannequin in the 1970s.

Unknown actors were made up to look like a particular character, while celebrities played themselves. Their faces were sculpted, and holes were left for noses and eyes. Films and audiotapes were made as the actors spoke scripted material. The effect of animation was created by projecting the moving image of the performer's face onto the sculpture while the audiotape was being played.

Live performers mix the static and dynamic qualities of such animated figures in a display of virtuosity. A robot mannequin is a live model who pretends to be a mechanical mannequin. Her performance is a complex layering of imitations: the model poses as if she were an actual robot, which in turn is posed as if it were a live model.[32] The delicious dance of perception across the line that divides fiberglass fake and human impersonator causes some passersby to stop for extended periods in front of the window, waiting for the "mistake" that will prove that someone is breathing on the other side of the glass. Said one model, "The extreme we aspire to is having someone stare at you through the window trying to figure out whether you're real or not."[33]

The robot mannequin style is highly mechanistic. In Howard Marx's description, "Models may freeze in position as mannequins and may hold a pose for up to a minute or so. Then, you can almost hear the gears whirring as they move into oddly mechanical steps, turns, shifts of the arms and twists of the head."[34] Robot modeling centers on movements of the arms, which are held long from the shoulders and cocked back at the wrist, and of the head, which rotates suddenly from one angle to the next and in all planes. When watching a robot mannequin work, one becomes conscious of how ordinary human movement consists of an acceleration, a stride point, and a deceleration: the robot mannequin appears to have only the middle phase. She moves rapidly and precisely from one position to the next, none of them naturalistic or in any discernible way functional; the movements appear simply to oil her joints. The robot face remains impassive as the model pivots like a jewelry box doll.

Diane Everett is a fashion model and a former Miss New Jersey whose career began at the age of fourteen, when she debuted as a robot mannequin on television to promote a designer's clothing. This was in the mid-1970s, when Brooke Shields popularized the notion of the precocious child model, when hordes emulated Michael Jackson's dancing, and when a television program starring the mimes Shields & Yarnell brought their form of fluid motion with sudden stops and rewindings into millions of living rooms. Everett recalls that her uncommon ability to do "the robot" generated excitement at her school, where being able to dance was a prerequisite to being considered "cool." MTV has kept the alternately fluid and percussive dance style popular.

As a teenage model, Everett had a steady stream of work both in the United States and abroad, enough to put herself through New York University in preparation for a career in broadcast journalism. Yet her robot modeling is what brought her the most fanfare and recognition. Her robot routine for the Miss USA pageant won her a spot on the news, and she has had scores of news teams recording her work in words, photographs, and on tape since then. Everett may be one of the longest-working robot models, having regularly performed six-hour stints for several years' worth of Saturdays and Sundays at the Gallery of Wearable Art in Soho. For Everett, robot modeling is exciting in the ways dance and gymnastics are, allowing her to show off her body, muscle control, and mental discipline; she likes best to perform in sleeveless clothing so her audience can see her muscles working. She also recognizes it as a rare opportunity for a model (who usually works in print) to control a performance. And she loves to watch the people who stare at her.

Audiences may stare for long periods, trying to determine what the creature on the other side of the glass is made of.[35] Alese Marshall, head of a West Coast agency whose models specialized in impersonating mannequins in malls, describes audience response: "At first they're startled when the models come alive, but then they applaud. If the model just shifts position, there's often a double take from a shopper who was passing and looks back as if to say, 'Did that manikin move?'"[36]

Everett says there are a couple of dead giveaways: the movement of her abdomen as she breathes and the texture of her hands and feet, which she keeps covered whenever possible to hide the veins, skin texture, and any irregularities in her nails. Yet most audience attention goes to her eyes, and when she performs she can frequently hear pairs of people testing each other, one to the left and one to the right side of the window, waiting for the infinitesimal blink that will tell them that she is living. "You're *there* to be scrutinized," she recognizes.

The eyes provide the most important clue to a model's flesh-and-blood status. In the 1930s a live model would enter the window "like an automaton and then remain completely immobile for a few minutes. . . . Amateurs in the know stood in wait for the inevitable quivering of the eyelids."[37] A tease-line to a feature in the *Los Angeles Times* on live mannequins reads, "If their eyes water, they're real." Model Josie Perbix confides, "You can't blink if you want people to think you're a manikin, but if you don't, your eyes tend to dry off—then you start to cry. I have more of a problem than some of the other models, so some shoppers wait for me to 'break' when the tears start to fall. I just slowly shift a hand up to screen my face, or drop my head slightly."[38] Many models who share Perbix's dilemma solve it with a pair of sunglasses to shield the movements and lubrications of their eyes. The disguise is simplified by the fashion, made popular in the 1970s, of topping show-window mannequins' noses with sunglasses.

Everett believes that only amateurs perform while wearing sunglasses, for the eyes are the central part of the performance and a cherished part of her own contact with her audience. She finds watching her audience as interesting as she imagines watching her is for them, and is always astonished at what is apparently instinctive to Colette: that people find standing still a never-ending source of fascination. She once tried wearing sunglasses for a performance, simply to evaluate the trend, but she found that they disrupted her concentra-

tion. The license to blink freely not only made her eyes tear but caused her to "start wavering back and forth." Everett believes that a viewer can instantly tell a good robot mannequin from a poor one by her eyework and by the kind of eye contact she makes with her audience. Everett stares directly at a viewer's eyes, nose, or eyebrows, trying to give the eerie impression that she is "looking right *through* them." Indeed, working six-hour shifts on an elevated platform, Everett has herself been witness to traffic accidents and stabbings, yet she has never been called—never been acknowledged—as a legal witness. As the mannequin in the window, she is officially there to be seen; it is individuals, not institutions, who are curious about what she in turn sees.

Without sunglasses, Everett readily lasts twenty-minute sets without a single blink. She has found that she can keep her eyes open and lubricated for the entire set by fixing them in one place while rotating her head in the fluid motions characteristic of the robot style. When the robot mannequin "fails" to blink, an audience can become frustrated; perhaps, having invested this much time in trying to establish the model's reality, viewers want a payback. They may even try to induce blinking. One model recalled that "one guy held a baby up to my face and kept saying, 'Look at the dummy!' Another time there were several of us modeling in a group on the lower level of a mall and some teen-age boys shot spit-balls at us from above. The first one hurt, because you're not expecting it. After that, you can hear them coming and brace yourself."[39]

Some viewers refuse to believe that the model is alive. Older people, Everett asserts, often have a hard time with the idea that Everett is actually a live model and continually protest, "A human couldn't do that." Everett plays with these unbelievers, occasionally trying to shock them. Yet even when she waves, winks, or blows kisses—all within the robot style—many still will not believe she is not made of fiberglass.[40] Other observers relate to her more as a doll than as a real figure, a reaction encouraged by her performance style: If she is wearing a long gown, she is able to shift position without lifting her feet from the ground. She simply pivots, like a jewelry box dancer. Even when audience members are quite close to her—for example, when she is performing in a store interior rather than in a window—they refer to her in the third person, as if she can't hear their comments (even derogatory ones). Everett's own skeletal feedback has a mechanical aspect as well: She compares its sound to the shifting of gears on a car. She says she can often hear the joints click in her neck and in one shoulder, and uses the click to gauge how far she has gone in a particular movement.

Everett has learned that, in trying to determine her reality—and then her expertise—viewers tend to behave toward her as toward a baby they are trying to get to smile or laugh. They wiggle their ears and "do the weird things that people—you know, *humans*—do." Everett has encountered flashers, mooners, people carrying funny posters or making funny faces, people wearing suggestive hats, and people who come back each week to try to distract her. She has seen babies grow up in front of her windows, parents bringing them back each week to "visit the robot." One small boy, perhaps three years old, had apparently been rehearsed at home in an impassioned love scene: he fell to his knees before the window in adoration, swooned and rolled around melodramatically on the ground, and blew kisses to her.[41]

On one level, onlookers may simply be testing the model's reality; on another, viewers seem to be trying to establish a mutual gaze, perhaps the physical essence of relationship, with the living mannequin. Everett's experience demonstrates that the crowd outside needs to make contact with the performer—and that the viewers, in turn, need to be seen by her. In certain ways, they are most seen by her when locked in a mutuality of a force that reminds one of the archetypal mother-infant mutual gaze: for while Everett prides herself on never having laughed at a funny face or other calculated attempt to make her lose her composure, she has a harder time maintaining it when she sees their startled reactions on discovering the "mannequin" is alive.

Everett recognizes that for her as well as for her audience, the eyes and how they are used instantly signify power relations. When taking on a new assignment, she likes to spook her new employers with her gaze, in part to prove to them just how good she is. As with other primates, the challenge of the gaze is emblematic of the struggle for power. Everett is determined never to be the one to laugh or to break the gaze first. Everett also uses her eyes as a metaperformance tool: to draw her crowd, she blinks more frequently, a signaling that something is going on; once a crowd has gathered, she holds onto it by keeping her eyes virtually motionless, increasing spectators' confusion and fascination.

Voyeurism and mutuality lie at the core of live mannequins' performance. Richard Schechner noted the "seductive and dangerous charm" of the mutual gaze between spectators and performers in environmental theatre.[42] Performance artists have also experimented with confrontation and participation. In a 1988 exhibition at New York's New Museum of Contemporary Art by British artist Stephen Taylor Woodrow, the so-called artwork stared directly back at those who had paid to be allowed to view it. Trussed up to the wall as *The Living Paintings* for seven hours each day, six days a week, Woodrow and two of his colleagues became "person-paintings"; they never smiled at or spoke to their onlookers, but they glared and scowled at them, spat and threw things, and accepted a spoon-fed lunch from museum spectators who "derived great delight from feeding the art." A New Museum staffer said that the living paintings were "adept at moving about in their suspended state, grabbing purses or plucking hats from unsuspecting gallery goers." P. K. Anderson wrote that *The Living Paintings* demonstrated that "suddenly, how one perceives art takes on an altogether new meaning—transformed from a reactive experience of staring at a static canvas to an interactive encounter with another human being."[43]

Display directors, quick to recognize the centrality of a reflexive vision in establishing the relationship between viewer and viewed, tease spectators' ocular hunger. Visual imagery and visibility figure prominently in display history—the heritage, perhaps, of surrealism. In 1952 Gene Moore created a series of three windows for Bonwit Teller in which scenes were staged, à la Magritte, within the pupil of an enormous eye. In the 1930s Dana O'Clare placed contorted mirrors in windows in order to force passersby to look at themselves in the glass. Another Bonwit window by Moore "incorporated a mirror below the window so potential customers could observe the unfortunate condition of their own shoes while viewing the pristine merchandise before them."[44] A Henry Callahan window for Lord & Taylor from the 1930s used the store's unique hydraulic lift to lower a scene so far down into the window that passersby had to strain close to the glass to see the "theatre" within. An audience that had to tiptoe and lean to see implicated itself. And the work of Candy Pratts in the 1970s frequently featured voyeur figures posed facing the rest of the scene, parallel to the street voyeur.

Sometimes the mixed reality that the spectator of the live mannequin senses occurs completely within the window frame, when a live person performs alongside ordinary mannequins. When Everett performs in a store window, she is often the downstagemost element of an entire stage set that includes ordinary mannequins. Although Everett has performed in all kinds of clothing, she finds that evening clothes most effectively mask the differences between live model and mannequin. At times, she has camouflaged herself among the mannequins, donning wigs to match theirs, mimicking their expressions, and making herself up to match them as closely as possible. At times, Everett draws from the mannequins in a more concrete form: she has snitched earrings from them in order to complete her own outfits. She kids about her relation to them: "Keep up the good work, guys"—or, "Get out of my way, you cramp my style. You're making me look bad."

Although she attempts to blend in with the mannequins behind her, Everett believes in the additional selling power a live performer brings to the store. The mannequin can promote the image of the store and communicate its general look, she acknowledges, but a live model can sell specific styles "right off her back." Everett believes that a "real body" (although, one might argue, a body sculpted deliberately through daily workouts) is a selling advantage over what she calls the "nonexistent body" of a mannequin because "no one has a body that looks like that." With a live mannequin, "It's like seeing the sculpture itself, instead of the slide of it." Her capacity for movement also distinguishes her from a mannequin: "I'm like an act, and they're just—there." For Everett performance includes a changed relationship to space—and to the audience—over time.[45]

Model-mannequin performances have also been staged for performers whose qualifications derive not from their talent for mimicking mannequins but from their having been chosen as the live models from which mannequins were sculpted. Rosalind Russell was the star of a 1953 publicity event at Bonwit Teller, performing alongside a mannequin that Gene Moore had modeled after her. Russell refused to perform in the windows at this midnight event (after her Broadway performance in *Wonderful Town*) unless Moore appeared with her. A shy man, Moore cast about "for a way to appear in those windows without looking foolish." He eventually decided to play the role of photographer and stood to one side of Russell with his Roloflex round his neck. According to Dan Arjé, Moore's assistant at the time, Russell strode from window to window, in front of an enormous throng, and tore away the wrapping paper covering each pane. Wearing a negligée that matched one worn by a mannequin in the display, she "camped"—some said, looking a bit like a drag queen—beside her mannequins, mimicking their poses and playing with them.

Manufacturers as well as display directors have appropriated the now-she's-living-now-she's-not motif that was central to Russell's performance. In the era of superrealism that began in the late 1960s, the trope has become a staple of mannequin brochure photography. For a sales brochure, mannequin manufacturer Ralph Pucci had model Aly Dunne improvise stunts with her mannequin for "fun shots"—which included her sitting on the mannequin, posing with it, and hugging it.

Perhaps the most celebrated man-mannequin performance in the display world is a life performance by Lester Gaba, a prominent mannequin sculptor of the 1930s, who, in perfectly re-creating the features of the model Cynthia Wells, appeared to have fallen in love with his mannequin.[46] The Cynthia mannequin "had an eerie, almost human quality, and unbelievable chic," Gaba wrote. "I was so fascinated by the finished product which looked very much like the live model that I ordered one just like her for my own apartment." Cynthia instantly captured the attention of Gaba's circle of acquaintance, illustrious figures in the fashion world. Within a day of first being sighted at Gaba's apartment, Cynthia was invited to an opening in a fashion salon. In a sense, it was her social debut, and she received one invitation after the next to elegant events, with Gaba as her escort. Cynthia had a full schedule:

> Elizabeth Arden, Howard Greer, and all of New York society sent her invitations to soirees, costume balls, dinners, cocktail parties. She dashed from "21" to El Morocco, from the Stork Club to the Colony— accompanied by me, of course. I was only the poor perspiring slave of a window mannequin who by some freak of fantasy had come to life—almost. Famous designers called to get permission to dress Cynthia. . . . Cartier, Tiffany, and Harry Winston loaned her diamonds for an evening out. One night, escorted by four detectives, Cynthia wore the fabulous "Star of the East" diamond valued at a million dollars to a ball. That was all she wore, for she was starred as Lady Godiva in a tableau. . . . She was featured in *Vogue, Town & Country, Ladies' Home Journal,* and she signed a year's contract to appear as the cover girl on *Beauty Fashions* magazine. I took her to Hollywood to make a movie with Jack Benny called *Artists and Models*—and Louella Parsons announced her engagement to Charlie McCarthy. Pola Stout wove fabrics so that Cynthia and I could have suits made of the identical material for her appearance on Fifth Av-

enue when she led the Easter parade one year. She traveled to Paris, London, Washington, Australia, Tokyo. She received fan mail, poison pen letters, poems, songs.[47]

According to Michael Southgate, an old friend of Gaba's, another "poor perspiring slave" actually carried the heavy plaster mannequin from place to place, for Gaba was a very slight man, but the anonymous muscle man never competed in the press coverage with Gaba for the role of Cynthia's beau. Southgate assessed Gaba's affair with Cynthia—as promoted by the press and apparently everyone who saw them together—as a publicity stunt to promote his mannequin business.

Southgate has seen many other man-mannequin promotions since Gaba's day, although these have been portrayed less as heterosexual matches made in heaven than as matings between a living woman and her alter ego. Their efficacy is testimony to the theatrical power of these mixed realities. Southgate recalled that Chelsea Brown used British talk shows to get "mileage out of her mannequin like you wouldn't believe: she'd take it on chat shows with her, she'd talk about how she dressed it in the morning, how she discussed her problems with it. It was her best friend: that was her angle." She used the mannequin as an aid to publicity for about a year.

Gaba wrote that Cynthia, not he, was the real celebrity of the pair. And in some cases the reality of the created figure can overshadow that of the live person. Ralph Pucci selected Aly Dunne instinctively. She "looked like a mannequin" to him: "She had that real long neck, she always was posing, her hips were thrown out, her legs were always in funny positions, her hands were expressive." A Disney staffer in creative development tells of

> this little boy who went to Disneyland, and first he saw the Pirates, and then he saw the General Electricity Show, and he asked his mommy—Are those people real?

And she said—No, they're not real.

And then he went to see Mr. Lincoln, and came out, and said—Is he real?

She says, No, he's not real . . .

He says—*Momma, am I real?*[48]

Computer scientist Myron Krueger noticed a similar effect, even with adults, in his artificial-reality multimedia works of the 1970s. Krueger developed an interactive video work entitled Critter:

You stand in front of a big video-projection screen. Your own life-size image appears—but you're not alone. A tiny cartoon character floats nearby on the screen, hovering in midair, tentative, clearly afraid of you. Stand still and the creature floats closer. Soon it lands on your arm, dangles from your fingers, climbs your shoulder. The computer-generated creature seems alive and aware of your presence. Finally it reaches the top of your head, where it dances a triumphant jig—and your video image vanishes from the screen.

That's when, according to the artist, "most people involuntarily look down at their bodies to make sure they're still there."[49]

This sense of overwhelming reality may be in part what makes mannequins effective selling tools: if you can lose yourself in the image of the mannequin, you will look as she does if you buy the clothes she wears. A display director for a Saks Fifth Avenue branch puts it this way: "A customer who is size 14 comes into the store and sees a dress on a tanned, size-5 mannequin; there is a blue light overhead and a palm tree to create mood. The customer goes into the fitting room with the dress. When she looks in the mirror, there's no tan, no blue light and no palm tree, but what she sees is that mannequin."[50] Suzanne Dolezal mouths the oft-repeated formula: that "store mannequins are a reflection of ourselves." However, it may well be just the opposite of Dolezal's Aristotelian formulation. *They create us.*

3 "Coition through a Glass Pane"

It was not a typical photo session. In fact, the implications of our March cover grew more ironic as our work progressed. We knew we were starting off with a "Twilight Zone" concept: reversing the roles of mannequins and people. . . .

We [got] down to the business of shooting a cover. The proper lighting was set up and our live model, Rhona, was positioned with the mannequins. The various comments of curious onlookers revealed a consistent fascination with the mannequins. "Look, that model looks just like those mannequins; you can hardly tell them apart!" was an often repeated remark. Then too, came the reverse observation. "Those mannequins look just like that girl!"

—"The Other Side of the Window: Mannequins,"
Visual Merchandising, March 1979

Violetta with her mannequin, 1990. Photo by Serge Krouglikoff. Courtesy of Adel Rootstein (USA).

Fascination is the hallmark word for window display; it crops up not only in informal conversations about windows and the theatricality of mannequins, but in journalistic and critical writings as well. Fascination has often seemed to take the place of analytical commentary and may be responsible in some cases for stifling it altogether. How might we discuss a subject that visually preempts the critical faculty? Of what does this fascination consist, and who is the one fascinated?

For Marxist critic Wolfgang Haug, fascination is the natural outcome of an economic system that places value on the appearances of objects—on "commodity aesthetics"—rather than on their use value. A customer pays for several things on top of the use of the object itself: the cost of advertising (or styling) and broadcasting a public image of it, which includes its display. In other words, people are fascinated by—and pay for—the aesthetic qualities of both the object and the selling process: in Haug's terms, "these aesthetic images capture people's sensuality."[1] Yet who are Haug's "people" and what is their notion of sensuality?

Laura Mulvey writes that in film, "fascination . . . is reinforced by pre-existing patterns of fascination already at work within the individual subject and the social formations that have molded him."[2] Fascination is no "natural" attraction to an object, but one conditioned by accreted aesthetic, erotic, and emotional experience, by events and objects one has been previously taught to regard as fascinating.

Identification is the term traditionally applied to the relationship in the theatre between audience member and principal stage character. Fascination, on the other hand, implies that the spectator simultaneously experiences affinity and a riveting disidentification—a compelling repulsion. We can see this dual charge that fascination bears in the writings on mannequins, a trope of American journalism as well as of a host of films and television programs centering on an uncannily "real" mannequin figure. That fascination should be more intricate than accustomed theatrical identification attests to the complexity of our relation to mannequins. Women, simultaneously the targets of arguably male-produced merchandising images and the objects of male visual consumption, may have a particularly intense relation to mannequins: they may both sympathize with them, as both are objects of a gaze judged according to male-defined standards of beauty, and critically assess such beauty in mannequins that they define as "other."[3] Although critics differ on the degree of power of the female spectator, as well as on the extent of her complicity in her own objectification, her ongoing support for the mannequin as a representational category is nonetheless suggestive.[4]

On the one hand, the story of the popularity of the mannequin as trope and in its material form tells of the desire by female viewers to seize control of particular *aspects* of the representation of women in the body design and staging of mannequins while declining—quite significantly—to try to alter the essential perceptual aesthetic of the realistic mannequin or of its staging. The story, however, also tells of the visual magnetism of the figures themselves—for the most part designed by men for a female gazer, herself not insignificantly the object of an internalized, possibly male, gaze.

The Mannequin as Popular Image, Trope, Object of Publicity

In his famous essay on the uncanny, Freud brought up a cluster of themes that help to explain the extraordinary attraction the window mannequin has historically held in popular culture. For Freud, "The uncanny is that class of the frightening which leads back to what is known of old and long familiar."[5] The arousal one feels in the presence of something uncanny shows ambivalence for an object simultaneously attractive and repulsive. How might these opposite sensations be experienced simultaneously? Freud hypothesized that the

uncanny often represents primitive fears and wishes that we have repressed and that we both desire and dread. The experience of the uncanny, for example, is common "in relation to death and dead bodies, to the return of the dead, and to spirits and ghosts," since we both dread death and crave to know more about it.[6]

The uncanny is centrally related to experiences in which we doubt our own reality, in which our sense of our identity comes into question. In the case of the realistic mannequin or of the robot mannequin that Diane Everett portrays, speculation about whether the performer is alive or not has fundamentally to do with determining whether one can trust one's own eyes and impressions, whether one's reality is reliable; if it is not, can it—and oneself—be called "real"? Thus, the doubling of identity in fiction—whether through a physical *doppelgänger* figure or through mental telepathy—tests or perhaps even erases the supposed boundaries of the self. A 1979 *Visual Merchandising* article in a special mannequin issue pointed out that one's own reality can readily come into question when confronted with a realistic mannequin, for it is not clear whether the human or the mannequin is the prior reality upon which the other is based:

> We who are familiar with the visual presentation industry know that realistic mannequins are sculpted after live models. But don't those finished mannequins become models for customers . . . "teaching" them fashion lessons and style trends? . . .

This [questioning] went a step further when we reversed roles and put shoppers in the window and mannequins outside looking in. When thought of in terms of the industry, this set-up is not as bizarre as it first appears. Indeed, customers do serve as models for mannequins, as customers' lifestyles, tastes and appearances not only influence new trends in mannequin manufacturing, but also constitute a critical factor in a store's selection, use and placement of mannequins. . . . The visual merchandiser must observe and study customers as if they too were on display.

So, ultimately, our [mannequin issue] poses the question of whether art imitates life or life imitates art. Perhaps with mannequins and people it's a case of both.[7]

For Jentsch, a precursor of Freud, the mechanical doll or automaton was the exemplary image of the uncanny: "A particularly favourable condition for awakening uncanny feelings is created when there is intellectual uncertainty whether an object is alive or not, and when an inanimate object becomes too much like an animate one." Jentsch also highlighted "the uncanny effect of epileptic fits, and of manifestations of insanity, because these excite in the spectator the impression of automatic, mechanical processes at work behind the ordinary appearance of mental activity." For both Jentsch and Freud, the appearance that "special powers" are operating behind the scenes in either an animate creature or an inanimate object helped to characterize the experience of the uncanny.[8]

In his 1817 story "The Sandman," E. T. A. Hoffmann evokes the uncanny as the primal terror of not being able to distinguish between the real and the imaginary, a terror that would later fuel many a *Twilight Zone*. The principal character, Nathanael, has suffered terrifying childhood experiences that may or may not have been produced by his imagination in freefall. Studying abroad, he falls in love with a mechanical doll named Olympia and forsakes his fiancée at home, whom he curses as a "damned, lifeless automaton."[9]

Every moment that Nathanael spends gazing through his window at Olympia, the "daughter" of his professor, is rapturous. He observes at the beginning that "she did not seem to notice me; indeed, her eyes seemed fixed, I might almost say without vision. It seemed to me as if she were sleeping with her eyes open." And yet, the more Nathanael stares at her, talks to her (her only reply: "Ah! ah! ah!"), and dances with her, the less he is able to tear his thoughts from her:

Without really knowing how it happened, just as the dance began he found himself standing close to her and she had not yet been asked to dance. Barely able to stammer a few words, he grasped her hand. It was as cold as ice. A deathly chill passed through him. Gazing into Olympia's eyes he saw that they shone at him with love and longing; and at that moment the pulse seemed to beat again in her cold hand, and warm life-blood to surge through her veins. In Nathanael's heart, too, passion burned with greater intensity. He threw his arms around the lovely Olympia and whirled her through the dance. He had thought that he usually followed the beat of the music well, but from the peculiar rhythmical evenness with which she danced and which often confused him, he was aware of how faulty his own sense of time really was.

In finding her hand warm as he touched it, Nathanael projects his own desire onto the doll. In distrusting his own sense of timing to favor hers, Nathanael accords the doll more reality than himself. Though he recalls that when he first touched Olympia's hand, "the legend of the dead bride flashed suddenly through his mind," he disdains his friend Siegmund's intimation, on behalf of several of their friends, that Nathanael has fallen in love with a doll. Siegmund must speak gingerly after Nathanael first rebuffs him:

It's very strange, however, that many of us have come to the same conclusion about Olympia. She seems to us—don't take this badly, my brother—strangely stiff and soulless. Her figure is symmetrical, so is her face, that's true enough, and if her eyes were not so completely devoid of life—the power of vision, I mean—she might be considered beautiful. Her step is peculiarly measured; all of her movements seem to stem from some kind of clockwork. Her playing and her singing are unpleasantly perfect, being as lifeless as a music box; it is the same with her dancing. . . . She seems to us to be playing the part of a human being, and it's as if there really were something hidden behind all of this.

As Nathanael's fate dissolves into pitiful doom, others who hear of Olympia begin to distrust their own mistresses: "The story of the automaton had very deeply impressed them, and a horrible distrust of human figures in general arose. Indeed, many lovers insisted that their mistresses sing and dance unrhythmically and embroider, knit, or play with a lapdog or something while being read to, so that they could assure themselves that they were not in love with a wooden doll; above all else, they required the mistresses not only to listen, but to speak frequently in such a way that it would prove that they really were capable of thinking and feeling."

Ambivalence is the keynote of portrayals of the relationship between human subjects and mannequins. Many polarities are aptly explored within this relationship: love and death, virtue and evil, reality and fantasy, oneness and doubleness, free will and being controlled from without (like a marionette). By the 1960s, mannequins had become a staple motif in movies.

The 1944 film by Hans Richter entitled *Dreams That Money Can Buy* contains seven framed episodes, each one devised separately by a surrealist artist. These are loosely held together by the dream interpretation that takes place in a makeshift psychiatrist's office. As a catalog issued in conjunction with the film summarizes, "Joe, a young poet in a desperate mood, determines to capitalize on his unique gift for interpreting one's inmost dreams. He settles down in a fancy office, selling to his clients whatever he molds from the material of their unconscious."10

The most celebrated episode, "The Girl with the Prefabricated Heart," depicts the love story of two department-store mannequins, who mimic and satirize the mechanical courtship of humans. The two principals and their cohorts, manipulated by offscreen puppeteers, are jerked back and forth or presented in quickly alternating photographs of set poses. The female mannequin, for example, is introduced primping and posing in front of a mirror: She is shown with her arms in the "down" position, then suddenly presented with her arms in the "up" position, as if they have been rotated

180 degrees in their sockets. We flip back and forth in dizzying repetition between the two images, a technique that simultaneously lends the mannequin motion and emphasizes its inflexibility, for it is capable of only two poses.

In silent mime to a witty song by John Latouche, the female mannequin is introduced to a male: "Just like in the movies, a mail-order male, sent by the Gods directly from Yale." She hears his proposal and takes his flowers and jewels, is draped in a white wedding gown, refuses his amorous overtures, and spurns him, calling upon her nearby girlfriends (also mannequins) to come to her rescue. Latouche's lyrics present this love story between two classically perfect creatures—equipped with all the education (for the male) and the accessories (for the female) that money can buy—as an emblem of our streamlined modern sensibilities: "Venus was born out of seafoam. . . . But the goddess of today is formed on the assembly line. . . . And to top off this daughter of Science and Art, she was equipped with a prefabricated heart."

The film plays off the human qualities of these figures against the clearly mechanical. Inspired by an idea by Fernand Léger, "The Girl with the Prefabricated Heart" beckons us to recognize in this satire of mechanical lovemaking how we succumb to the safety of mechanical forms for our most intimate acts. When the male mannequin encounters resistance to his pursuit, he chooses a well-worn backup strategy, an easy choice in an age of modern advertising. The accompanying song-narration describes the plan:

> So Nature and Art will not win her
> I'll ply her with diamonds and pearls;
> But bracelets and rings are practical things,
> Things that appeal to the mind of a healthy and well-balanced girl.

The female mannequin resists his ardor in the idiom of one too used to department store prettiness to engage in untidy acts of love. When he asks her if he may kiss her, she answers indifferently, "I suppose so." But quickly she objects: "You're mussing my hair. . . . Watch my new clothes." In this burlesque of love-as-act-of-purchase, of purchase-as-rehearsal-for-love, we recognize our own participation as buyers and sellers of love and romance, as well as of a commodified beauty, in situations in which people and inanimate objects may function variously as objects of and props for human feeling.

It is then all the more disturbing when the bodies of the characters become mere things, no more worthy of romantic love than shards of badly imitated sculpture. Rejected by his beloved, the suitor "fell to the ground . . . quite lifeless." A human actor would collapse from the middle of his body, but the loss of love is signaled in the mannequin by the sudden display of how brittle this assembly line lover is: Falling backward over a chair, his head drops out of his stiff shirt collar and onto the ground. Tears run down his disembodied face.

If we have identified with this creature's story enough to laugh at it, recognizing in it our own, we are bereft at the episode's end, feeling ourselves neither alive nor dead, but simply inanimate: The uncanny in "The Girl with the Prefabricated Heart" lies in our inability either to pull away from the characters and to treat them as objects or to see ourselves as wholly merged with them.

The polar relation between love and death in "The Girl With the Prefabricated Heart" is emblematic of contemporary journalistic treatments of the department store mannequin. For as much as the mannequin is a sales instrument, a means for marketing both a particular article and a specific store's image, it has become a popular literary icon as well in magazines and newspapers. A typical feature story either provides a behind-the-scenes look at the creation of a glamorous image or explores the origins and how-to's of an industry that the reader has rarely thought consciously about—a tourist's-eye view of an alien workplace. Occasionally, a "news" story treats the debut of a new mannequin design as both the unveiling of a new product and the birth or modeling of a new way of being for the human species.

The *New York Times Magazine*, *Life*, *Vogue*, *Time*, *The Saturday Evening Post*, even *Smithsonian*, are among the popular publications that have dedicated feature stories to mannequins. *People* has regularly included stories on new industry developments, fetishizing mannequins in much the same manner as human celebrities. Glamour shots of mannequins and the people associated with them have been featured in such publications as the *New York Times* and *American Way* magazine—and in many issues of *People*, which once presented them in a "most beautiful people" feature.

Feature articles on mannequins—the bulk of what has been written on the subject—offer a rapidly predictable emotional progression. In the beginning, the writer is fearstruck and fascinated by the sublime resemblances between mannequins and humans. Describing a Jerry Hall mannequin, Greg Collins teases us with his own attraction to her: "The three of us are standing around a Jerry Hall mannequin, modeled directly from the famous model and Mick Jagger companion. It looks just like her, too, without, of course, clothes, hair or arms. But these few minor cosmetic deficiencies do not take away from her—I mean, it's . . . Not that I'm really attracted. I mean . . . Damn it! The thing's weirdly erotic."[11] The writer may move then from considerations of the mannequin's formidable exterior to speculation about its thoughts and desires. Suzanne Dolezal found that "while mannequins may project chic and well-being on their pedestals in Saks and Hudson's, an aura of mannequin misery hangs heavy in the air at Mario's," a mannequin refinishing studio. Owner Mario Messana is "apparently oblivious to their silent screams."[12]

The tone of these articles is frequently surprise. In numerous reports, writers discuss their awe for such aspects of the figures as their immense height or their lifelike (or better-than-life) qualities. A 1983 story depicted the mystery figures as "slim, beautiful and young, and time brings no wrinkles to their brow or cellulite to their thighs. Their hair is always immaculate and their nails never break." Some authors are shocked

*Aly Dunn with her manne-
quins. Courtesy of Pucci.*

to realize how thought-provoking mannequins become once they are made an object of conscious examination. Rochelle Chadakoff begins her story: "If you do notice a mannequin, something is wrong—it had a hand amputated by a clumsy browser, a slipped wig or it is bare and bold and looks slightly bizarre."[13]

Typically, mannequin stories open with a riddlelike account of the mannequin's supposed emotional qualities or with enigmatic hints about her glamorous appearance or lifestyle. A 1977 *New York Times* story depicted its main character's life as short, but with a payoff in luxury: "Her wardrobe has dozens of designer dresses, marvelous furs and jewels, and she's at home at some of the best addresses in town. She has a retinue of helpers to dress her, arrange her hair and refresh her makeup."[14] There is always a catch in these stories, something that helps the reader guess that the character being lauded is inanimate. In one instance, this spoiled creature rarely smiles. In other narratives, she refuses under all conditions to respond to human overtures, remaining instead aloof and silent.

As writers imagine fiberglass figures as mortals, they develop concerns about the mannequin's "lifespan" and its eventual demise. In some cases, the length of service is cut and dried: two years, five years, seven years tops. In part, the preoccupation with mannequin obsolescence acknowledges that these are fashion figures and hence subject to outdating in terms of style or "for lack of durability of ladies' ideas about what a lady's figure should be."[15] But that practical consideration scarcely explains the anthropomorphic focus on the length and quality of the figures' "lives."

Some accounts of mannequin lifespan suggest that the figure has not simply become passé but has truly aged. The aging process may be described in terms of a fading career that begins (if the mannequin is lucky) in a high-visibility fashion window, then goes downhill as she is relegated first to a store's prominent interior spaces, then to more obscure ones, and finally to budget departments: "They ride high one year, or maybe two or three. Then, poof, before they know what's hit them,

they're in supporting roles, or in the back of a closet, or shipped off to some village store. The stars become has-beens, fading into near obscurity simply because they don't project what the fashion world would call 'today.'"[16] Robert Benzio, display director at Saks Fifth Avenue, spoke of sorrowfully spotting in a store window a favorite old mannequin that he had helped design. He wondered why she hadn't been "retired" with dignity.

From observations about mannequins' wrinkle-free surfaces, writers typically proceed to speculation about the figures' inner worlds, about their response to the immobile, unchanging, voiceless conditions of their lives. At a lecture in Philadelphia, a Greneker representative gave "a colorful outline of the lives and loves of the girl in the window display." And a column for the industry publication *Merchants Record and Show Window* is written from the point of view of the mannequin herself: she is "secretly laughing at this [admirer] or with that one, wondering as to the thoughts of this young steno or that old spinster, resentfully observing the amorous glances of some self-styled Romeo, mischievously reading the thoughts behind the smiling eyes of that gay young man-about-town, with never a change of expression in her always-lovely face."[17] "Lovely Annabelle" scoffs at the ministrations of the "very unromantic and coarse second assistant" and queries whether she should simply "topple over and end it all." She longs for the tender touch of the display director, "her hero," who gives her "that sweet caress, which he so unwittingly executes in the due process of lifting her bust onto her new found hips" and who during his last visit gave her a "gentle tug at her trunks, that playful pat on the breasts" without which she feels incomplete.

In *The Art of Window Display*, Lester Gaba paints a picture of Cynthia as a moody date, who at her first party sits "in disdainful silence, refusing to talk to anyone." Cynthia is at once a sexually enticing and remote enigma and an object of pathos who evokes thoughts of death. She is "a mystery, a woman of silence who never opened her mouth and said, 'I'm only made of plaster!'"[18]

In a brochure, manufacturer Robert Filoso based an entire marketing campaign on the treatment of the female mannequin as if alive. His intense "Eye Spy" collection showed mannequins that were designed for display settings where they were meant to be partially concealed. Some of them blocked their eyes with an elbow or a set of tautly splayed fingers. Filoso provided the mannequin "Judy Garman" with both a mission and a set of job skills to give any buyer confidence in her ability to bring off her double role as undercover spy and merchandiser: "Judy Garman's mission, should you decide to accept her, may be to spy on you, or to fill your specific assignment. Whatever her job, she will remain undercover, but you can't help [but] feel her presence as she is always in the spotlight." And, like a good spy, she could wear many disguises. Garman could "take on any identity required; can be disguised in furs, coats, gowns, dresses; any attire needed to fulfill your assignment." Her eyes were a "penetrating brown, subject to change with painted colored lenses"; her hair color could change "according to assignment request." Garman was (or dressed like) a true professional.

The wish for mannequins to speak—or the knowledge that they don't—is a recurring motif in resolving the human-versus-object quandary that plays itself out in feature articles. A 1981 interview with Nellie Fink concluded with her half-joke, "I've always said I'd never leave this business until the day that [the mannequins] start talking back." A 1984 article on Adel Rootstein began, "They talk and they pout. They play leapfrog or spin hoops. They pirouette down a runway. Or sit—legs rakishly spread—on a bench. Indeed, the only thing that separates them from anyone else in Adel Rootstein's showroom is the fact that they remain mute when Rootstein asks—as she's apt to ask an unexpected intruder—'Hello, are you a mannequin or a human?'"[19] And a 1941 feature article showed a picture of a mannequin positioned as if excluded from a trio behind her, with the catty line "Talking behind my back?" as caption.

In feature articles on the mannequin, writers present their subject self-consciously, dropping hints of sexual competitiveness between writer and mannequin. Greg Collins, writing for *Gentleman's Quarterly*, observed: "The German word *männeken* means 'little man.' Boy, were they wrong. These days, it stands for 'big woman.'"[20] In magazine scenarios, the female mannequin is typically read by the male writer as eroticized: Keith Dunstan found a mannequin in a store window "sitting . . . exactly in the manner which my mother used to tell my sister never to sit." The sexually charged atmosphere of the mannequin factory was also brought home by Cliff Bostock, who said that the sexual aura that surrounded him gave him an uncanny sensation that he had walked into an "eerie place": "besieged by naked mannequins posing languorously, smiling seductively or haughtily, one has the feeling of having wandered into a place where an orgy of international deaf mutes is about to take place."[21]

Male writers' self-consciousness—their overt questioning of the role that they must play "opposite" these creatures—is even more evident when they confront male mannequins. Collins quaked at the sight of a "well-defined" male mannequin named Joe, whose "stomach is so rippled it looks like a venetian blind," and was daunted by the mannequin's phallus: Michael Southgate told him, "'Now that we're using male models, the men have changed shape completely. The average man's figure was a thirty-eight chest, thirty-two waist, with a thirty-four inside leg. Now we need at least a forty chest, or perhaps a forty-two, with nothing bigger than a thirty-inch waist.' I calculated that the last time I had a thirty-inch waist, I was 11. 'And they like a thirty-five or even a thirty-six inside leg.' What's an 'inside leg'? I wonder. I hope he means 'inseam.' Joe, here, has a prosthetic pubic mound that looks like a light fixture." Collins seems hyperconscious during this meeting with the male mannequin of how he measures up; for Collins, the mannequin's body is the normative one, next to which his own is lacking. The feature stories written on Lowell Nesbitt's "Man of the '90s" mannequins for Pucci also seem to suggest that if men want to keep up with the heftier, more athletic, and explicitly virile mannequins, they'd better head out to the gym—otherwise, they're in danger of having sand kicked in their faces.[22] The implication is that these mannequins are love objects for women, not stylized versions of the men's own bodies.

Even security mannequins may be treated as surrogate mates for the female customer. "Gregory," a male mannequin available for general purchase, was aimed primarily at a market of lone women. Sold for $499 clothed, $449 unclothed, Gregory occupied the passenger's seat of your car and discouraged would-be attackers. His "masculine" appearance was an integral part of his design. As the "Meet Gregory" ad read: "Gregory's stern appearance is no accident. His rugged cleft chin, square-set jaw, firm expression, and broad shoulders telegraph to criminals that this is a man to avoid." Perhaps best of all, Gregory wore what you wanted him to: "Gregory comes dressed in a gray cotton turtleneck, dark gray slacks and belt. . . . You can garb him in sports, casual, or business attire. Or put him in a tux for formal occasions." A column in *Smithsonian* magazine satirized innovations by suggesting that security mannequins serve a useful social purpose not by protecting married women when they must drive alone at night but rather by stirring up "a little marital jealousy" when these women rode through town "accompanied by a man-size replica of Paul Newman or Steve McQueen."[23]

Whether in spite or because of its sexual charge, the mannequin may also become a site for a battle between the sexes. The bad news about Nesbitt's muscle-mannequins was, apparently, that "these new role models still won't take out the trash." Another writer lauds mannequins because in obvious contrast to live women they "will never demand salaries, gain weight, start a union, get pregnant or grow old."[24]

It is an effort, for male and female writers alike, to wrench themselves out of a voyeuristic and erotically charged mode, but as articles progress the mannequin's objectness wars convincingly with its humanness. In a

1983 article, Susie Foster wrote with mock modesty about the means by which the weighty creatures are kept upright. Some of the support rods, she wrote, require "the soles of shoes to be butchered so the rods fit through, others—er—have support rods through their bottoms, meaning that clothes must be slashed at the back for fitting." In the industry itself, this type of support is unflinchingly labeled a "butt rod."

Likewise, Greg Collins seems chagrined to see how mannequins are typically handled—one hand around the neck, the other unsentimentally under the crotch. His squeamishness on behalf of the object derives from what one might feel if a human were carried from place to place in this fashion. Even more extreme is the writer's reaction to the bodily fragmentation mannequins undergo for dressing, storing, and shipping. Images of death and creatures strung precariously somewhere between death and life abound: "[We are] tramping down a series of narrow winding staircases in the old castlelike building [of Saks], where the mannequins are quartered. It is a real Phantom of the Opera trip. The hundreds of naked, hairless and armless mannequins in the room—all lined up shoulder to shoulder in wooden stalls like a cowshed's, their arms hanging around their necks in bags (for space reasons)—do not comfort me any."[25]

Part of the notoriety of the 1937 *Life* story on Lester Gaba's Cynthia may have come from the contrast between her gay social life and her sordid dismemberment at the end of a glamorous evening. The alluring photo-essay depicted Cynthia choosing from her many social invitations in the morning's mail, then showed the couple enjoying a formal dinner and a theatre performance of *Madame Bovary*, taking a carriage ride around Central Park, and stealing a goodnight kiss at the Gaba front door. At the end of the photo-narrative, we see Cynthia prepare for the night's retirement by allowing Gaba to dismantle her and store her parts in black sateen bags, "where Cynthia spends her private life." A series of four shots shows Gaba taking Cynthia apart, Cynthia naked and hairless, Cynthia from the waist down, and the bulging black bags that contain her. The fitting consummation of a romantic weekend—the dismemberment of the mannequin—is meant both to titillate and to horrify. The Gaba weekend with a mannequin is a tale of sex and death.

Death imagery provides a counterpoint to romantic and sexual longings. Dominique Autié, in her introduction to the historical survey *Mannequins*, described the figures as "immortal corpses" and spoke of a "complicity between the mannequin and death." A visitor to the Disney manufacturing site for the robotic Audio-Animatronic figures that animate such rides as Pirates of the Caribbean and The Country Bear Jamboree called it "a robotic Emergency Ward."[26] Another writer found the sight of a mannequin storeroom "like a ghostly Buchenwald": "There were shelves of arms, shelves of hands, shelves of legs, thighs. . . . There were cupboards full of hairless, naked females, some white, some brown, some black, and all thin."

Ortega wrote persuasively about the difficulty we have in deciding whether to treat human effigies as objects or as creatures. Though he was referring to Madame Tussaud's figures, his words apply equally to newcomers to the mannequin workshop: "Wax figures defeat any attempt at adopting a clear and consistent attitude toward them. Treat them as living beings, and they will sniggeringly reveal their waxen secret. Take them for dolls, and they seem to breathe in irritated protest. They will not be reduced to mere objects. Looking at them we suddenly feel a misgiving: should it not be they who are looking at us? Till in the end we are sick and tired of those hired corpses."[27]

Disidentifications
The host of regulations that have arisen in the twentieth century governing how mannequins may be portrayed is evidence of just how dangerous the creatures' image is perceived to be. Most regulations seem geared to control the passerby's perception of the store's morality. In the early 1920s the Women's Christian Temperance Union

protested against the use of realistic mannequins in the windows, particularly inasmuch as the figures were sometimes "naked" in full view of the public. Conservative objectors in succeeding decades have followed the wctu line, finding the figures themselves indecent, all the more so as they begin to sprout nipples and navels, and show more skin. For the protesters, the mannequin is as much a threat to public decency as a human woman displaying herself broadly in a public place with the express desire of being seen; the mannequin is translated as *a woman seen.*

Until the 1940s, common practice in Boston store windows proscribed the use of extravagant lipstick and nail polish on mannequins. And a New York merchant "was hauled into court" for assembling mannequins in his windows without their having the benefit of slips or girdles. In many parts of the country, it was illegal to undress or dress mannequins in view of spectators.[28] Dan Arjé recalled that when he worked as Gene Moore's assistant at Bonwit's in the 1950s, a window dresser could get a ticket for undressing a mannequin in the window with the shades up.

Many display artists began to paper their windows as they worked, a technique that is still common, less for modesty's sake than to create suspense about what's going on behind the curtain. Even in 1898, L. Frank Baum had advocated screening the window while working on it—again, not for decency but to reap the promotional benefit of the mystery and of passersby's ingrained voyeurism. Baum advised painting a sign on "common muslin" that announced, "Watch this window" or "We are preparing a surprise for you" or "This window is dead to-day, tomorrow it will be alive with bargains." Though it is no longer a legal issue, Bloomingdale's actually requires that windows be covered while mannequins are being cloaked.

Although some regulations were imposed by the stores, others were standard practice established and enforced by the local merchants' associations. The Fifth Avenue Association, a group of New York merchants who had banded together to maintain the high-brow image of the avenue, enacted one of the most renowned injunctions, prohibiting the use of motion in windows. Benson has emphasized that the department store, although generally "the embodiment of urban bourgeois respectability . . . [was] simultaneously an arena for clashes of class-specific ways of behaving."[29] Moore recalls that the Fifth Avenue Association periodically sent around a list of its regulations (which he—and possibly only he—got away with systematically ignoring). According to Dan Arjé, motion in the windows—whether from animated figures or objects, such as are still used in many Fifth Avenue Christmas windows, or from live window performers—was believed to reek of the questionable morality of theatrical presentation. Perhaps it was precisely because motion had long been touted as an easy way to draw attention that the Fifth Avenue Association forbade it: it seemed "cheaply sensational."[30] The Association's watchdog presence extended from the windows of the store out into the street; whatever took place under canopies also had to be above board.

Nudity continues to receive the most attention as a controversial window technique, disturbing both passersby and serious customers (and board members).[31] In the late 1960s, Salvatore Marra staged abstract mannequins by the Swiss firm Schläppi in the windows of Alexander's fur salon. The furs were lightly draped around the figures but left open in the front. The mannequins were crowned with neon hair, which was powered by transformers inside their heads. The artist regarded them as sculpture, but some of the store's constituents couldn't help but see them as unsuitable nudes.[32]

Mannequin history is rife with anecdotes about viewers who have read sexual content into windows, though it is not at all clear that the nude mannequin universally signifies sexuality. A display by Guy Scarangello showed two mannequins embracing. His intention, he later said, was to suggest a friendly, romantic atmosphere; the gesture was read in another spirit, however, by the powers that be. The strategy Scarangello typically used to head off panic at any suggestion of sex was to slide wedding bands on the mannequins' fingers;

those simple props somehow sanitized the situation.

Scarangello's relation with his bosses is typically jovial and teasing, and many of the controversial effects he stages are playful attempts to tease a response out of the store's management. Perhaps he tries to goad the general public as well. Scarangello proudly tells of a gigantic fish that he had painted across the front of the Gucci store. The fish was adorned with male and female figures, the female topless; he was all set to put a bra on the figure once the management (as expected) objected. "I anticipated that kind of thing," he chuckled. He remembered thinking that day, "Gee, it's ten o'clock, and something must be wrong—nobody is calling me."

The other target of pungent protest against specific window displays is religious imagery. The Archdiocese of New York raised Cain over a Barneys window when Scarangello cast as nuns a trio of abstract Rootstein mannequins in simple black Gianfranco Ferré gowns with a flouncy white trim. It was an obvious play on the associations of the dress, but one that the Archdiocese found unseemly in a commercial display. According to Scarangello, the Archdiocese sent protesters and threatened that its nuns would boycott Barneys (!) if the windows were not immediately struck. On a like note, Bloomingdale's received calls complaining that the appearance in the windows of fashion T-shirts with crosses imprinted on them was an inappropriate endorsement of Catholicism and urging that the only way to be fair would be to include T-shirts with Stars of David as well.

Death is the one domain that display directors admit is inappropriate to their medium.[33] Bob Currie had planned a funeral window for Bendel's but was stopped by the store president, Geraldine Stutz, before it was installed. Simon Doonan once succeeded in bringing a funeral window to the public in the Los Angeles Maxfield's window. Scarangello, who saw in Doonan's display a breach of basic decorum, feels that the use of death and grief in a window setting "borders on the irreverent" and that display reaches its limit when it has the power to hurt the customer. Currie and Scarangello contrasted the window space with the art gallery and considered the latter better able to treat human suffering without making fun of it.

Many different kinds of empathy arise between mannequins and spectators. Often female passersby can cast themselves into a sort of triangle with the mannequin and a person in apparent authority over her, such as a display artist or a window photographer. Sometimes the live woman competes with the mannequin for the favor or preference of the display man—making the man the trophy of a game played in the name of feminine captivation. As Willo Font takes his weekly photographs of Bloomingdale's windows, passersby compete with the mannequins for his attention. A woman blocks his view of a mannequin, adopting its pose and saying, "I'm much prettier than her" or "I can do that much better than her." Occasionally Font takes the picture, just to get the woman out of his hair, but because he sets his camera for long exposures for window shots, these photos usually come out blurred: the camera is geared to record mannequin, not human, beauty.

Sometimes woman and mannequin are allied against display man, a game that the live woman "wins" by protecting her "own kind" and thus surpassing her. Jim Mansour was arranging a mannequin in the window when an elderly woman entered the store, wanting urgently to speak with him. "You've got to let me take her home," she said. "She's so unhappy." Mansour replied, "Who is?" The lady gestured. "This mannequin that's in the window here." He turned to look. "Which one?" She pointed the mannequin out to him. He tried to reassure her. "Really? What do you mean? I'm going to put a really great dress on her." The woman insisted, "No, sir, I'm serious. I've seen her for a long time now, and if I take her home, she'll be happy with me."[34] Mansour was eventually able to convince this "beautiful, queer" old woman that he would take good care of the joyless mannequin. When he went to finish dressing the mannequin, however, he noticed a small lacquer "tear" appearing to run out of its eye—a mistake in manufacture, and the apparent catalyst of the woman's response.

This tender desire to save the mannequin from the heartless display artist crops up with surprising frequency. Font recalled a free-for-all that began when one of his assistants started to spray Windex on a Bloomingdale's window before photographing the display. A passing woman wheeled around in her trench coat and hissed, "What are you doing? That's my sister over there," apparently referring to a Cher mannequin wearing a long blonde wig in the nearby window. She lunged at Font's young assistant, and Font tried to break them up; then a male passerby joined in, apparently trying to keep Font from beating up the two women. The final participant was Font's other assistant, who had arrived late for work.

Many passersby view the display artist's treatment of the mannequin as reflecting a negative attitude toward women. Historically their claim has a good deal of merit. For the Surrealist Exhibition of 1938, surrealist artists used mannequins to explore psychosexual themes, many of which were harshly and antically misogynistic. Man Ray, Joan Miró, Kurt Seligmann, Salvador Dalí, Andre Masson, Maurice Henry, Marcel Duchamp, Oscar Dominguez, and Max Ernst made department store mannequins into objects of decay and depravity by covering them with snails, matting their hair, painting colossal tears on their cheeks, and enclosing their heads in bird cages. As Man Ray wrote, "In 1938 nineteen nude young women were kidnapped from the windows of the large stores and subjected to the frenzy of the surrealists who immediately deemed it their duty to violate them, each in his own original and inimitable manner but without any consideration whatsoever for the feelings of the victims who nevertheless submitted with charming goodwill to the homage and outrage that were inflicted on them, with the result that they aroused the excitement of a certain Man Ray who undid and took out his equipment and recorded the orgy, not in the interests of history but merely because he felt like it."[35] Surrealists, who were renowned for their images of woman as object and as slave, regarded mannequins as the "ideal woman"—silent, beautiful, and ceaselessly receptive. Critic Thomas Hess wrote:

"By the 1940s, shop-window dummies became the Surrealists' best friends and loved objects; they were chosen for their fashionable glamour, their sex appeal, and their passive deportment."[36]

Contemporary display directors vehemently and without exception reject accusations of misogyny, but passersby persist in linking specific images of women that they perceive in the window with the intentions and belief systems of the men who created them.[37] Guy Scarangello recalled a Christmas window that he designed for Barneys, which featured a female mannequin in a scanty French maid's costume standing in a kitchen with two fully clothed male mannequins. The window was part of a series, each frame of which was supposed to represent a different room or section of a house. According to Scarangello, this window inflamed a whole "parade" of women, who would stop him on the street and pester him, insisting, "This is a woman who has to earn a living, and she's going to submit to this man, and the man is the head of the house." Shrugged Scarangello, "They had a whole scenario that I never dreamed about! They had projected a whole thing! I didn't mean it to be sexist. This could have been a gal who was part of a catering service, and this was just sort of an amusing kind of costume that she was wearing for that kind of thing. But, no! They had placed her as *help* in the house, and that the master of the house was going to seduce her, or it might have actually been part of a sexual kind of thing, and it went on and on."[38] "The feminists," as Scarangello characterized them, wrote letters and distributed fliers in front of the store denouncing the windows. They demanded—and got—a meeting with the manager. They perceived the window as depicting violent attitudes toward women; according to Scarangello, they imagined a scenario in which the female figure was a married woman with children at home who desperately needed the job with the catering service and couldn't afford to quit.

Scarangello professed bewilderment that the mannequin should even have been read as a dramatic character: "She's a mannequin in a window! How do you know she's all of these things: number one, she's married; number two, she has children; and number three, she needs to submit to the man of the house because she needs the job?! . . . For me, this was just a sexy little gal in there—like the clichéd French maid." The men in the window wore business suits, and one had an overcoat on, as if he'd just come inside. Scarangello claimed it just as likely that these were guests at the party as that they were in-house dominators. He may have been working both sides of a serpentine street in his protests: it would be hard to suppose that when creating the window Scarangello failed to recognize the perceived dramatic tension among his carefully costumed figures as the element that would snare passersby.

Display directors rarely face such recriminations when gender roles are reversed: a sign, perhaps, either that men do not look closely at windows showcasing women's clothing or that there is more room for teasing in the expanse between men and the subject and images of display. Scarangello once produced a controversial window for Barneys in which a set of figures was posed with a black leopard, then a popular prop in displays. A male mannequin towered above both the leopard and one of the women, who was reclining; the male mannequin carried a whip. "All of the feminists were irate," he recalled. He had intended, he said, to have the whip understood either as a formal element of abstract composition or as something that would be used to tame the *leopard*, not the woman. Yet he found a simple solution: he took the whip from the male mannequin's hand and gave it to one of the female mannequins. There was no further trouble.

Gene Moore recalled a similar incident that involved a series of back-to-school windows that he created for Bonwit's. He had obtained some textbooks to use as props and, in one window, had carelessly (he said) opened a medical textbook to a page that showed a detailed diagram of the female genitalia. When the display provoked comment, Moore "fixed" the problem by going into the window, picking up the book, and reopening it to the spread on male genitalia. The protests ended.

The feminist backlash against mannequin stagings seems to center less on the *manufactured* image of the woman than on the *displayed* one, on things-apparently-done to the female figure. The mannequin is no creature of thrilling flesh for feminists, as it was for the Women's Christian Temperance Union; instead, it has become an object of domination and control. Richard Currier recalled a window in which he had physically joined one mannequin to the next in a grouping by draping them with a signature gold Chanel chain. Angry letter writers perceived his construction in terms of female bondage and even slavery; Currier, however, denied any such intention. His claim is fortified by his consistent declaration that mannequins are not surrogate women but merely "hunks of fiberglass." Binding them with a chain is no more suggestive than stapling related pieces of paper together, Currier insisted; mannequins are simply the props that carry the clothes well, and visually connecting them encourages the viewer to see more of the clothes in a single glance.

Such an attitude must be regarded as at least in part disingenuous. Even granting that Scarangello was innocent of planting the subtext that "the feminists" read into his controversial Barneys scene, it is scarcely credible that he would not have known that a woman in a French maid's uniform is a charged image for contemporary women.

Creating a similar confrontation, Simon Doonan designed a set of Christmas windows for Barneys with a circus theme: one window showed a knife thrower and his female assistant, another included an image of a woman sawed in half. Doonan's flat response to the protests: nonspecific apologies that people were offended, but a firm refusal to change anything, because "these things do happen in the circus, and these windows were about the circus."[39] Both Doonan and his protesters acknowledged that the images were problematic; only the protesters saw no reason to repeat them.

Display directors can get themselves into hot water with their public when they insist that they be allowed to take material from social reality but then demand that their work not be considered in the context of that same reality. When Gene Moore portrayed a bag lady and a wino in a 1983 Tiffany's window, the public reaction was volatile. A *Daily News* reporter found it inexcusable for a luxury store to profit from the depiction of members of an oppressed group; for the public, "the major cause of . . . anger was the contrast between the jewelry in the window and the plight of the homeless woman and wino."[40] Moore removed the clay figures by Robert Keene McKinley from his window tableau, leaving only props: the woman's slippers and the featured necklace. In an interview, Moore suggested that some of the activist groups that joined the bandwagon in protesting the windows may have turned his display into an opportunity to publicize their own issues. He reported receiving a phone call from a protester the morning after he dismantled the display. "You spoiled everything!" the caller reproached him. "We were planning to picket in front of your store with bag ladies, and now we can't do it because she isn't in the window any more!"

In contrast with the truism applied to traditional theatre and filmmaking that a play or movie "succeeds" if the audience is unaware of its having been directed, audiences of window display seem hyperaware of the expressive function of the window, even though the form is art for commerce rather than art for art. Some viewers assume that even "mistakes" are intentional. Bloomingdale's routinely fielded calls during the street theatre years from puzzled passersby wondering, "What does it all mean?" A more critical segment of the audience is happy to furnish the display manager with the benefit of its acute perception; a Doonan Christmas window left one caller "disturbed that one sword was a saber, the other an epée, not a match in the fencing world."[41]

Even early audiences of window display were watchful critics. Sports scenes were particularly prone to criticism from passersby in the know. In 1935, Albert Edward Hammond advised his readers, "Where the figures are placed in positions to represent a given movement in the playing of a game, such as the driving of a golf-ball or handling a bat or fielding in cricket, it is vitally important that no loophole shall be left for criticism."[42]

Relatively early in his career at Tiffany's, Gene Moore began to make a trademark of second-guessing his audience's readiness to second-guess his own rigor. He conducted a test in 1962 to see just how closely viewers observed detail. Moore glued a set of rusty old keys to the plate glass of a window, all but one pointing in the same direction. He got several "helpful" responses, and he began to regularly insert conscious "mistakes" into his windows, insisting that they are a prime category

of what a passerby searches for in a window display: "Someone will notice if a harp's strings are out of order. A harpist or a harpist's daughter will come in, ask for the store manager, and announce the error. People look hard at store windows . . . and since Tiffany's windows are so small, people look at them even more carefully, examine each detail." In her book on Moore's work, Judith Goldman wrote, "The test was soon a trademark: the planned irregularity became a regular occurrence, a way to add drama and invite participation."[43]

Moore has trained his audience to search for the mistake—the one object placed "wrong"—in his abstract designs of kitchen utensils, candy canes, and ice cream cones. In the case of mannequin windows, however, there is not yet a tradition of something being formally askew. Oddities are simply read as bows to surrealism, and to that movement's predilection for alter-

A rare "death window": a dialogue of shrouds by Simon Doonan for Maxfield Bleu. Courtesy of the artist.

A "mistake" window by Moore, 1962. Courtesy of the artist.

ing the female form. Hence, the intention of the display director is presumed to encompass all that is in the window.

Mannequins—even when placed in unaccustomed postures and situations—seem to invite an anthropomorphic projection that whatever they appear to be doing, they *are* doing.[44] Display lore includes a tale of a 1946 Gimbels window that presented a cocktail party scene. Though it was unusual at the time to show mannequins "drinking," when a mannequin fell over in the window, passersby are said to have assumed it was because she was so drunk that she had passed out.

Display directors can be maddeningly or mercurially insistent that what their audience perceives in the window isn't what is there, that what is there is only what the director intended. A window that Moore prepared for Tiffany had a set of holes through which fingers came popping out. He was looking at the display one day when Walter Hoving walked by and said, "Gene, you sure did some dirty windows this time." Moore rejoined immediately, "Mr. Hoving, you sure have a dirty mind."[45]

Often, however, display directors execute only incompletely the image of what they want, so that *no one* ever sees what the display director sees. Michael Southgate of Adel Rootstein was called by an excited Candy Pratts at Bloomingdale's one day to come and see an installation in progress in her favorite, the corner window. He saw a backyard scene centered on a mannequin, posed upside down, with her head in a bucket of water; her soft wig dripped realistically. "What do you think?" Pratts demanded. "She looks like a mad woman trying to commit suicide!" Southgate returned. Pratts corrected him. "What do you mean? She's washing her hair in the garden." To Southgate, Pratts's "enthusiasm for the whole ambiance" of the scene had blinded her to what was actually visible to the audience, "a corpse with rigor mortis that has gone upside down."[46]

Martin Pegler, an industry commentator, writes that the display artist's choice of a mannequin has the power to suggest to a store's passersby, "This is who we are.

This is who we cater to."[47] In exclusive stores, at least, that is the ethos. In stores that depend on less expensive merchandise, display directors often seem to divorce themselves from the first part of Pegler's exemplar and claim higher taste than their patrons: "This may be who *you* are but this certainly isn't who *we* are."[48] Display people are regularly chided by others in the industry for their unwillingness to put aside their high-fashion image when selecting the appropriate mannequin for the store. The snide comment commonly repeated is that every display man thinks he should work with Rootstein mannequins. Robin Lauritano is unusually frank when she describes the Filoso mannequins she inherited from her predecessor at the Canadian boutique Le Château as being "too sophisticated"; Lauritano promptly discarded them.

According to Guy Scarangello of Gucci, specialty stores must be even more careful than department stores about projecting a consistent image. Specialty stores buy fewer types and makes of mannequins, choosing instead to impersonate the store—and its ideal customer —in a type that is quickly defined and always visually accessible.

As a display principle, the need to mirror the customer was acknowledged at least as far back as a 1926 display manual:

Harmony between the wax figures used for window display purposes and the merchandise shown on or in close conjunction with them is essential because the customer is influenced to look upon the model as a replica of herself (or himself), and if it is incongruous or out of keeping, this desired effect is immediately lost. A clothing store, for example, may have secured the highest-grade wax model for a window display of men's wear, but it will make an expensive suit of clothes look cheap and unattractive if the model does not resemble the type of man who is accustomed to wearing such apparel. Similarly, in a women's wear display, if the complexion and type of the wax manikin do not harmonize with the costume, the effect on sales is bound to be depressing.[49]

Advertising had made personalities—or their images—available for consumption since the 1920s: conversational-sounding advertising copy in print and radio advice programs with titles like the "Voice of Experience" and "Your Lover" claimed to help "people cope with a modern, bureaucratized world in which authority and vivid personal relationships had become attenuated."[50]

If the mannequin is indeed the customer's point of identification with the store, sound psychological strategy demands that mannequins reflect their customers in some way. Such mirroring provides the customer with a signal that he or she belongs in the store. A 1985 study by two cognitive psychologists showed that customers' perceptions of a store's suitability to their needs was determined to a large degree by their perception of "who else shops there." The relevant categories, for both men and women, included a perception of a "high class" clientele and a clientele that was the shopper's "type."[51]

Along with the images of its customer and of itself that the store hopes to project, the merchandise itself completes the framework that determines which mannequin should be selected. "What [it] boils down to is taking the time and expending the energies to find out what the merchandise will be, how is it intended to be worn, how will it be worn on the mannequin—how will your customer view it?"[52]

Display directors typically link the composition of a mannequin to the emotional or visceral qualities of the merchandise being marketed. In the 1930s, the new cellophane mannequins were deemed best "for displaying lacy evening clothes, diaphanous lingerie and bathing suits." In the late 1970s, activewear was displayed in lively poses on mannequins that had tanned skin. Sophisticated clothing required mannequins in "quieter" poses with subtle makeup and lighter skintones.[53]

Henry Callahan, in his Saks years, may have been the display director best known for adopting a complementary approach to mannequin selection. According to Scarangello, Callahan believed that there was a one-to-one correspondence between a particular dress design and the mannequin that would best project it. Even now, in a watered-down version of the Callahan ethic, Saks buys certain mannequins that are used only in conjunction with particular designers' lines.

Clyde Matthews, though writing to live fashion models, might just as well be advising the stager of mannequins when he treats presentation as "a means of visualizing merchandise." He urges that "a successful showing of a mode necessitates that you animate your showing with the proper spirit to match the particular garment." Street dresses "should be modeled with an air of casualness and freedom." Sport clothes demand that the model "[slip] in and out of realistic attitudes," which is "merely a matter of play-acting so important to the effectiveness of a model's technique." He advises, "Pretend that you are excited at the thought of engaging in the sport which the costume represents," and suggests that models carry props "such as a beach ball, badminton racquet or skis . . . since it will engender the proper spirit in you and enable the buyer to visualize the ensemble in its sphere of action."[54]

The mannequin that at once conveys the human quality of the garment, embodies the personality of the store, and encapsulates the ideals of the consumer is the realistic mannequin. It is also the mannequin most likely to ignite a competitive instinct in the passerby and to offend those who are sensitive to the reality that is mirrored by that image.

4 Realisms

By actual inquiry, I have found that while the average person cannot tell what makes a figure look natural, the reverse is true when it comes to telling what makes it look unnatural. It is simply that the unnatural part of the figure, no matter what it may be, calls attention to itself, just as a deformity does in real life. The man with two legs walks past unnoticed, but the man with one leg and a crutch catches the eye at once.

—Irwin G. Culver

Irwin Culver was a mannequin manufacturer of the 1920s, when mannequins received their first push to "approximate human beings." But Culver's observations on the natural and the unnatural are perfectly consistent with what mannequin manufacturers today, after decades of accelerated passion for realism, remark: even the most sophisticated clients—industry insiders, that is, not just on-the-street viewers—are more articulate in expressing what is "off " with a figure than in identifying what is "on," what makes it appear so real. Realistic details escape the eye—and evade analysis.

The real is so elusive in part because it replicates the essential anxieties of the very century during which the mannequin has undergone such radical changes in conception and realization. Orvell argues that "a major

shift occurred within the arts and material culture from the late nineteenth century to the twentieth century, a shift from a culture in which the arts of imitation and illusion were valorized to a culture in which the notion of authenticity became of primary value." During this period, "the question of what was 'truthful' [metamorphosed into] the question of what was 'convincing.' "[1] And so the quest for the "real" became the star search for the "realistic."

Realism is no single-faced puppet. Our ideas of what appears most real to us vary with the times, the technology, and our recollections of realisms. And the imperfection and relativism contained in realism are precisely what make it a compelling aesthetic. Mannequin historian Marsha Bentley Hale enumerates the factors that determine the body attitudes of mannequins in a particular time: whether a model is used; the materials available; the sculptor's way of representing the human body commercially; the fashion styles of the period. Changes in the politics, social life, arts, and technology of the culture are other influences.[2] The history of mannequin realism that follows is an attempt to pin down the give and take between successive ideas of what constitutes a believable representation of human presence. It is precisely the imperfections in realism and its relativity that make it a compelling aesthetic.

A History of Female Realisms

Before the 1920s, mannequins were routinely called dummies. Hale believes that the display mannequin evolved from four once-separate types of figures: the dressmaker's form, the lay figure or artist's model, the fashion doll, and wax sculptures.[3] Originating in the mid-eighteenth century, the dressmaker's form was the most significant of these precursors. A "form" is an exact model of a customer's measurements (or, later, in the age of ready-to-wear, of a standardized size), reproduced on a shaped torso that was used to free the customer from fittings. The most celebrated form was that displayed by Count Dunin at the Great Exhibition of London in 1851. Dunin's mechanical figure was composed of seven thousand pieces of steel and copper, connected by sliding metal tubes and wheels that could be made to expand or contract to "represent the deformities or peculiarities of form of any individual." The many articulated parts meant that the form could also adopt virtually any position. Dunin's mechanical mannequin was the ultimate body surrogate for fittings, for it could be used as a tool not just for outfitting one individual but "more especially in cases where great numbers [were] to be provided for, as in the equipment of an army, or providing clothing for a distant colony."[4]

Both Dunin's figure and the more conventional dressmaking forms prevalent during the nineteenth century were prized not for the capacity to represent character or human presence but simply for replicating the measurements of a specific individual in a portable, constantly available form. There is no evidence that in the creation of these figures attention was paid to capturing the likeness of the original model in any way that would have been significant beyond the needs of dressmaking.

Even the response to the needs of dressmaking was limited. Dressmaker's forms were not expected to account for postural idiosyncrasies nor for the effects of motion on the fit of clothing. These were not even values for dressmaking, so they had no place in the construction of models. Dressmaker's forms began to be used to display as well as to construct clothing around

1840, but they were not intended to represent humans, much less particular individuals; they were traditionally presented with white paper cones in place of heads. As ready-to-wear became a more profitable type of manufacture with the opening of the first shirtwaist factory around 1890, dressmaker's forms were pressed into much heavier service as display props.

During this period the general sentiment about using forms to display wares rather than merely to fit them could be summed up in Nicole Parrot's words: "What couldn't be seen didn't need to be beautiful."[5] Dressmaker's forms had been essentially legless and headless torsos, focusing on measurements between the shoulders and hips. Few adaptations were made when these forms began to be used in a display setting. Until around the turn of the century, manufacturers saw no need to sculpt legs underneath the long gowns displayed during the period. Attention went to developing the realism of the "noble parts," the visible aspects of head, neckline, and arms; torsos sat on purely functional spindles.

At the 1894 Paris Exposition, German manufacturers introduced 200-pound wax figures. A far cry from the pure functionality of the headless dressmaker's forms, these figures appropriated as many genuine human features as possible, producing an overall effect alternately described as realistic and grotesque. They sported real human hair, meticulously inserted a few strands at a time into their wax heads. Eyelashes and eyebrows were equally authentic, and teeth were supplied by manufacturers who did business with dentists.

Papier-mâché-headed mannequins at the turn of the century were fitted with "extremely realistic glass eyes." Hale notes that because of the "great contrast between the primitive papier-mâché and the almost frightening realism of the glass eyes, it was as if live people were staring out from behind masks." The principle was taken to the extreme in the era's "Mechanical Olympia" figure, which had movable glass eyes. The strategy was then "considered a catchy way to enhance merchandise display" but has since been abandoned as "too realistic."[6]

Twenty years after the 1894 Exposition, wax mannequins were used in many American display windows, launching a long period of neck-up realism. And where manufacturers' attention focused, so did advertising. During the 1920s, mannequin advertising centered on the figures' superrealistic faces, easily molded in malleable wax. A realistically executed face is the realism boasted of in the "humanized wax figure" advertised in 1920 by the L. A. Feldman Fixture Company. A catalog of wax figures by the premier manufacturer of the day, Pierre Imans, typically showed two versions, side by side, of each of its offerings. On the right-hand page sat or stood the full figure of the mannequin, dressed in the flapper-style costumes of the period and set within a luxurious chamber or on a palatial staircase. The figure rarely faced full front but gazed with a turned chin over a cocked or elongated shoulder. The facing page showed a cameo-style enlargement of the mannequin's face and bust that resembled a portrait of a society figure. It was taken to show both as much of the face as possible to potential admirers and only as much as was flattering to the subject; none of the faces was shown facing flat front.

The face-first realism of the 1920s is attributed by some to the popularity of European waxwork exhibitions, by others to the new silent films.[7] Perhaps the rapidly evolving status and perception of women as they struggled to gain suffrage and entrance to universities helped to center attention on highly focused, portrait-like depictions of the face.

Mannequins were also presented as being capable of portraying emotion. Filene's held a contest for the best title for a window filled with mannequins, each of which was styled to represent a different emotion. Although the mannequins shared the same space, they did not explicitly relate to each other, but sank deeply and separately into thought, concern, and other introspective poses.

The malleability of the wax figures contributed to the evolution of realism as a display value. Wax figures were in many ways decidedly impractical—heavy, cumbersome, and given to melting in the windows. The lucky—and the strong—store owners remembered to move the mannequins before the afternoon sunlight hit. The same impressionability that imperiled these figures, however, made them adaptable to any whim of the display director. The fact that the "ladies would melt [was] a useful trick sometimes, but catastrophic at others. If, for example, you wanted one of the waxen beauties to carry a handbag and she wouldn't, you simply put a lighted match under her hand until you could bend the fingers into handbag-carrying shape." To the extent that the manufacturer left bodily realism to chance, the properties of wax and display men's ingenuity took over. The downside was that constant surveillance was necessary. Irving Eldredge, manager of window display at Macy's, left the New York heat for a week after setting up a window with a glamorous railroad travel theme, complete with "three wax ladies, modishly dressed for traveling in Macy clothes and surrounded by a nice collection of Macy luggage." Returning from his vacation, Eldredge found a far different display, "not the sprightly girls he'd left behind, but three very melancholy ladies. The heat had melted their wax necks, and their heads had dropped of their own weight until they reached the secure resting place of all tired heads."[8]

"Animation" in a turn of the century figure meant simply that it was available in facing-front, right-foot-forward, and left-foot-forward positions, and with a head that looked right, left, or straight on. Realistic figures could be distinguished from the "dummies" of the past by their postural versatility, by the chance that passersby had to see them in many different guises. Interchangeable limbs in different positions became available. Many of these were made of a flexible rubberine, which could be shaped to many different postures and made to grip props; the versatility of the figures was advertised as a way of offsetting their higher cost. The very knowledge that change was possible gave the figures a sense of reality. "Interchangeable arms" were the key feature of a new product on the market in the 1930s, a most adaptable sports figure: "One pair of arms is suitable for use with the figure when employed for showing bathing, ski-ing, or athletic wear; another pair can be used for boxing, wrestling, and punch-ball positions; a third pair for golf and hockey, and single arms for the different pairs can be combined for a tennis position. This figure is one of the most natural yet produced."[9] Shoppers could return to the store to see the same figure in many different stances, activities, and relationships to its setting—that is, "doing" different things. The realism was effective not because the figure looked equally at ease in boxing, swimming, and tennis poses, but because it was essentially the same figure: it "lived."[10]

Once attention was given to the face, personality became associated with the mannequins—a personality that would transcend changes of body pose, or *attitude*. This led to the sense of a character that persisted throughout different poses, attitudes, and activities and was reinforced by the display principle of *repetition*, in which viewers have an opportunity to perceive the same face in different positions in space.

The push toward realism gathered momentum in Paris in the 1920s by centering interest in the mannequin's face. In contrast, by the 1930s, American realism meant that mannequins made reference to a common cultural stock of faces that actually bore little resemblance to the faces of the American consumer: "Most European mannequins came from Austria, France and Germany. They didn't look like American women of any period. Most of them looked Germanic, like the old bisque dolls. Others represented the Austrian, German or French conception of what American women looked like, which was worse."[11] Once realism was seen to center in the face, the natural next step was to choose faces that all could agree were "real," that is, that belonged to someone living: celebrities' faces would be molded onto more or less "standard" bodies. Realism, of course, is a dicey category: even when the faces have been taken from real people, body sizes at Greneker have been, according to Martha Landau, standardized in line with national statistics to make the mannequins easy to order clothing for. Both the head and the body are abstractions in this kind of manufacture. The head is a fragmentation, the body a reflection of a nonexistent "average."

During the 1930s American manufacture developed its own identity under the hallmark of realism, producing such innovative sculptor-manufacturers as Cora Scovil and Lester Gaba. Scovil manufactured the first plaster figures, decreasing the weight of a typical mannequin from two hundred to twenty-five pounds. This kind of practical change—more manageable weight, improved durability, simplification of preparation and maintenance—often enhances the popularity both of a particular mannequin and of mannequins in general during periods when they have fallen from favor.

Scovil's new figures were modeled after famous movie stars; Gaba's were lighthearted caricatures of New York socialites of the day. Both were modeled after real and recognizable people, and were a marked contrast to the "stay-at-home types" they replaced. Gaba presented his realistic mannequins as the great middle road between the "dummies" of the recent past and the "Art mannequins" currently raging through the display industry, and his figures served as a foil for acerbic critiques of the imperfections and artifice of contemporary women. According to a 1933 feature on his first collection of famous mannequins—dubbed the Gaba Girls—the artist had "decided to make them look 'as much as possible like real girls' (and twice as natural!), to strike a compromise, if possible, between lady wooden Indians and Sur-réaliste clothes-horses." In the author's estimation, the realness of the Gaba Girls depended on their believable skin tone and texture, their easy postures, and perhaps most of all, "how little Mr. Gaba relied on conventional prettiness—for the features are as irregular as your cousin Helen's."[12]

The writer missed no chance to quip about the unrealistic aspects of Gaba's craft: "The eyes have intelligent expressions (even Mr. Gaba must occasionally sacrifice realism to Art)." Another writer picked up on Gaba's proud trick of making one of Cynthia's feet a half size larger than the other, "a not abnormal human difference."[13]

Display people also got their jibes in, not at the mannequins, but at the self-manufacture of the live women whom they were to copy. For some years display people seized every opportunity to point out that while mannequins may look fake, live women don't exactly rise whole on the seafoam. In 1926, William Nelson Taft wrote in the makeup section of his display manual that "the lips should, of course, be made sufficiently dark, to appear natural—or, in the case of women's heads, as unnatural as many in life actually appear."

A 1946 *Saturday Evening Post* article treated Gaba's creation of Cynthia as the "impetus to the era of realism," as indeed it may have been in America. Cynthia was praised for her realistic hands, arms, eyes, and ears, for the wealth of "quite lovably tangible" features she displayed. Yet it is doubtful that this attention to Cynthia's "noble parts," and the desire to imbue her with such a distinctive personality, could have happened as quickly without the prior example of the French Pierre Imans mannequins, with their attention to capturing detail and mood in the face. As manufacturer Katherine Keller Stubergh recalled, "Everyone in the display business aspired to equal the Imans figures."[14]

Some critics hold up mannequins, like fashion, as mirrors of the social and economic worlds. Under this view, mannequins are "realistic" insofar as they reflect either experienced or perceived realities of a given period. During World War II, for example, mannequins were made shorter, the length being taken out of the legs—not because women had shrunk but because of materials rationing. Clothing of the period was also restricted in yardage and trimmings to save on fabric that might be needed overseas. After the war Mayorga Mannequins premiered a collection of "Welcome Home Mannequins": the female and male held their arms outstretched toward each other, while a small girl looked up eagerly toward her "father."

Hale is particularly interested in the relation between society's beauty ideals throughout the twentieth century and the reflection of these ideals in mannequins' bodies and faces. Other writers endorse her observation that there may be a relation between the social and economic experience of the time and the look of "realistic" figures. A writer for *Fortune* noted that during the Depression, figures had come down a notch from the "elegant or snooty" expressions of the 1920s to wear more informal clothes; the most attractive look one could hope for was "pert" or "gamine."[15]

Nicole Parrot registered the wide array of social types that were portrayed in mannequins before World War II, when sculptors "established a portrait of the society of their age." Many are types we would chafe to see in our own time: "Buxom Bertille—size 46—smiling and elegant in spite of her curves, stood arm-in-arm with a flat adolescent while pigeon-toed children ran around between them. A proud beer drinker, with a bald head and a pot belly conversed with a cheeky urchin in a cap and well-brilliantined sideburns. Young, old, fat, thin, monocled aristocrats, sporting types, were all to be found in shop-windows. . . . Aggressivity, wit, charm and vanity are all cast in wax and found suitable to present muslin dresses or tweed suits with gaiters." Any social type that one might reasonably expect to see in the store or on the streets outside it was a fit subject for a mannequin. In the 1940s the tradition of social realism was carried on in a modified form by Mary Brosnan's firm, whose mannequins were designed by Brosnan herself and her sculptor Kay Sullivan. Brosnan's mannequins were modeled from specific people but generalized to represent broad social types. Brosnan might "use a debutante or a college girl or a Croton matron, take liberties with her in clay and come up with something which might be any debutante, college girl, or suburban matron."[16]

During the 1970s display artist Bob Currie consciously patterned some of his mannequin stylings in the windows of Henri Bendel after some of his customers and told of a circular pattern of influence between the images he created and the customers who had inspired them. Currie recalled wrapping the heads of his window mannequins in cloth, more as a propping than as a costuming idea. Customers poured into the store, wanting to buy the innovative turbans they had seen in the window. Currie was ordered to design some—quickly—for sale.

In a colorful variation on the customer-reflection theme, the owner of a prominent Fifth Avenue boutique called Martha repeatedly ordered custom wigs from D. G. Williams modeled on her own hair. The manufacturer Edward T. Cranston recalled that Martha would spend a good deal of time selecting the mannequins she wanted, and then hand him an envelope filled with a lock of her hair: "So, we made all the wigs the color blonde she happened to be at that period." (Martha was later criticized by designer Bill Blass for the "floozy blonde wigs" she had placed on the mannequins.) Realism in Martha's case meant that the store's patrons could buy not the image of the tasteful customers but (a copy of) a piece of the glamorous owner.

If social realism breaks through the physical borders of neck-up realism, a third brand of realism strives for shock through anatomical realism, particularly in body parts about which tappable social sensitivity persists. Gene Moore claims credit for giving mannequins distinct navels. Many manufacturers have jumped to claim the introduction of nipples as their own innovation. That anatomically correct innovation has encountered particular resistance in stores, some of which have filed down or—a longtime model's trick—concealed with Band-Aids the nipples of mannequins manufactured in an indecently explicit state. Pucci's "Man of the '90s" mannequin was so unambiguous genitally that when its picture appeared in magazines or on television, the proverbial fig leaf had always to be in place. This "descriptive" male mannequin was a new kind of shock, for most anatomic breakthroughs had involved increasingly graphic female mannequins. Nevertheless, some viewers clearly prefer an absolutely faithful reproduction of all external body parts on the mannequin, even though they can't be reshaped, tucked, or otherwise molded in the layering on of clothes. Dominique Autié is only one

of many writers to complain that mannequins do not have "real" genitalia.

Jean-Pierre Darnat included tongues in his Darnat Girls in the late 1940s. Other open-mouthed mannequins have yawned, laughed, grinned—but this particular variety of caught-in-the-moment realism is relatively rare. Manufacturers have time and again tried (and usually failed) to make girlish freckles or a manly stubble look like something other than acne in an immobile face.

With the development and refinement of plastics technology in the late 1940s and 1950s, much more detailed sculpting was made possible. Paradoxically, during the immediate postwar years the pursuit of realism seemed to be at an all-time low. Gender differences had always existed in mannequin design, but certain periods have highlighted those differences far above others—and far above other bases for differentiation. During the 1950s, male and female mannequins were as polarized as Tarzan and Jane. Female mannequins had "tightly pinched waists, full hips and brazenly thrusting bust, while the 'Tarzan look' . . . was popular for males—'athletic men with V-shaped silhouettes, hair combed back in slight disarray.'"[17] Martha Landau recalled that the mannequins that Greneker made in that decade, when Gene Moore was the company's chief idea man, were so beautiful, so exaggeratedly "feminine," that they were intimidating. Far from trying to copy exactly the features of the live model, sculptors selected only those features that corresponded to their visions of perfection. Model of the day Suzy Parker was pretty enough to be made into a mannequin—except for the mole on her face. The features of other models were chiseled down, omitting freckles, regularizing nose shape, and smoothing other imperfections. In Landau's words, the mannequins of the 1950s were "too perfect to be human." Gene Moore, however, prefers those mannequins' poses to the posturings of the 1990s: "They looked like ladies, instead of ladies being tramps or tramps being ladies, [like] today."[18]

In a reversal of realistic design, people were styled in

the 1950s to look like mannequins—and mannequins deemed realistic were those that looked like models who happened to look like mannequins. After 1947, when Christian Dior introduced his ultrafeminine, full-skirted New Look, "live models appeared to emulate mannequins rather than the reverse. With 'wasp' waists and emphasized busts [and padded hips], they took on mechanical poses similar to plastic dolls with rounded shoulders."[19]

After the war, figure shapes were sturdily homogeneous. To achieve a half-size look, display people stuffed wadded tissue paper in the bust and hips of a size-12 mannequin and drew smile lines on the face with a gray eyebrow pencil. The notion that the normative size was a thin woman's and all others mere modifications of it proved long-lasting. When Landau tried in 1973 to persuade Maury Wolf, head of the merged

From an eight-window series by Gene Moore, "The Making of a Mannequin." Courtesy of the artist.

Wolf & Vine/Greneker, to manufacture half-size mannequins for the large market that existed for them, he responded, "Inside every fat woman is a thin woman trying to get out."

Since the late 1970s half-size figures have found a secure place in the market, yet much of the 1950s ethic endures. Although half-size, petite, older, and ethnic mannequins have become common, they are almost always stylized as a compromise with the dominant aesthetic—tall, thin, evenly proportioned, and whitened. Half-size mannequins by Greneker are "what every large girl would like to be: beautifully proportioned." Petites are universally several inches taller than the women for whom they were designed to show clothes, because "clothes simply look better on taller figures."[20]

In the early 1950s Gene Moore had expressed at least one wish for realistic display, that mannequins might one day "be made to stand without the aid of a rod and base." That advance arrived during the 1960s, helping to provide renewed momentum for the realistic mannequin. Manufacturer Robert Filoso said that the mannequin "became a real person." The watershed event was Adel Rootstein's manufacture in 1966 of the Twiggy mannequin. Possessed of an instinct for choosing models just before they become international stars, Rootstein captured Twiggy in fiberglass and introduced her to an international public just as the live model became prominent on the British, French, and New York modeling scenes.

Twiggy had a gawky, 5-foot-4-inch, flat-chested, size-6 figure: the choice of her body type—as a clearly radical alternative to the poised, more filled-out woman just preceding—was one shock, and one key to the impact of the mannequin: "As the Beatles were to music and Churchill was to politics, Twiggy was to fashion."[21] Her age and status contributed further to the appeal: the mannequin, like the seventeen-year-old live model, was a coltish adolescent, not a mature high-society woman. A final jolt came from the type of poses that Rootstein chose for the mannequin line. Twiggy stood

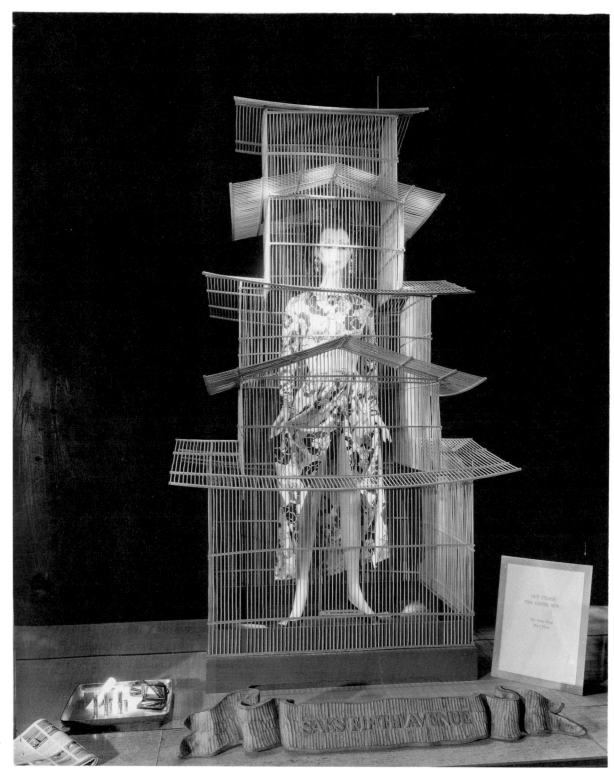

Window showing all too clearly the exoticized, marginal status of ethnic figures in high-fashion windows. Photo by Nick Malan Studios. Courtesy of Saks Fifth Avenue.

The young Twiggy, with her revolutionary mannequins, 1967. Courtesy of Adel Rootstein (USA).

with her knees and toes turned inward, chin pushed forward, and hands balanced protectively against her thighs; as the manufacturer put it, "Twiggy never stood erect and no mannequin has stood erect since."[22]

Rootstein's next mannequin after Twiggy became almost as famous in display history. This was Donyale Luna, in the manufacturer's words, "a coloured New York model whose sinuous prowl and extraordinary long-fingered gestures made her the most sought-after catwalk model in Paris—and an electrifying presence in a shop window: she also happens to be the first black mannequin." Luna, perhaps even more than Twiggy, ignited a revolution in poses, set as she was "in a seductive 'feline' stance."[23] Most of Luna's poses showed the

Luna. Courtesy of Adel Rootstein (USA).

mannequin, weight forward, as if preparing to pounce or landing after a long backward jump. All of Luna's poses came with exceedingly articulated, almost claw-like fingers.

Contrary to Rootstein's boast, Luna was not the first black mannequin, but people of color had typically been represented by white figures—with the facial features of white women—whose surface had been altered to resemble Asian, Hispanic, or black skin. A far-seeing Lester Gaba may have created for a Harlem store in 1938 the first mannequin not only with black skin but also with black features, after the store's owner had "complained to [him] that there were no real Negro type mannequins available." The omission of this innovation in most visual merchandising histories reflects both the contemporary unpopularity of Gaba's design and the industry's almost universal acceptance of Rootstein's claim of priority. In a 1980 letter to the editor of the *New York Times*, Gaba conceded that "unfortunately, there was little demand for these ethnic models, and they were dropped from the line—although I think Bergdorf Goodman bought one, which appeared in its windows briefly." Greneker claims a 1962 black mannequin, and display historian Robert Hoskins maintained that a later Rootstein mannequin, "Toukie Smith," which was issued in 1973, was the first to have truly black features.

But Luna was, at any rate, the first widely recognized black mannequin, and her manufacture prompted several other companies to follow suit. In 1968, Decter issued a collection of eighteen black mannequins, "all with Negroid features, including high cheekbones and broad noses."[24] At first, many people found Luna inaccessible. A British newspaper complained:

> In any shade she's a rangy emaciated six footer with a tiny head, hands like trailing willow branches, legs that go on for ever and about as far removed from us low-bottomed British pear shapes as Escalope de Veau au Fenouil is from roast beef.
>
> Is it merchandising madness? Have clothes become so weird that only weirdies look good in them?[25]

Billed in Detroit, ca. 1935, as "The World's Premiere Showing of the First All-Colored Mannequin." Courtesy of the Mannequin Museum archive.

And some white women had a difficult time imagining why they might want to look at black mannequins. Said a 32-year-old typist from Blackpool, "Colour bar or or no colour bar, no white woman in the world wants to identify herself with a black girl."

Contrary to expectation, black mannequins never quite caught on, even in many black neighborhoods. Martin Pegler offered an explanation:

> Fortunately, high-fashion is color-blind when it comes to the color of the mannequin. . . . However, in some merchandising communities—in the Midwest and parts of the South, a black or oriental might not create the desired store image of catering to high-fashion. In some areas a black is a black and an oriental is an oriental and fashion be damned. In other communities—the black shopper may not relate to this ultra sleek, ultra polished black lady in the window. She just isn't her kind of people—she's just in black make-up. Even when you use ethnic mannequins you must consider, again as always, whom are you selling to—and what does she see herself as.

One solution was to experiment with abstract mannequins, the "neutral carriers of glad fashion tidings, . . . the three dimensional backgrounds for the merchandise without any political, racial or religious axes to grind."[26]

The "real people phenomenon" hit the live modeling world during the same years, and character models were routinely used to sell products. By the mid-1960s, "advertising agencies discovered to their apparent surprise that humor could sell their clients' products—everything from beer, cereal, and toothpaste to banks and insurance, and then found out that this humor produced even greater results when it was delivered by 'real people' faces with whom the consumer could identify."[27] These so-called real people were actually character types: professional models who posed as if they were not. In time, this phenomenon may be responsible for the use of actual real people—that is, nonprofessionals—as models. Esprit photographed its own employees and their families wearing the new line for its 1985–86 catalog. The Gap has made the use of real people a consistent feature of its advertising. In 1972 Macy's, Gimbels, and Ohrbach's co-sponsored a fashion show for which each store promised to supply ten nonprofessional models. Fashion designers who weren't willing to take that risk continued to cast professional models in the roles of real people (placed within a glamorous international setting), an effect critic Kennedy Fraser found "strangely jarring."[28]

A renewed clamor for broader representation, of age groups as well as ethnic groups, began in the 1970s after a period of strict idealization. The impulse is part of the mimic-the-customer aesthetic of realism—and a function of retail's need to stay afloat in difficult times. In 1988 Robert Filoso issued "Classic Drama," which he claimed to be the first line of mannequins that depict older women (that is, ages 42–48). He said, in deference to market needs, "After all, it is the baby boomer or older age group that women's designer fashion is really intended for . . . the women who have the style and the drama and the money to carry the designer look off very, very well."[29]

One of the most potent experiences of Martha Landau's career was her first sighting of the "Contessa" mannequin, designed by Henry Callahan, in a Lord & Taylor window in 1972: "This was the first step . . . away from the beautiful, disdainful, don't-touch-me gorgeous creatures that we had been doing. First of all, she wasn't a be-bopper—she was a woman in her mid-thirties. And she had this marvelous bump on her nose." Landau, who had been working in the mannequin industry for seventeen years, called the Contessa the first mannequin she had ever seen that "looked like a human being."

Adel Rootstein strove to make her mannequins more reflective of a street reality than had previously been available in the industry. She said, "I wanted to make mannequins relate more to fashion photography and journalism because fashion was coming off the streets, as opposed to coming down from aristocracy."[30] Ralph Pucci said that when he joined the mannequin company

A 1970 window featuring a black mannequin, spot-lighted and placed at an extreme edge of the composition. Photo by Nick Malan Studios. Courtesy of Saks Fifth Avenue.

The mature woman's mannequin, "Classic Drama," designed and produced by Robert Filoso. Collection of author.

his father had started and began developing his own ideas for mannequin collections in 1976, he wanted to draw his ideas directly from what was happening on the street: the athleticism and the expanding interest in and availability of designer clothing for men.

Twiggy and Luna paved the way for the most contemporary trend in realism, founded on the notion that the whole figure—not merely the "noble parts," or even each part rendered with strict anatomical fidelity—must convey a feeling of overwhelming reality, convincing spectators for at least one dizzying second that they may be standing next to a real person. This illusion would be achieved by suggesting movement through pose and through the display artist's staging of the mannequin in a way that felt "real": Did the mannequin stand in a pose that made physical sense to the viewer? Would someone stand that way wearing that type of clothing?

And yet this brand of realism also pushed the boundaries of "natural" behavior: the more outrageous, extended, unambiguous the pose, the more "realistic" it was taken to be, even though few people might adopt these extreme poses.[31] One journalist wrote in 1981, "Super-realism is the catchword of the business today. And though they would deny it, those in the trade go to great lengths to ensure that their showroom displays elicit involuntary exclamations of shock and disbelief among their clients. To them, such comments as, 'but they look so *real!*' mean that they have succeeded." Dominique Autié wrote of a desire on the part of the manufacturer "to confound" the viewer. The realistic mode in mannequin design might be likened to taxidermy; Donna Haraway pointed out the aspects of enchantment that are inherent in this essentially realistic mode of representation: "The power of this stance is in its magical effects: what is so painfully constructed appears effortlessly, spontaneously found, discovered, simply there if one will only look. Realism does not appear to be a point of view, but appears as a 'peephole into the jungle' where peace may be witnessed. Epiphany comes as a gift, not as the fruit of merit and toil, soiled

by the hand of man. Realistic art at its most deeply magical issues in revelation."[32] Paradoxically, when a mannequin looks "real," it looks not like what it is, but like a living person.

As brands of realism come and go, innovators attempt to discover what kinds of anatomy, posture, and body attitude could look as convincing in a still figure as in a living one. In 1906, Baum wrote that "ease is the keynote of artistic posing. The figure must first of all have an appearance of absolute repose. If it has that it cannot help being both natural and graceful. Of course there are many striking positions that are full of grace and perfectly natural, but it must be remembered that with the human figure these attitudes are not sustained. They are spontaneous." Stillness had to look intentional on the part of the figure and be part of a natural position to look "real." As Erving Goffman pointed out in *Gender Advertisements*, it looks natural to be still in a naturally still position, like "sleeping, pensive poses, window shopping, and importantly, the off-angle fixed looks through which we are taken to convey our overall alignment to what another person—one not looking at us directly—is saying or doing."

Much of the contemporary perception of reality comes from the sense that the still mannequin could take off at any moment into movement. In the Rootstein mannequins, this quality is best conveyed by muscle definition, by the easily apparent body sense, from looking at a taut knee or a straining shoulder, that the figure could shift its weight or change its position. In the Rootstein era, the highest form of realism has become the exact duplication of a human model. Rootstein may be responsible for the trademark advertising motif of featuring the live model alongside "her" mannequin; the object is to confound the viewer, at least temporarily, to make her wonder which of the two is the model, which the mannequin—and upon discovery, to wonder why she hadn't known all along. Filoso and Pucci profit from a similar advertising gambit: a mannequin is marketed as a faithful reproduction of a well-known model and is named—often, by both first

Dance-inspired mannequin from Pucci's series "Mysteries of Motion." Courtesy of the manufacturer.

A mannequin in suitable repose, 1958. Photo by Nick Malan Studios. Courtesy of Saks Fifth Avenue.

and last names, such as Pucci's "Aly Dunn"—after its live inspiration.

Adel Rootstein's mannequins are a far cry from historical figures who *could be* people—any people. They *are* people, existing ones. Although she sometimes used people off the street, the British manufacturer expressed a penchant for models who "influence fashion" in some way—though she declined to approach Princess Diana, who Rootstein felt would be a choice in poor taste. As the display man Dan Arjé put it, a Rootstein male mannequin is "not just a handsome, Arrow collar face: [he has] character, individuality . . . [He looks] like *somebody*."

Although both Rootstein and Filoso advertised an identity between model and mannequin, they departed from their live models in distinctive ways. Robert Filoso was interested in the "pretty" aspects, the softer features, of the faces he sculpted. He was quite selective of the details in his representation of a face and readily admitted, "I pick the *nice* things out." Manufacturer Ralph Oestricher of D. G. Williams similarly boasts both of the precise duplication of his model and of the mannequin's improved qualities: "Our sculptor not only captures the facial features of a specific fashion model, but our make-up artists duplicate her make-up exactly as she wears it. Often, with subtle changes invisible to the untrained eye, we find ourselves with cosmetically improved mannequins that look more glamorous than their real life counterparts."[33]

And the Rootstein mannequin, despite its industry reputation, is likewise a representation of selective reality. Creative director Michael Southgate maintains that many aspects of the original model are omitted or altered in order to produce the perfect mannequin. The company always strives for realism but sometimes must take a step backward because a particular feature, although an accurate reproduction of the original, doesn't make for a "glamorous figure." According to Southgate, "A figure is more like fashion photography than a real person: in fashion photography, the things you don't want to see somehow get glossed out, and that's really

what you're aiming at with a mannequin—things like imperfections in skin, even freckles, the little fine lines around the eyes which are perfectly normal, perfectly natural, but once it's there in fiberglass it becomes unattractive. Don't ask me why."

Southgate tells of the scenes he habitually plays out with corporate customers who scan the figures in the showroom and say, "Well, they're very nice, but we don't have any customers who look like that." Invariably, Southgate replies, "Who the hell wants mannequins who look like the customers? Have you *looked at* the customers?" For Southgate, accessibility is a trade-off for glamour: the kind of accessible, touchable beauty that many women long for would result in a mannequin that no one wanted to look like.

Paradoxically, fantasy plays an important role for the company that is best known for its realistic figures. Southgate muses, "Credibility can only go so far. And it isn't a con job: it's what's acceptable. Human beings—and now I'm getting a bit philosophical—are fascinated by stylized images of themselves—from as long as the beginning of time. Greek sculpture is not 'real.' Rubens' fat ladies are not 'real': they don't have any veins or cellulite. Everything is stylized. . . . People like dolls from the time they're children; they're brainwashed with dolls. We love glamorized images of ourselves." For Southgate even a runway model is not real, because she gears her attitude, movement style, even the tautness of her leg muscles for effect. For Rootstein's Nellie Fink, going beyond realism gives the viewer an opportunity to become part of the picture: "You must create a fantasy that makes the viewer want to be a part of it. And after all, isn't fantasy what we're all looking for?"[34]

As Rootstein staff members point out, a figure must depart from the living model to convey the impression of realism. Otherwise manufacturers would simply cast the model from life rather than expend the effort and money to chisel out an inevitably less accurate likeness. And life casting does in fact play a role in mannequin manufacture. Lloyd Squiers, a sculptor for Greneker, regularly calls his girlfriend into the studio to cast her

An anatomical shot from Rootstein's 1990 brochure for "Violetta," showing the naturalness possible when a still pose is selected (same mannequin as on page 50). Courtesy of the manufacturer.

"Muscular realism" in this mannequin series entitled "Intuition." Courtesy of Hindsgaul Worldwide.

Semirealistic mannequin head. Courtesy of Greneker Mannequins.

slender, graceful hands for a new mannequin line. Casting of feet is also a fairly common industry practice. In the 1940s, Lillian Greneker cast faces by "placing an extremely lightweight plastic material on the face of a living model. The plastic is so fluid that the subject is able to smile while her likeness is being caught by a camera. After retouching, the plastic mold is superimposed on a paper model with a resulting manikin head that bears considerable fidelity to the original subject." In a further refinement, Greneker developed a technique whereby photography and sculpture were combined in order to achieve the most realistic effect: "I started by having girls come in and we'd sculpt their heads. But this didn't work. You just can't paint sculpture. Now we're really backing up a photograph instead of painting a piece of sculpture. We make a life cast of the girl's face, then photograph her and print the photograph on the fabric which is the mold of her face."[35] In general, however, the techniques that have been used to cast whole bodies, or even faces, have been found to produce unattractive results. Paul Wolff of Decter Mannequins describes the difficulties in the company's experiments with casting a model's face directly: "You have a problem in that if you lay the heads back or forward to make the cast, all the muscles either go back or forward because of gravity. It's not a realistic look."[36]

Southgate maintains further that viewers' prior experience of mannequins leaves them easily convinced that a stylized figure is realistic. These same viewers would be shocked (and dissatisfied) to see a George Segal-like casting-cum-sculpture in a window in place of a realistic mannequin. The balance between the real and the fantastic is an almost impossibly delicate one.

Real Men

The history of the male mannequin consists of a protracted series of dismal embarrassments to the industry, largely the result, it appears, of male discomfort with even an idealized version of the male form's being regarded as an object of display. An article about the

Photo of direct body casting, published in The Detroit News, *ca. 1930s. Courtesy of the Mannequin Museum archive.*

new, sexy displays in the late 1970s discussed how display directors could avoid discomfiting their customers in other than profitable ways, at the same time advising how displays might be adjusted in case of a problem with customer or passerby response. Anticipating trouble, one New York boutique showed a men's "sensuous silk robe" on a female mannequin instead, posed in a suggestive bedroom setting. The owner feared that some men might be "insecure" about wearing such a garment and reasoned, "What could be more seductive than a woman in a sexy tunic draped over black satin sheets?"[37]

Underneath that apprehension probably lay another: the garment would not sell if it were displayed on a male mannequin. A man who would hesitate to wear such a soft garment for fear that his masculinity might be called into question would also be sensitive to the biggest problem realistic male mannequins have in selling clothes: they strike most viewers as effeminate. Southgate has remarked that no position is tolerable to

male viewers, who are skeptical of both of the masculinity and the realism of the poses: "If his hand is on his hip, they say men don't stand with their hands on their hips." Boys are subject to the same fears: E. Stephen Barker urged display artists to "find manikins for younger boys that also have an athletic appearance, for a 'sissy' look will turn off this group."[38]

Customers have had reservations about the realistic male figure throughout display history. "Selling the males is much harder," Southgate observes. "You can sell 500 female mannequins to a store, with no problem. But you deliver ten males, and everyone from the managing director down to the elevator operator has something to say about them. 'This one looks like a rapist.' 'This one is a murderer.' 'This one is a fag.'"[39] Whether a criminal or—the much more common (and no less freighted) perception—a homosexual, the image of the male mannequin almost always repels the intended audience. Barker wrote that the presentation of merchandise on realistic figures elicits a response in the viewer that is all about his or her own lovability: "They work because the customer looks at the presentation and says to herself, 'That's me! . . . I can look like that. . . . I want to look like that because if I do, I'll be loved!'" Barker's assessment may help to explain the power that the fear of effeminacy has for male viewers of realistic male mannequins; lovable, effeminate men appear to be loved not by women, but by other men. Perhaps this is why, when male mannequins made their appearance in display windows in the 1930s, they were grouped in vast numbers, sometimes thirty or more in a bank of windows: a group of male figures may have been calculated to send a stronger message of rugged male camaraderie and to be less threatening than a single figure.

Men's stores have traditionally used headless dressmaker's forms to show off the merchandise. Without heads or discernible personalities, forms gave off an aura of good tailoring and respectability, and seemed more appropriately humble, tastefully indifferent to their appearance. Forms are still the dominant means of displaying men's clothing.

*Pierre Imans early male
mannequin. Courtesy of
the Mannequin Museum
archive.*

and Show Window inquired informally why male mannequins had taken so long to be accepted; the consensus was that few mannequins "symbolize[d] in appearance at least the he-man type of the modern, well dressed American."

For the male American public, the representation of masculinity was a critical feature of realism. Wax mannequins that were imported from Europe in the 1930s—unlike most fiberglass mannequins today—were anatomically correct and were sized "small," "medium," and "American," according to the size of the genitalia. Normative bodies had to be self-consciously masculine, though figures regarded as comical variations from the norm were less closely identified with rugged masculinity. According to Hammond, "Expression as well as pose often needs to be considered in relation to the merchandise: for example, the figure for sports wear should generally have a conspicuously masculine expression, while the 'outsize' figure is more natural if the facial expression is jovial rather than intellectual."[40]

Between World War II and the late 1970s, male mannequins suffered a spell of particular disfavor: "The only place you saw the full male figure mannequin was in a seedy, run down 'Rent-a-Tux' operation where some slick haired, mustachio-ed gigolo from the thirties stood in frozen astonishment—over-dressed in ruffles and brocades. . . . The full mannequin was out of favor because it was too pretty—too soft in pose or too rigid in bearing. . . . If the pose was 'manly'—it also meant it was awkward and stiff, and if the pose was relaxed—the figure appeared too limp and dainty."[41] According to Martin Pegler, male mannequins during this long stretch were just as "pretty and aloof" as the female figures, making them death to sales.

During the late 1960s and the 1970s, when the portrayal of women in fashion photography continually extended its boundaries, men's modeling remained codified and stiff. Francine Marlowe outlined the four basic types of characters a male model might play in print work:

The unpopularity of men's mannequins may be attributed in part to the problems of reproducing fairly and accurately a man's features in a form that is not supposed to look posed or made up. Albert Edward Hammond observed in his 1935 book *Men's Wear Display* that "it is of only comparatively recent years that wax figures have been brought into general use in men's wear shop windows." In the same year Cora Scovil introduced her movie-star mannequins, a striking contrast with the more homely models that had preceded them, and helped to break the "57th Street Tradition" against full, headed mannequins: Bonwit Teller bought six of Scovil's figures. In 1937, the *Merchant's Record*

1. The Elegant Sophisticate "has pronounced cheekbones (in fact, he has a collection of fine, aristocratic-looking bones from head to toe) and a self-assured air that can, when the camera demands it, border on the arrogant."
2. The Rugged Outdoor Man "is superrugged, with broad shoulders, a broad brow, and a look of strength mixed with sincerity. One glance and you feel he was born to ride a horse."
3. The Juvenile, "wholesome-looking, well-scrubbed, with a ready smile, he's the All-American boy next door, or the eager young fellow starting his first job." The Juvenile may grow into the roles of either Elegant Sophisticate or Rugged Outdoor Man.
4. The Character, the interesting face that doesn't fit into any of the previous categories: "What makes a character a Character type is the fact that he looks like the public's idea of the so-called common man." The Character model deals in exaggerations and contrasts: "If he is short, he may have a photo of himself [in his portfolio] alongside an extremely tall, leggy girl."[42]

The character of the male model is established in part by how he is staged, the type of clothing he wears, the pose he assumes, the props and environment of the scene, the social world he is placed within, and the style of the photograph. The Elegant Sophisticate is usually staged to show "how trim and supple he is," while the Rugged Outdoor Man is presented in action shots that show off "his powerful physique." The type in turn reflects back on the merchandise, showing the potential consumer what kind of person would wear that garment or use that object. Deviations from these strictly mythologized forms spell threats to the image of masculinity and hence to salability.

When superrealism dominated the manufacture of female mannequins, particularly during the late 1970s, men's mannequins followed suit—and did worse than ever. Some manufacturers added chest and even underarm hair to the mannequins, as well as mustaches; others tried using glass eyes again. And Adel Rootstein

went out of its way to use nonprofessional male models, "say, a mechanic or an electrician," to produce an image that would have more appeal to the American market.[43]

Richard Currier finds that the more "real" one tries to make a realistic male, the more "like a mannequin" it looks, whereas a female mannequin looks "real" the more one messes with its hair and makeup. With male mannequins, "you can never make them stand the way *men* stand; you can't." In this regard, male mannequins mimicked poor taxidermy, in Donna Haraway's words, a form of "upholstered death."

Starting with "Workout," Ralph Pucci's line of active figures introduced in 1978, most designers have tried to keep male mannequins from seeming effeminate by making them look athletic, much the way Ted Shawn had beefed up the image of men in dance four decades earlier. That strategy won Pucci a reputation as the first contemporary manufacturer to treat male mannequins as "real people."[44] Pucci's athletes suggest the boxing–vaulting–tennis playing figures of three decades earlier filtered through the whole-body aesthetic introduced by Rootstein: athletic activity is enjoyed by whole bodies and selves, not merely by tightened forearms.

When display artists wanted more versatile masculine figures that could be used to display merchandise other than active sportswear, Pucci developed "Varsity," a collection of mannequins in relaxed, after-sport positions; the poses and moods of the figures suggested activity just completed, rather than asserting themselves, as did the athletic figures, in the midst of such activity. Pucci maintained, "We own the fashion men, as Adel Rootstein owns the fashion women."[45] These athletic males that gave the Pucci company financial and creative credibility were not strictly realistic mannequins but rather "semirealistics," as the industry dubs them: they had sculpted hair rather than wearing a wig, and in most cases they wore no makeup. Each mannequin, a sculptural or architectural version of a human form, had a "real body, but sprayed-out colors, to tie in to the decor of the shops." Bright primaries, or black or white

Handstanding mannequins from the "Workout" series, which also included mannequins in diving, jogging, vaulting, and bicycling poses. Courtesy of Pucci.

stone finishes, were common, rendering the Pucci mannequins in some ways *less* realistic than the athletic mannequins of thirty years earlier.

Disco may have contributed to consumers' increased comfort in the 1980s with softer, more graceful, and even vulnerable male bodies in mannequins. Martin Pegler observes that the mannequins of 1978 no longer had to conform to the "bruiser or jock" image; they had become "finer scaled and more graceful in a continental sort of way. The disco-oriented male shopper can relate to the slender young man in the window who wears a scarf with flair and casually drapes a jacket over his shoulders."[46] The unisex look of the early 1970s also helped soften the rigid masculinity-femininity barrier. "Maleness" was "reconstituted" so that the essential dichotomies that had previously assigned men to one side and women to the other—primitive/cultured, natural/spiritual, unclothed/clothed, vulnerable/controlled, subordinate/dominant—became more porously bounded in fashion photography of the 1980s.[47] Late in that decade Rootstein introduced "Ross," a figure, as the company press release reported, that

> turns its back on brawn and looks forward to an age of new values—to an era where men are men without having to prove it and machismo is a bygone word.
>
> Abandoning the hustle and bustle of the eighties, the new "soft man" looks ahead to a more suave and sophisticated decade. Men are elegant and refined—the biceps have been replaced by the brain.
>
> The collection [comprises] four new poses created around two men—Tristram and Tom—reflecting contemplatively on the successes and failures of the past decade. . . .
>
> Ross is the thinking man's collection.

The celebrated 1990 Lowell Nesbitt Collection male mannequins—a group of brawny and explicit poses styled after classical and hypermasculine Greco-Roman sculpture—were more popular as art pieces in stores than as dressable mannequins, suggesting that a figure is more acceptable if it is presented as art rather than as a realistic depiction of a live man. Realism may need to be abstracted for certain male audiences. Jim Mansour of The Limited ordered a couple of hundred Nesbitts shattered specially at the manufacturer's—limbs severed from the torsos, faces smashed—to enhance the illusion that they were art-historical ruins.

Even contemporary Rootstein mannequins vary between male and female figures in the level of realistic sculptural detail and definition: though female and male hands may take the same positions, female fingers are more articulated and separated, perhaps reflecting the cultural stereotype that hypermasculine upper body movement emanates more from the shoulder and elbow than from the smaller joints of wrist and fingers.

For some industry commentators, the trouble with male mannequins can be traced to a nagging conservatism with poses, particularly in an era in which poses serve to suggest movement. For sculptor Tanya Ragir, "sculpting male mannequins is the most difficult. There's a real problem with the notion that a man who moves is effeminate. So a male mannequin is going to sit with his legs spread and his fists—lots of fists—closed. The most you get [in terms of touching male mannequins] is hands over the shoulder. There's so little you can do. . . . With a woman you can do anything. With men, you start swinging a hip or shifting a rib cage, and pretty soon it's considered effeminate."[48] These restrictions are in part a reflection of a common perception that showing clothing, modeling, and being looked at are women's jobs. Model Rod McCray believes that runway work for a male model entails less "showing" than for a female model. In street fashion as well as in formal fashion presentation, men have been supporting characters. One account of a 1990 fashion show for Jean-Paul Gaultier observed that the classical hierarchy of the ballet stage prevails as well in the fashion world, where women are shown off by men: "The models came out in pairs. A woman in a black-and-white floral-printed leotard and stockings that kept sliding down—no garters—accompanied by a man who walked along pulling them up for her."[49]

The new, "soft" man, "Shy Boy" by Patina-V. Courtesy of the manufacturer.

The Lowell Nesbitt "Man of the '90s" mannequin. Courtesy of Pucci.

eyes [surveyed] the audience as though challenging opponents to debate. He shifted his weight from one foot to the other and his expression changed with the sense of his words. He almost seemed to breathe. The impact was extraordinary."[56]

Within the visual merchandising industry, hyperreal figures are used primarily to promote specialty merchandising for short periods. Their exposure is limited partly because of their still-high expense, and partly to conserve their novelty. Many in the industry believe that, at least until the novelty wears off, the figures can grab the passerby's attention long enough for the merchandise to make a significantly greater impact.

And yet, in an odd turnabout on realism, the effectiveness of hyperreal mannequins seems to stem not from identification and projection, but from fascination with their technological wizardry. Realism may reach an upper limit beyond which further anticipated improvements focus attention on fragmented details rather than on a sense of the whole. In this context, hyperrealism functions as a form of abstraction, casting an erratic glow on the inescapable debate over the relative merits of realistic and abstract mannequins.

Michael Southgate, a friend of the 1930s pioneer of realistic mannequins, Lester Gaba, smiled to think that Gaba's Cynthia met her end in a Long Island garage, where her creator was trying to resurrect her as an animated figure. Her motor overheated, and she blew up. Maybe you can push realism only so far.

5 Street Theatre

For 150 years the trend in manufacture was toward greater homogeneity and standardization of products, and the retail industry followed a complementary impulse to make store operations as large-scale and as standardized as possible. In the 1970s that trend suddenly reversed as a host of influential boutiques sprang up in London, Paris, and New York, bringing with them a market for more specialized merchandise and a more individualized image for the consumer. These boutiques put a new spin on the venerable practice of offering multiple types of goods and services under a single roof, focusing on the most up-to-the-minute trends: "for the first time, stores installed jukeboxes, offered unisex apparel and combined unrelated merchandise lines like health foods and casual clothes under a single roof."[1] Larger stores readily followed the boutiques' profitable example.

Fashion designers like Diane von Furstenberg and Calvin Klein became models and spokespeople for their own lines of clothing. This personalization may have helped consumers cope with the suddenly bewildering array of choices that faced them, though it may have been calculated to make them feel that they were "acquiring not mere things, like sheets or blue jeans, but a little piece of the person whose signature those things bore—a few essential drops of that person's life, looks, wealth, success, and fame."[2] Market needs—for a multisensory, theatrically enlivened experience and for a reconstituted personhood through the act of shopping—had at last caught up with a set of time-tested merchandising strategies to create a unique form of window display called street theatre. The form derived from two techniques that were widespread in American display—the grouping of mannequins to simulate affective interactions, and lifestyle merchandising.

Realism in Seventies Display Staging

Lester Gaba recommended in the 1950s, no doubt with a wicked sparkle in his eye, that display men stage juniors' clothing on a single female mannequin, with lots of young male mannequins—or photographs of boys at least—nearby. "Boys," he reasoned, "are a girl's chief interest." D. G. Williams posed a couple so that the woman appeared to "straighten" the man's tie. In the 1960s, the manufacturer Wolf & Vine introduced "The PAIRables," a set of glass bases that could be slid together to permit two mannequins—"without natural rapport," as the brochure kidded—to be staged more closely together. The brochure's pitch was based on the pleasure the display person derived from mating mannequins. It offered, "You can separate them . . . if you have the heart!"

Simply placing mannequins close together is enough

Mary Brosnan "Bow Tie"
party scene, manufactured
by D. G. Williams, New
York. Courtesy of the Mannequin Museum archive.

to suggest a relationship between them. Decter has exploited this principle of association in its own showroom, staging one adult mannequin as "family elder"
to a more recent collection of children's mannequins.
During the 1970s consciously created "groupings" animated mannequin showrooms and windows, as mannequins were specifically designed to be sold in sets and to
be staged in relation to one another. Rootstein claims to
have started the trend with "collections of women who
seemed to talk and touch—a radical departure from the
traditionally isolated, regimented figures."[3] In 1974
Time called the trend toward groupings—or what it defined as "clusters of interacting mannequins"—the latest display fad. In 1979 Hindsgaul reported that "we

feel a definite swing to the grouping concept in the ini-
tial design period." Manufacturers gained tighter control over display artists' choices, a trend that continued
for over a decade. In 1981 Helen Burggraf predicted
that passersby would see "a continued emphasis on realism, natural poses and poses that suggest movement,
and 'conversational groupings' (several mannequins designed to interact with one another)."[4]

In promoting their groupings, manufacturers appealed to viewers' desire for realistic representation, not
just of the individual in physical movement, but of the
emotional exchanges of social life as well. Figures did
not merely stand amid others, they related to the figures
around them. A press release for Rootstein's "Classy
Lady Long Legs" collection in 1984 described how
these figures related among themselves as women, and
how different they appeared when linked with a man:
"The figures, particularly those with raised arms, lend
themselves naturally to linked and rhythmic groups of

two and three. With each other they're intimate, secretive. With a man, proudly detached." In Rootstein's "Body Gossip" collection, the mannequins were "self-aware, almost narcissistic." Their body language suggests that "there is something knowing between them . . . a little scandal, a little wickedness."

A Decter sales letter may best explain the wide appeal of groupings. The "Young Americans" collection featured a "newlywed" couple of mannequins crossing a threshold, as well as a couple that held hands gently, standing back to back. The letter that introduced the collection exclaimed, "What we have brought to you is a *marriage between mannikins and emotion.*"

Mannequin manufacturers had long attributed emotions to their creations, but in the past it was up to the display people to determine how those emotions might be played out. With the concept of groupings, display directors purchased not only individual mannequins but staging ideas. Rootstein offered a couple in its "Style"

A pair: Chris and Catherine. Courtesy of Adel Rootstein (USA).

collection—"Catherine," who stretched her legs out in front of her on the floor, supporting herself on her palms behind her, and "Chris," who straddled her, his mouth edging toward hers.

"Rhythmic repetition" was an influential staging motif during the seventies and eighties. Figures that were identical both in face and in pose would be set close together, often in trios, to maximize the visual impact of an outfit, or of a set of related separates. For the "Walk and Talk" line, Rootstein combined rhythmic repetition with the groupings concept: "Six very friendly girls, stepping out together, chatting and giggling. Designed in two tight groups of three, they're perfect for showing off co-ordinates—dress, pants, skirt, sweaters, jacket, all taken in at a single glance." The groupings were specially developed to go with coordinated collections of relatively inexpensive clothing, rather than one-of-a-kind items that made a stronger statement.

The big—though by no means new—idea of 1970s realistic staging was "lifestyle merchandising," which banked on what Stewart Ewen has astutely called "the cash value of the imagination." Lifestyle merchandising, according to Guy Scarangello, is the showing of a person's entire world in a display. A person's lifestyle, in merchandising terms, is "the life environment of a particular person." The term *lifestyle* started to be thrown around a good deal in fashion and advertising circles in the mid-seventies. Blair Sabol noted in 1977 that "lifestyle seems to be the hot-sell of late," and that newspapers had regularly begun to publish whole "living" sections that featured not only fashionable clothing but modish furnishings and foods. Fashion designers began holding fashion shows in their own homes during this period as well. Lifestyle merchandising illustrates the relation between a person's character and his or her setting. It implies a relation between people and objects. Robert Kowalczik, a Saks display man, finds that issues of intent and the mannequin's relation to the merchandise are essential for him: "When one of my assistants . . . dresses a mannequin, my first question is, 'Where is she going?' She's not just standing there in the store—

A situation window by Henry Callahan, showing how and where clothes might be worn in social situations, 1958. Photo by Nick Malan Studios. Courtesy of Saks Fifth Avenue.

she's jogging, she's at the club, she's on her way to a cocktail party."[5]

The same principle had once been called "dramatizing the merchandise." A 1937 writer gave this example: "Consider a window showing men's topcoats. A well arranged background of autumn leaves would be harmonious enough but it would add no extra incentive for buying a coat. But change the autumn leaves to a blown-up photograph of a football game. At once your imagination begins to work; you are transported to a place where (1) you will enjoy yourself; (2) it will probably be chilly, (3) people for the most part will look well dressed." In 1948, one writer reported that "displays which show merchandise in use or in the kind of surroundings in which it may be used, are called realistic displays." On one level, the use of mannequins at all for the merchandising of clothing constitutes a type of realistic staging because it lets the viewer see how the garment looks on *a* human body, if not the viewer's own. Ties were considered to be "most appealing to the customer when displayed knotted and pinned under shirt collars. Hosiery on foot forms catches the eye quicker than when folded."[6]

Vendors who anticipated lifestyle merchandising saw that they could sell more of an item by invoking a situation in which it can be used pleasurably, in which it is needed, in which it can enhance one's image. Lifestyle merchandising was simultaneously enhanced and subverted by the revolutionary movement that seized New York display during the mid-1970s. At once, street theatre displayed elaborate scenes of daily life—or at least the high points—that implied strong relationships both among figures and between figures and their environments—and that systematically ignored the merchandise.

"Street Theatre" Display

In May 1976, *New York* magazine reported on a run of "new-wave windows" that had been seen around town—at Bloomingdale's, Henri Bendel, the Lexington Avenue boutique San Francisco, and the Halston bou-

tique. The windows used mannequins in situations that were often déclassé, unflattering (according to contemporary modes of visual presentation), or downright macabre:

> Mannequins hanging out in a dyke bar! Classy ladies surrounded by mountains of garbage! A high-fashion corpse stretched out on the floor! Is this the *Enquirer*? Are these the latest fashion-*vérité* photos in *Vogue*? Neither. They're just a few scenes from Henri Bendel's window displays that are causing pedestrian crowds day and night.
>
> These new-wave windows are a kind of street-theater, making comments on the news of the day—the garbage strike, the sleeping-pill syndrome, the latest fads and hang-ups—and sometimes even mocking the very customers the windows are designed to attract. They're sit-com and melodrama for the acquisitive class, and they're attracting as big and devoted a claque as Chevy Chase and *Mary Hartman, Mary Hartman*.[7]

Industry spokesmen credit the writer of the *New York* piece, Rosemary Kent, with coining the term *street theatre*. The handle stuck, both for the public and for the display industry, and it was used extensively to describe the trend in New York windows between about 1974 and 1979. Street theatre windows reflected an important confluence of many passions—the heightened visual quality of culture, demanded by a generation raised on television; the valorizing of self-regard, as in a mirror or store window, that disco culture brought; the increasingly incestuous relation between art and commerce; the growing celebrity status of fashion designers; and the extraordinary productivity of visual and theatre artists as they explored issues of fragmentation, depersonalization, multiple realities, and fading presence.

One distinguishing feature of street theatre windows was the presentation of mannequins in discernibly theatrical scenes that highlighted relationships, conflicts, and actions and their consequences. Kent accurately characterized these situations as "sit-com and melo-

"Dead" mannequin at Henry Bendel. Window designed by Robert Currie, 1974. Photograph by Tim Herr.

drama." Many windows dealt with explicitly violent or sexual themes—insanity and physical transformation, through such modes as drug use, suicide, and pregnancy, took center stage. And, reflecting the rise of body art during the late sixties and early seventies, actions done *to the body* (of the mannequin) were in the foreground. Publicity for street theatre displays played up their sensational qualities: "Will corpses sell Halstons? According to the merchants—yes. These picture windows sell like crazy. More important to ask is: will the new windows go too far? Be banned in Boston? Become X-rated? Tune in tomorrow. These windows are certainly the kinkiest commercials in town." Another

writer warned, "If things go on this way, minors wishing to window-shop may soon need to be accompanied by a parent or guardian."8

Body artists had changed the focus of artistic activity from artist-working-on-object to artist-working-on-self. In 1970 Dennis Oppenheim staged a five-hour performance entitled *Reading Position for Second Degree Burn*, about which he wrote: "The body was placed in the position of recipient . . . an exposed plane, a captive surface. The piece has its roots in a notion of color change. Painters have always artificially instigated color activity. I allowed myself to be painted—my skin became pigment. I could regulate its intensity through control of the exposure time. Not only would my skin tones change, but . . . change registered on a sensory level as well—I could feel the act of becoming red. I was tattooed by the sun." Oppenheim's 1970–71 film project *Gingerbread Man* captured the artist's ingestion and digestion of the title figure; the material of the "final work" was "micro-projection-feces 6' diameter x 3000 enlargement."[9]

Body art made the body the omphalos, both subject and object of the work. Conceptual artist John Baldessari "loved the thought of an artist going into an organ bank instead of an art store for supplies." Like Oppenheim, most body artists used their own bodies as material. Ronald J. Onorato recorded that "by 1970, [body artist Vito] Acconci withdrew from the space around himself and focused on the physical reality of his body instead." Acconci "presented himself as agent behind the artistic activity, revealing and highlighting 'I' as subject, as in 'I make art,' and the art object's status as a stand-in for the artist. The artist, not the art object, became the target for self-imposed activity, as well as the target for the viewer's attention."[10]

Acconci's 1972 performance *Seedbed* featured the artist audibly masturbating underneath the floor of New York's Sonnabend Gallery as he vocalized the sexual fantasies he "buil[t] up . . . on viewers' footsteps."[11] The artist's progression through arousal and climax is typical of the primal physical processes performed by body artists, many of whom concentrated on themes of sex and death. Bruce Nauman made two slow-motion films, *Bouncing Balls* and *Black Balls*, showing his testicles moving and being painted black.

The body art of Chris Burden dealt with "physical endurance, pain, death risks, death imagery, and a moral dilemma for the spectator or sponsor." In 1971, Burden "stuffed himself into locker number five in the Art Building of the University of California at Irvine, and there he remained, entombed . . . for five whole days. The locker was two feet high, two feet wide, three feet deep—adequate for a student to store his art materials in, but when the student *is* his art materials, a real crunch." Other Burden works included "getting himself shot by a rifle at Irvine, crawling almost naked through glass in Los Angeles, breathing water in Chicago, being kicked downstairs in Switzerland and licked by flames in Austria." Eleanor Antin took daily photographs for a month during a slow-working diet in a piece called *Carving*, "as if she herself, rather than a natural process, were a sculptress of her own form."[12]

Max Kozloff suggested a source for the treatment of bodies as artifacts in body art: "Crimes that violate bodies depend, in one degree or another, on our propensity to turn people into things." The doubts we have about the reality first of fiberglass figures and then of ourselves are also expressed by body art, which, as Kozloff described it, reverses Pygmalion: "Instead of the fable of the stone statue that changed into a living body, we now have the story of the animate body that doubles back into inanimate art."[13]

Performance artists who create personas—following Marcel Duchamp's invention in 1920 of his female alter ego, Rrose Sélavy—use their own bodies to a profound degree in their work, creating art of themselves in a studio shared by an audience, if sometimes an unaware one. Lynn Hershman created "Roberta Breitmore," a persona that played itself out over a period of years. Colette's "Justine" was another art-life performance dependent upon the body of the artist as medium.

Like persona performances, street theatre windows did not simply talk at their audiences in the old way. The art-audience relationship was altered. Aside from the "mistakes" that Gene Moore left in his windows as bait for curious onlookers, little had been done before the street theatre windows to demand the participation of the passerby. With the emphasis in street theatre displays on the consequences of action—the portrait of the sleeping-pill overdose, the murders—passersby were implicated as witnesses. People were also reported to linger, on the average twice as long, at street theatre windows.[14]

Much of this response was consistent with the postmodern aesthetic and its demand that the viewer participate. Dick Higgins wrote that in postmodern performance art "one cannot sit back, like the old ladies of Boston at a Tchaikovsky concert, with eyes closed and breasts heaving, waiting to be ravished emotionally. Rather one must be like the witness at a ritual or crime, or like the public at a boxing match, being both in tune empathically with what one is seeing and mentally dealing with the tactics of each move. One will be lost if one looks for passive thrills."[15] Higgins's choice of the image of witness to a crime could not have been more appropriate, given the subject matter of many of the windows. Viewers were needed to decipher the action and to repeat the story—indeed, to verify its occurrence. Bertolt Brecht's ideas about audience involvement lend a theatrical precedent to this altered notion of pedestrian spectatorship: "The audience [should] no

longer have the illusion of being the unseen spectator at an event which is really taking place."[16]

Photographer Duane Michals said that drama can be created in a photograph by the dialectic between what one sees and what one hopes to see. This dialectic can create a "drama of person": "It's not the photographer's eye; it's the photographer's mind; so that the eye is always just the machine, but it's the mind that translates that figure." Street theatre displays demanded this kind of extended interplay between what one saw and what one made of it. Display artist Victor Hugo described the place of the audience in his work: "Really most of my windows are like a happening. It's up to the people who view these presentations to interpret the occurrences. A person must intellectualize because I give them clues to what's going on, but I don't tell them everything. Finally, the last factor in all my windows is people, it's their reaction that actually finishes my work."[17]

A "body story": a nose-job window—perhaps inspired by Andy Warhol—by David M. O'Grady for San Francisco Clothing, New York, 1976. Photograph by John Peden.

Candy Pratts's ideas about the viewer's relation to the display extended even to the architecture of the windows. When Pratts arrived at Bloomingdale's, elaborate valances bordered each window—a Bloomingdale's trademark. Pratts speedily removed the valances so viewers, instead of merely peering into a fishbowl, could feel the action spilling out onto the sidewalk. Windows could also appear to invite the viewer into the action. One window showed "Great Americans" at the dinner table, while several mannequins clustered in a corner. A place at the table was left empty, as if awaiting a "chosen" mannequin—or a spectator.[18]

Pratts's displays, reported a Bloomingdale's in-house publication, "[force] the passerby to stop and fill in the blanks, completing the 'before and after' sequence of events. While this freedom of interpretation delights the imagination crowd, it understandably challenges the more passive shopper. They call in asking, 'What does it mean?'" This caught-in-the-act quality was characteristic of both fashion and other forms of photography that documented staged events, and of the body art of the period. Photography also had long been used to record various forms of public deaths, and a whole genre of "grotesque" photography in the early 1960s grew out of the melding of artistic and documentary photographic traditions. This genre focused on "photojournalistic imagery of violence, social aberration, suffering, and death" and documented the aftermaths of these occurrences. The "evidence" photograph was the heir of crime photography: "Obviously it was impossible to photograph most crimes when they occurred. So forensic photography and photoreportage of violent crime were devoted initially to consequences: the fate of the victims and, whenever possible, the doom of the culprits."[19] Tabloids were a more sensational medium that storyboarded a fictional past event, weaving a narrative around still shots. By the 1920s, the *Daily Graphic*, a confessional "news" paper, introduced the composograph, "a photograph of models posed in a dramatic reenactment of 'what was believed to have taken place.'" These after-the-fact traces of an event assumed the status of art and underscored the idea that art was a process or act—as in performance—more than an object. Chris Burden redefined the artwork as the "residue" of an act when he said, "Art is really about ideas rather than a thing. What makes it art is the materialization of the idea. I do art by acting out the idea; other people do it by making an object. People get it all confused; they think that a painting is the art. But the art is actually when the artist was making the painting. The object is the residue."[20]

No longer as respectful, polite, or inviting as windows had traditionally been, street theatre windows explicitly aimed to shock and disarm their audience. The impulse to shock corresponded to trends in other visual media in a period of intense visual oversaturation. The iconoclasm of the street theatre movement, Simon Doonan believes, was heavily influenced by the punk movement, which was "about re-evaluating everything, . . . about not becoming overly concerned with bourgeois ideas." Doonan also sees punk as the source of much of the violence and destructiveness evident in windows showing "women getting mugged, people tying girls up on motorcycles, [and] smashing TVs."[21] The intense living for the moment that punks favored was also reflected in the trashiness of street theatre display, which conjured the most sensational topics of the day in the most precipitous fashion possible. Photographer Deborah Turbeville, who has both worked in and strongly influenced display, explains: "When you do store windows, you have to use a shock manner to call attention to the display. There's so much visual pollution everywhere that it keeps us from really seeing what's in the windows. Even movies are into this shock thing, partly to keep our attention from drifting. The display people are terribly aware of this and of what's going on. They're the fastest to pick up on new visual things."[22]

During the street theatre era, looking was prime audience sport. Kent reported that "one Park Avenue hostess pile[d] her dinner guests into the family limousine for window-hopping tours." Candy Pratts recalled the scene on Thursdays, when she and her staff would change the windows and serve popcorn to "window groupies" who would throng outside the store to watch. Throughout her tenure at Bloomingdale's, "little gangs of New Yorkers, members of the creative community, would tour the town on Wednesday and Thursday nights when the windows change."[23] Willo Font, Bloomingdale's display photographer, recalled the special evening strolls that people would take after dark when he was documenting the windows. Many people would linger outside to critique the displays, telling Font what they did and didn't like and demanding that he pass their comments along to the display people in the morning. Marc Manigault's "voyeur" windows at the boutique Riding High played on the activity of looking. He set up one scenario so that the spectator had to peek through wooden blinds to see it. The spectator was not, however, the only voyeur. One band of three tidily attired mannequins was peeking at another grouping, dressed in black silk lingerie. The two groups of mannequins were separated by another set of wooden blinds, placed perpendicular to the exterior one.

The makers of street theatre delighted in providing or admitting multiple views of a given situation for the passerby. When Pratts came to Bloomingdale's in 1974, she knocked out dividing walls to create two triangular windows banking Lexington Avenue at 59th and 60th Streets. These quickly became her favorites; they presented radically different perspectives on her "situation dramas," depending on whether the viewer stood on the street or on the avenue. Font was so taken with the compositional and social complexity that Pratts had created that he developed a new photographic style to document the way the windows worked. Previously, windows had been photographed straight on, and in a way that would provide the most complete, most glare-free account of what had actually been placed in them. With Pratts's inspiration, Font began photographing the windows as a film director might, showing the scene not only from the points of view of various passersby, but also as each *mannequin* "saw" the others in the scene. Font says his work of that period was in a kind of

"comic book style." For one window, he'd start by shooting the whole picture, then shoot the broken chandelier in the middle of the floor, then the face of one woman searching out the other, then an isolated group of women whispering in the corner, and finally an open purse with a lipstick peeking out—"and then you would try to figure out what caused all this commotion." In contrast with ordinary documentary display photography, the order in which the photographs were viewed became important. Font recalls that after Pratts left Bloomingdale's in 1979, the people who remained were less interested in details or in point of view, and he reverted to "whole shots" again.

In the revolutionary street theatre windows, merchandise frequently played no more than an incidental role. For her infamous steam bath window, Pratts positioned turbaned mannequins (presumably naked) in individual enclosures. The merchandise ostensibly featured in the display was swimsuits, which were "draped casually on hooks" on the tiled wall.[24] Whereas traditional display design had followed from fashion style, during the street theatre period—a particularly uninspired era for fashion—display finally bought its own wings, to the dismay of orthodox display people. Traditional windows had made the merchandise the star; with displays that treated the mannequins themselves as primary players, new values for tableau performance were born. According to Bob Currie, display was adapted to the demands of storytelling as "showing became only a vehicle for telling."

Currie, then directing display at Henri Bendel, is credited with the introduction in 1974 of the street theatre style. According to Michael Southgate, Currie was the one who "changed the shape" of display, who "took away the beautiful mannequins with the perfect spotlight, with the lovely accessories at her side, which Henry Callahan had made a format for the world." Currie had started out in interiors, not fashion; at the age of fifteen he was a furniture mover for a large interior design company in New Jersey. Eventually, he advanced into display work with the company. His work was discovered by Bendel's after he had freelanced a window for designer Norma Kamali's boutique. Currie knew that a second-floor window needed to call on extreme measures to draw attention: his Kamali window was centered on a traffic horse with blinking lights that he had stolen from the middle of the road in the dead of night.

When he made the move to Bendel's, Currie said, he made a conscious effort to do with mannequins what had not been done before: "When I came into the field, I looked at every store in New York City, and I figured out what was missing. And what was missing was any sort of life, any breath of life, or any reference to humanity: there was always a very stiff figure, with some sort of reference to Paris or whatever." The scenes

The Pratts steam bath window for Bloomingdale's. Collection of author.

evoked a time and a place and a mood, but not a life. "To me, they were very dry and very dead. Also, the mannequin was very dead in that it had painted lips and false eyelashes and straw wigs. And I thought, 'People don't look like that.'"

Currie began to change the makeup and wigs on the mannequins every time the windows were changed, and he designed each head treatment to reflect not only what went best aesthetically with the garment but how the character modeling it would be likely to present herself, given what she was "doing" in the window: "If a woman is going to wear a black dress, she is going to change her makeup for mourning, for the black dress, and she is going to change her hair." Currie also drew on the everyday experience of the women he saw around him, both at Bendel's and elsewhere, for ideas for his situations: "All of my hints came from the street —seeing women on the street, going to the laundromat,

going to the grocery store—or from dreams (because dreams are a part of life)." His women were often presented "disheveled."[25]

Like few before him and fewer after, Currie was free to choose clothing that gave him ideas for his windows. As long as he featured work by the designated fashion designer, his own taste and imagination governed most else. Typical of display directors who were given such latitude, he reported that there often was little planning and much improvisation: "We never knew what was going in the window until a week before."

Currie's process of installing a window display reflected his practice of suiting mannequins to fashions in a believable way. Currie traveled through the store, selecting clothes and then finding complementary stockings, shoes, and accessories. Although he might not yet know which mannequins would wear which pieces, he "knew what the hair was going to look like because of the clothing." With his uncommonly large staff—five or six assistants to strike and then install the two windows each week—Currie would line up each primary article of merchandise and the entire stable of mannequins. All the members of the display staff contributed their ideas because "the pose of the mannequin could either kill the dress or make the dress. So, I would look at the line of the dress. For instance, if it had a very big, say, a bat-wing sleeve, I would choose a mannequin whose arm was up, so that you could see the volume." For Currie, the fixed value was the mannequin's pose; the variables arose from the interplay among pose, garment, makeup, wig, and interaction with the other mannequins. Currie emphasized that the close patterning between the design of the mannequin and the design of the garment actually gave the mannequin the appearance of life: "The clothes helped the form. There's movement in fabric; there's not movement in fiberglass."

L. Frank Baum wrote in 1906 that to "a clever trimmer . . . the form is not a lay figure, but a living, breathing being. Under the hand of the careless trimmer the best jointed form is but a 'dummy' capable only of wooden attitudes." For Baum, to inspire a dummy with living attributes was not so much to regard the figure as living, but to treat it and imagine responding to it *as if* it were living, supplying (or "accessorizing") it with all that it might need to fully realize the social role it is *dressed* to play. Imaginative display artists have developed this Stanislavskian "as if" further, creating for themselves a creature that aspires to life (as, of course, they might envision her, not as she might see herself), first in lifestyle merchandising and to a more extreme degree in street theatre. Right within the Baum tradition is a Bloomingdale's mannequin stylist who stated that he regarded himself as his mannequins' personal manager.[26] Currie's principal method of creating life from fiberglass was based on harmony of design between clothing and human form.

Currie was known by some for a "specialty of portraying violence" in his windows. At the fabric emporium Clarence House, Currie boarded up one side of the window. The window was "stamped Danger, bristled with razor wire, and was littered with the bones of the last adventurer who tried to get through to the strange flickering globe above its pedestal of nails. With its macabre imagery, the display seemed more like a still from George Lucas's latest film than an advertisement for a fine fabric house, despite the brocades in the background."[27] As Currie remembered, "I was very influenced by old Hitchcock movies, and so there was a lot of murder." Orvell notes, however, that disaster simulations were popular as far back as the mid-nineteenth century. Coney Island, for example, replicated "the Fall of Pompeii, the eruption of Mount Pelée, the Johnstown and Galveston Floods, not to mention a burning four-story building that was repeatedly set ablaze and extinguished." And realist literature of the turn of the century had shown off the contemporary obsession with "life not literature." The subjects that captivated people of the period were marked by "blood, sex, money, grime, garbage, immigrants, and killing snowstorms— a recognition of areas of experience previously excluded from polite literature." Similar subjects animated the fictions of street theatre—and perhaps for a similar purpose, the outing of previously private subjects.[28]

Currie was celebrated for his wildly "everyday" fictions. One famous window featured call girls, in a luxurious early-morning bedroom scene, catching their last few winks while wearing eyeshades. In another window, "the dummies in at-home clothes were making a scene in the kitchen with champagne and spaghetti. But everyone knows Bendel's customers don't eat fattening things like spaghetti. It's another of Currie's scenarios that seem to feature spoiled, bitchy women."[29] Marilyn Bethany wrote that Currie may have been responsible for a new display and social image of women: Currie's "Jean Muir–clad woman aggressively seated in a puddle may have been the first sighting of eighties 'attitude.'" According to Ruth Miller Fitzgibbons, Currie "proposed to put mannequins that characterized (or caricatured) the selected clientele at Bendel's into 'everyday' situations—celebrating the banal, exploiting haughtiness with mockery, expressing personal fantasies. Some of his celebrated scenes have depicted super-chic Park Avenue-types walking their fish, a poison vial drama in which one dummy picked the wrong potion, [and] three starlets with a lecherous producer caught in a compromising act."[30]

Currie generally prepared several more mannequins with costume, makeup, and wig than he actually used; a few would always be "edited out." His situation windows typically had about eight figures, the most important of which was chosen not so much for artistic as for technical reasons—it could best support the weight of the others, which were leaned onto it in the casual, slouched positions that were new and ubiquitous in the 1970s. (Currie had always felt that mannequin stands were "giveaways.") Around the central supporting figure the others were grouped based in part on optimum support but more importantly on how each mannequin "related" to the others.

The groupings always had dramatic content as well as technical expediency: "I . . . knew that in order to create interest in that space, . . . mannequins had to be placed together, and . . . the groups had to be identified as groups, and they also had to be opposing another group. So, often there would be one mannequin and eight [in another group]; or, three mannequins and four." He always treated the mannequins "as if they were human"; they were never simply elements in an abstract composition. Sometimes the "opposition" between the two groups was more in the nature of "a conflict; sometimes it was a conversation." For Currie, drama and merchandising went hand in hand: the arrangement of mannequins as members of a discernible social group helped passersby to perceive the unity of a clothing collection.

The perception of a slice of life made situation windows different from what a photograph would capture: "The camera has its own eye, and it is the eye of something that is stopped. . . . In the case of what I was doing [at Bendel's], it was a moment from a story. And, I've never seen a photograph that I connected to anything. I see it as an object, really. [My windows] were about a momentary pause in a life or in a situation." A photograph "has no beginning or end," whereas in Currie's scenarios, "it was coming from somewhere and going somewhere, and you just caught it." Performance was implied.

According to Currie, it was only about a month before the style of display that he had initiated was copied by the ever-trendy industry, most notably by Candy Pratts, the new display director at Bloomingdale's. Pratts had been snatched away, at the age of twenty-five, from her three-year display position at Charles Jourdan just as Bloomingdale's was trying to change its image from an interior furnishings palace to a fashion house. Pratts's appropriation of Currie's images quickly became a running joke among the display staff at Bendel's: "You should see what Bloomingdale's did this week!"

A silent dialogue grew up between the two stores, enacted through the medium of the display windows. Currie maintained that because the stores were managed so differently and on such different scales Bloomingdale's was able to copy only *some* of what Bendel's did. For one thing, "I was at an advantage in that I wrote my own ticket in everything," whereas Bloomingdale's could get mired in bureaucratic decision making. Currie's "revenge," he said, was to stage displays that he knew Bloomingdale's, with its sometimes cumbersome scale, could never pull off. Once he removed the glass and put a car in a window. By the time the press and media caught up to street theatre, Currie had moved away from that style into a more abstract, architectural aesthetic, leaving Pratts to claim much of the credit.

Perhaps more than any other display artist working in the street theatre style, Pratts relied on clearly evident sources. Deborah Turbeville spotted the resemblance to her own photographs: "I must say, it makes me feel strange to see my pictures coming back at me through these windows. A while ago, Bloomingdale's did a scene in which everything was covered with sheets and newspapers and there were girls in summer clothes. I was really stunned; it looked so much like my pictures in *Vogue* last June—the empty summer house and the haunted women wandering around." Dorothy Seiberling found some of Pratts's windows "unmistakable variations on Deborah Turbeville's photographs, replete with angst-happenings and limbo-languor." Pratts knew Turbeville's work well, for she had both commissioned and appeared in it. In 1974 Pratts invited Turbeville to create a series of background photographs for a shoe window at Charles Jourdan. Turbeville took Pratts and several other models to the Wolf mannequin factory in Chelsea and photographed them costumed as dummies —complete with padded bodies, bathing caps over their hair, and white paint covering their faces, for a "kind of lobotomized look." Turbeville placed her models in boneless, ragdoll positions in the factory, in some cases "plopp[ing them] down like puppets, without feet."[31]

Another indisputable source for street theatre was the photography of Guy Bourdin and Helmut Newton, whose scene-of-the-crime shots also depicted live models and mannequins in compromising positions. One Newton photograph shows a nude model, sprawled face down, on the roof of a Central Park West apartment building, her limbs thrown out awkwardly. The shards of a champagne glass and a toppled chair lie around her. Broken champagne glasses had been a long-standing motif in the display work of Gene Moore, and Pratts and display artists such as Victor Hugo also capitalized on the shock value and the sense of human presence that this potent image of destruction provided. Street theatre design was influenced even more forcefully by the sense of a body that had been *acted upon*— that had been, as in body art, simultaneously the subject and object of an action.

The way Pratts and her staff treated the mannequins, the body had literally been acted upon. Barry James Wood wrote that Pratts, "determined to make her mannequins expressive, . . . defiantly taped, rebolted, and screwed them into postures and positions they were never expected to assume. Many fellow display people thought she had discovered new, more flexible mannequins, not realizing that Pratts's own ingenuity was responsible."[32]

Robert Hoskins, Pratts's assistant during her years at Bloomingdale's, was responsible for the nuts-and-bolts work of reshaping the mannequins. Pratts was, Hoskins said, a brilliant thinker in visual and dramatic terms, but not a trained display person technically capable of handling realistic mannequins with the attention to detail that she always envisioned.[33] Hoskins's forte quickly became the leaning of mannequins, thereby disposing of the support rod and the elaborate wiring whose visibility from the street had plagued display directors aiming for a realistic effect. Through handling the mannequins every day, Hoskins became familiar enough with the balance of each one to know its capabilities. Whereas Currie made a single mannequin the fulcrum of his multifigure displays at Bendel's, Hoskins leaned each mannequin separately. Leaning gave the figures the same effect of naturalness that such manufacturers as Pucci were striving for around the same time with slouching and "after-sport" positions, and it seemed to create an atmosphere of greater realism.

Every Bloomingdale's mannequin was made to lean, each according to its own construction and balance. After playing with the unsupported mannequin, Hoskins could pose her securely by working against the direction in which she naturally plummeted. Rootstein mannequins were by far the leading players in street theatre display, at least partly because the manufacturer's ready advances in realism made the mannequins well suited to ultranaturalistic stagings.[34] Hoskins, however, credited a more practical appeal: unlike most others made at the time—and even now—Rootstein mannequins were engineered to have a low center of gravity and to balance easily.

Hoskins was also responsible for manipulating the Bloomingdale's mannequins into the positions that so startled others in the display field. Part of the impetus for his unprecedented experimentation must have come from Pratts's refusal to compromise. She recalled telling staff members who insisted that a pose couldn't be achieved to go back to the shop and *find* a way to make it work. Hoskins began to loosen the mannequin's arm from its socket and fill in the gap with newspapers, "which is what made people walk around and say, 'I've got that mannequin, but she doesn't do *that.*'" Hoskins would sometimes pair limbs from one mannequin with the torso of another. In one window, a mannequin wearing a chiffon evening gown lay luxuriously, her head on a rectangular satin pillow, her ankles crossed delicately, her knees supported on a matching cylindrical pillow. One arm stretched languorously above her head. Hoskins remembered that she was "all taped together" under the dress—and that "she" was probably actually an amalgam of various mannequin parts.

Sometimes only the "necessary" parts of a mannequin were actually used—a throwback to the "pragmatic realism" of the Victorian period, which dictated that only what was actually going to show on the clothed figure had to look realistic. In one Bloomingdale's window, two mannequins were shown kissing in a romantic scene before a fire. The man's arm was taped to suggest that he had it around the woman, yet the whole arm didn't show. Hoskins recalled, too, that the mannequins were used only from the waist up.

Pratts's staff functioned as executors of her idea, much the way assistant directors and stage managers do in large opera houses. Pratts assembled the four or five "guys" who were her prime assistants, who understood what she meant with a minimum of verbal direction, and who didn't have to be guided step by step. She explained in visual terms the "situation" each mannequin was in. She did not speak about the internal life of the mannequin, what the character might be thinking or feeling. For one window Hoskins recalled that Pratts "[just] said to me, 'Have a girl seated on a cube, holding a man's evening slipper behind her, looking at the girls in the corner, who are relating to her, and then just put the other man's evening slipper on the floor.' That's all she said to me. I didn't understand what she meant, but I understood what it looked like. And the rest didn't seem to matter."

Pratts would frequently "act out" for her coterie of window trimmers how she wanted her "girls" to act in the windows. According to Sally Heinemann, "Candy Pratts, who studied merchandising at the Fashion Institute of Technology, doesn't sketch and prefers not to write memorandums. So she tells her stories to those who actually install the windows."[35] Although Pratts only later studied acting at the Herbert Bergdorf Studios in New York, she brought a sensitivity for the issues that plague directors of naturalistic theatre to her display work at Bloomingdale's. Exits and entrances were crucial. Pratts's mother had always taught her that "attitude *is* a conversation. When you walk into a room, before you even say Hello, my name is Candy, you establish who you are, what you want to get out of this room, and where you're going."

Mannequin characters' pasts and futures were critical. In what Robert Hoskins called the "seedy hotel window," a faintly brothel-like reconstruction of a 1930s hotel, Pratts directed her staff to suggest each woman's history, "which comes out by the way she is wearing her clothes," by what accessories she is wearing or carrying.

Pratts wouldn't allow mannequins simply to *be* there; they had to have a conscious purpose, an "action": "I always used a mannequin as a human. It was 'she.' . . . We talked about them as people: 'She's in bed and she's waiting for Valentine's Day,' so it wasn't, 'Oh, here's a great pair of thighs.' . . . It was, 'She's on the roof trying to get a suntan.'" The seedy hotel window was also noteworthy for its detailed realistic propping: one mannequin "smoked" a cigar, mail had been placed in the lobby mailbox, and Pratts had even specified which novel one of the mannequins should be reading. An electric fan blew lazily in the background, and a passerby who placed an ear against the window could hear the radio playing faintly.

Pratts's attention to human detail and signs of presence extended even to windows that did not use mannequins. In what Hoskins termed a "very Candy" home furnishings window, a telephone was displayed off the hook; on the sofa, a black linen handkerchief, with a phone number painstakingly embroidered on it, had been "carelessly" thrown. Pratts's enthusiastic staff extended the technique even to interior displays: "All the guys wanted a piece of the action. . . . Nobody ever just threw a pillow any more; they all wanted to do a bed, with a pillow, and a glass with the Perrier water, and a cigarette with the lipstick mark: Everybody was going the whole nine yards."

On some level, the mannequins played out not only the roles that Pratts cast them in but aspects of Pratts's own life as well. During the years she was at Bloomingdale's, Pratts has said, she did only two things: design windows and party. In numerous interviews, Pratts has said that she prospected for ideas in her own active social life and reproduced her own experiences and observations of human movement and behavior in the windows: "As a woman, I bend, I stoop, I sit, I lean, I spill, I bump. I do 300 things. . . . If I am at a party and someone spills a glass, or bends over, plays backgammon, or is in the kitchen, it's the possibility of a window for me. . . . I memorize the way he or she is standing. If someone flops back in a chair holding the phone receiver and chatting, it's a feasible position, and I will eventually use it."[36] One window showed a mannequin from the back, walking diagonally toward one upstage corner of the window, apparently discarding evening accessories as she went; they streamed in an elegant trail behind her. She had been out partying all night, Hoskins explained, and had come home exhausted: "This is the disco era, remember."

Pratts also reflected the life of the streets back through the windows. Jack Posner noted that she used the windows "as a forum for social and political comment (women's lib, gay lib, sexual lib, worker movements, etc.)"—and the more controversial the topic, the better. Rosemary Kent had in fact defined street theatre in part as display that "[made] comments on the news of the day."[37] Occasionally, display people competed for the news: both Bloomingdale's and the Halston boutique featured windows inspired by the drug bust of Louise Lasser, the star of the television series *Mary Hartman, Mary Hartman.*

The explicit physicality of the mannequins was another mark of Pratts's realism. Her work was part of the cultural tide toward more explicit sexuality. The political pornography tabloid *Screw* appeared in 1969, and by the 1970s nudity was common in movies. But even within that permissive context, Robert Hoskins observed, "Candy brought a sexiness to the mannequins . . . that was very provocative." Whenever she could get away with it, Pratts staged "nude" mannequins. She was once ordered to put a nightgown on a mannequin that had been displayed sensuously on a bed set between Diane von Furstenberg sheets—at least a strap had to show to let passersby know that the mannequin was wearing something. Hoskins chuckled, "There's no such thing as a nude mannequin." A bedroom scene with several lounging mannequins—not explicitly interacting—was one of several Pratts windows that provoked accusations that she was promoting lesbianism.

Pratts may have been Bloomingdale's most demanding display director ever. A Pratts mannequin would "not . . . get one makeup a season, . . . [but] a new makeup every time" it appeared in the window, and she regularly sent the wigs out to be restyled—not to a display wig house, but to a stylist for human hairpieces. Each mannequin always received a complete manicure and pedicure. Pratts had her staff painstakingly coat each lower lip with five coats of lacquer to add a special, haunting shine to the mouth, and removed all eyelashes. Mannequins' lower eyelids were shaded brown to give the effect of a slight shadow from the lashes.

At times Pratts seemed to be engaged in a contest with Rootstein. Her manipulations and reconfigurations of Rootstein mannequins caused occasional embarrassment for a company that claimed to produce whole art works, which—unlike the work of many competing companies—couldn't be tampered with or altered without destroying the entire figure.

Sometimes Pratts succeeded in influencing Rootstein's design. Hoskins always arranged mannequins according to where their glances appeared to be directed. His attention to eye contact between the mannequins helped give the situations that he staged their feeling of reality. Eventually, Rootstein agreed to paint the eyes to focus in the direction most useful for Bloomingdale's stagings. In giving such attention to the eyes, Pratts changed the relationship between mannequin and viewer. Before street theatre stagings, Angela Taylor noted, mannequins had "gaze[d] dreamily just past one's head from department store windows"; street theatre mannequins that were portrayed as dead or unconscious or in locked focus with each other "gaze[d] somewhat less dreamily."[38]

At the same time, Pratts often obscured the faces of her mannequins, a strategy that Hoskins said focused attention on the activity being performed—on action rather than on being. The contrast is similar to the postmodern distinction Dick Higgins draws between acting and enacting: "Edmund Kean *acted* King Lear; today we *enact* our rituals of performance, stressing the materials of performance more than our own identities." Higgins postulated that the identity of the postmodern performer is predicated upon action: "Character is rela-

tive, not absolute. One *is* what one *does*. . . . One extends one's identity by doing a variety of things."[39] Like other display designers of the period, Pratts, who called her windows "happenings," linked window time with viewers' own time. A kitchen scene included a raw egg that had been dropped on the floor and had to be mopped up each night and replaced. Fictional and actual spoilage coincided.

For Pratts, the theatricality of her situations did not derive merely from a focus on the body, an emphasis on realistic details of individuals and groups of mannequins, or subject matter drawn from contemporary life. Rather, theatricality emerged from the experience she intended for her viewers, in which the process of discovery was critical. Pratts acknowledges that display is essentially a static form, but she believes that it can partake of the dynamism of theatre by planting multiple levels of both detail and meaning. If a viewer passes a window three times in a day, Pratts believes, the window should have a new charm each time: "The idea was always that there was something in the windows that you didn't see right away, where the girl held a bunch of nails in her hand or a note was on the floor." The capacity of the audience to engage in that process of discovery turned window trimming into street theatre, "the performance of a display." Eventually, after Pratts had affirmed in several interviews that the windows were meant to develop through prolonged or repeated viewing, people began to make a point of returning to the windows to reassess their earlier interpretations.

Pratts always acknowledged her debt to the extravagant displays of Victor Hugo, whose work at the Halston boutique between 1972 and 1976 contained even more self-referential elements than her own and—perhaps because he installed the windows himself—exploited his own role of being "on display." Like Colette, Hugo played the merchandising that normally was associated with window display against the merchandising of the artist, treating his own persona as sexual object. A sign in one window read "Victor Hugo for Sale" and included the phone number of his studio.

As Pratts made herself known on the party circuit, Hugo—lover of Halston, friend of Warhol—was known particularly in gay and art circles. The gay magazine *Blue Boy* photographed Hugo in the Halston window wearing a jockstrap. One Hugo window used symbols— eggs fried in Crisco—that he says the gay community would have immediately recognized as references to sexual practices then popular. For another window, Hugo strewed the glass from shattered Sparkletts water bottles, an image of destruction that he associated with his heavy involvement in cocaine at the time.

Hugo sometimes changed his windows over the course of the display's run to create the sense that events were occurring in real time. A 1976 window attempted to re-create a newsmaking bomb scare at La Guardia airport. One night, Hugo returned to the window and "destroyed [everything] as if there really had been a bombing." As he told it, "this was done for only one night to make it more dramatic. So, at five in the morning an unsuspecting woman called the police, telling them there had been a bomb in the window because she had seen all the mannequins torn apart, clothes torn away and the display in total disorder."[40] Realistic detail, as in the seedy hotel window by Pratts, was integral to the display: the clock showed the time, six-thirty, when both the bomb and the "bomb" exploded. Another display—a "pregnancy window"—involved even more elaborate intercession by the artist. At the beginning of the week, a mannequin lay in a hospital bed. In the middle of the week, Hugo himself "delivered" the baby and placed it in the mannequin's arms. He asked the husband of designer Diane von Furstenberg to act as the godfather. Jackie Rogers used a similar strategy at her New York boutique. Ten masked mannequins and a maid depicted the progressive dishevelment of a group of party-goers: "The display was changed day by day. By New Year's Eve, the maid's uniform was falling from her shoulders, and a cigaret dangled from her lips. The male guests had removed their tuxedo jackets and were obviously getting chummy with one another."[41]

Within a couple of years of its genesis in New York

windows, street theatre had spread to other American cities, including Los Angeles, Chicago, and San Francisco. The industry publication *Views & Reviews* helped to spread the style, as did publicity from the *New York Times,* the *Wall Street Journal,* and *Better Homes and Gardens.* Richard C. Minto, manager of the Chicago store Carson Pirie Scott & Company, describes a 1976 window series, "Out on the Town," that he created: "In the first window were several ladies beautifully dressed with a chrome and glass background. The next window showed them at a theater ticket booth. The next had one man and two ladies at a bar. The fourth showed them at the theater; the fifth at dinner; the sixth at a discotheque; the seventh out of doors in the moonlight. The last window showed the lady at home with her Alka-Seltzer and an icebag on her head."[42] As street theatre spread to "the provinces," Rootstein's Michael Southgate remembered, "people were appalled, fascinated, interested by it," though "there weren't many who had the opportunity to apply it."

The notoriety of the windows grew, but some critics balked at calling them theatre. Story artist Mac Adams, known for his photo-mysteries—"sequences of pictures which often seem unrelated, until one spots a telltale clue"—criticized Pratts's windows: "The trouble with Bloomingdale's windows is that they're just interesting situations. There aren't emotional underpinnings to draw you into the scene."[43] Hoskins acknowledged that much of the drama was left to the audience to create; the feverish pace at which the Bloomingdale's staff worked left little time to consider all the dramatic consequences of their displays. Given the difficulty with which many display directors talk about their intentions and the alarm and surprise which they exhibit upon being told passersby's interpretations of their work, this seems plausible. Some shock windows seem aesthetically *dependent* on their creators' refusal to consider too carefully beforehand the possible interpretations of their stagings and their expectation that audiences will linger and perhaps overinterpret the displays.

The excesses of street theatre seemed to provoke a

new, more abstract, "architectural" approach to display. Once discovered by the media, the form was quickly glamorized and its quality dissipated: "So many stores and directors picked it up, put it in their windows and most of them very badly. It simply became bastardized. Many times, and easily enough, the merchandise lost its elegance; and a situation which offered potential creative good taste often produced poor taste. Other directors never felt it was their place to impose on the viewer his or her values or lifestyles. There was no need to present sex, bi- or uni-, or drugs or politics or religion. And in fact, some felt that it was not just a matter of presenting it, but that it was a matter of imposing it because it did appear front and center in the windows."[44]

Many, like Macy's Joseph Cicio, could hardly wait until the wild period in display was over: "I've had it with all the neurotic little dramas so many display people are pushing," he said. And some celebrated the death of street theatre a bit prematurely. Pamela Senerius Gramke recalled in 1977 an earlier, more elegant style of display: "Remember pinning and draping, the exactness with which the mannequin was oh so carefully clothed? Some of this was lost, and lost without direct effect when street theater was in vogue. With a window so intricate in its propping; with the customer's eye traveling to so many elements of the window; and with the props vying for attention with the merchandise, such disciplines easily went unnoticed by passersby."[45] Gramke's criticisms were both moral and aesthetic. Even the progenitor of the street theatre style, Bob Currie, looked back on the period with some embarrassment and found many of his window displays "too intimate," the work of someone "without regard" for the private moments of life. He was grateful that the head of the store, Geraldine Stutz, prevented him from installing a funeral window: "She was right." Madness was a persistent theme in Currie's display work at Bendel's; he once wallpapered an entire window, made scratches with nails through the wallpaper, and posed a "crazed" mannequin behind it with strips of wallpaper clinging to her fingernails. Yet he reported invariably

feeling remorse after doing an "insanity" window.

During her four and a half years at Bloomingdale's, until she left in 1979, Pratts was the queen of street theatre display. Of all the artists of street theatre, Pratts is the only one who says that the excitement generated by that form of display might be revived. Street theatre, Pratts asserts, was not strictly a seventies phenomenon, dependent on the enthusiasm for experimentation in artwork and in many people's lifestyles. Though she does not readily credit her influences, neither does she claim originality, as some of her colleagues working at the same time tend to do. She is quietly aware that fashion in display is recycled and recyclable: "Look what happened in the fifties."

Indeed, no "innovation" in display is without its precursors. More than a generation before these young art-

Playing on the desire to peek, a Gene Moore window for Bonwit Teller. Courtesy of the artist.

ists, Gene Moore had begun presenting display as something that takes place in dialogue with the viewer. Alice Saarinen wrote: "Moore sets up a visual dialogue with the window-gazer. He is a brilliant conversationalist, at all times in control of timing and response. He snares your interest with a provocative generalization. Then, sure of your involvement, he counters with a *riposte*— the visual equivalent of a well-turned phrase, or an epigram, or a pun. He has manipulated you so cleverly that you feel a glow of pleasure and a smug self-satisfaction as you suddenly 'get it,' when the joke or the story comes through. If Gene Moore were to stand on the inside of the windows, looking out, he would see secret smiles on the faces of his spectators." Marilyn Bethany credited Moore with being the one who "introduced the concepts of satire and social commentary into window sets."[46]

Moore's commitment to mannequins bridged the anti-mannequin trend of the 1960s and gave the display industry new ways of suggesting and using human presence. Long before Pratts, Moore was concerned in his Bonwit Teller displays with showing situations "with clear and understandable relationships among the props and mannequins. I wanted there to be an obvious reason for the mannequins to be there. I wanted them involved in doing something, not just showing good posture to best show off what they were wearing. If I had a room, I wanted the feeling that someone had just come in or just left—a handkerchief on a dresser, some item dropped or left behind. Out of such relationships I could bring that make-believe world to life. And without those possibilities I would have been bored to death." Moore's attention to the human presence in the window was integrally related to his predilection for showing the backstage of the psyche: the items left behind as one hurried out the door are a metaphor for the thoughts that can be captured in daydreams but not in words. A 1960 window series showed heads of classical Greek sculptures, each with a top quadrant sliced out. Inside the quadrant Moore "placed a piece of merchandise indicating what was on that person's mind. In one

head was a watch—he had time on his mind—one was a female head with a diamond ring—she was contemplating marriage—and one had a butterfly pin—he had butterflies in his head."[47]

A story could be told by a person's documents and effects. In a March 1964 window series, Moore created, with the technical help of his accountant, federal income tax statements for concocted New Yorkers:

For the first window on Fifth Avenue I blew up a copy of the 1963 Instructions for Preparing Your Federal Income Tax Form 1040 to serve as background art and arranged in front of it a timely still life: a bottle of aspirin, ice bag, pile of pencils, erasers, tax forms, and lots of extra red tape. The next window introduced New Yorkers to the hapless Yves Mal Chance, filing a joint return with his wife. Shown in the window was his Schedule A-Exemptions form, on which he claimed medical expenses of $20,159.67, some of it from hospital and insurance premiums and payments to doctors Jones, Smith, and Brown, but most of it ($20,000) a "diamond bracelet prescribed to calm wife's nerves." Near the tax form and more spilled aspirin was a telephone directory open to pawnshop listings.

The third window depicted the dismal situation of a truly woebegone New Yorker, Ruth O. Astimit. She gave her occupation as taxpayer, her Social Security number as 123-45-6789, and her address as the impossible "corner of Park and Fifth avenues." Ruth's total income for 1963 was $233,463.76, all of it from "dividends, interest, rents, royalties, and pensions"; her taxes due were $180,071.18. Other articles in the window let on that she had spent all her money on a jewel, a gold bag, and a cigarette case. With four cents left to her improbable name, she had few alternatives. Two were shown in the window: a pistol and a noose hanging nearby.

The backstage of the psyche was perhaps more buoyant and charming in Moore's day than in Pratts's. Even suicide was funny. Nevertheless, his techniques revolu-

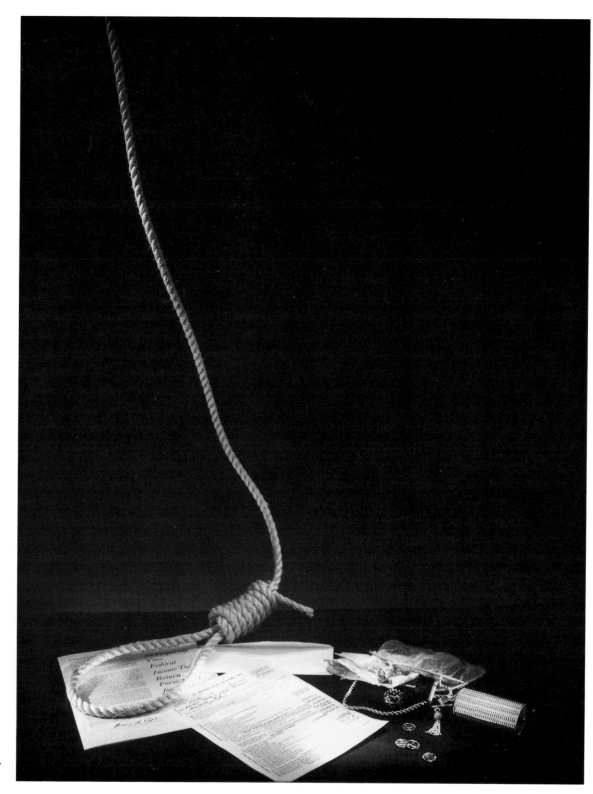

A whodunit tax story window by Gene Moore, 1964. Courtesy of the artist.

An interior display reveals the outlook of its manne-quin, 1962. Photo by Nick Malan Studios. Courtesy of Saks Fifth Avenue.

tionized what could be shown in a window. From mannequins who danced or reclined or appeared in startling situations to displays that incorporated been-there details, Moore's work may well have made street theatre possible. A full generation before street theatre he mounted his "Great White Robbery" display at Bonwit Teller: "a display for white merchandise that starred a masked mannequin who, gun in hand, stole articles of white clothing from other mannequins. A wanted poster, 'Wanted White,' appeared on the side panel of each window, complete with a sketch of the bandit, her alias ('Swim White, alias the Seal,' for example), height and weight, identifying features, and 'last seen in the vicinity of' whichever department sold the merchandise in question."[48]

Moore has been hounded by the press during and since that period when display was regarded as public art: "With lots of new young people in display, lots of articles about it in newspapers and magazines, and even television coverage, I found myself more and more being called the guru of window display—not my favorite word, but then I didn't choose it, and it usually means only that people use my ideas. Flying mannequins, mannequins lying down, mannequins in scenes of dire peril; diamonds in dirt, gin in fountains; windows that startle or amuse and windows that tell stories: I get cited for doing those and other things first as well as for bringing S and M to window display, an honor I could do without."[49]

How could Moore's windows and street theatre windows have conveyed so much activity while using stationary mannequins? Writing on a related topic, the choice of subjects for advertising photography stills, Erving Goffman noted that we can view these shots as part of a stream of extended action if what we see appears to be a climax of the longer stream, if the subjects "are captured in those acts which stereotypically epitomize the sequence from which they are taken." Sensational street theatre scenes often caught the action at its crest: the drug overdose, for example, *has* occurred, leading us to wonder what brought the woman to it and what will happen to her in the end. Our identification with the character represented by the mannequin helps us complete the narrative.

Another principle Goffman outlined to help show motion within stasis is to "draw on scenes that are themselves silent and static in real life: sleeping, pensive poses, [and] window shopping."[50] The display industry, particularly at the level of manufacture, has long capitalized on these naturally still poses.[51] Street theatre added the still states that the manufacturers had edited out—stupor, sexual exhaustion, and death.

Street theatre succeeded in grabbing the passerby's attention in part because of the perceived "marriage between mannikins and emotion" that Decter had promised in its "Young Americans" collection. Banking on street theatre's appeal, manufacturers could market emotional groupings of mannequins to display directors in more conservative regions of the country or to those who might not have the time or the temperament to cook up relationships among mannequins themselves. The manufacturer could thus retain control over how its product was used and perceived, the kind of control that Rootstein lost during street theatre by making a mannequin that was both easy to balance and realistic in its parts.

Challenged by street theatre and the increasing professionalization of the display industry, manufacturers began to push groupings, taking the dramatization of mannequins into their own hands. The increasing muscularity of mannequins, as well as the greater specificity of their poses, made it difficult to make any arm adhere to just any socket—muscles rode over the break line. The greater the realism or specificity of the pose, the more the manufacturer cut off the display artist's options—unless the artist was as skilled as Hoskins at reconfiguring mannequins. As the street theatre period ended and the pendulum swung toward abstraction, the balance of creative control returned to the manufacturer.

6 The Abstract Mannequin

What is surprising is that now that the mannequin is no longer an exact copy of nature it has more life.
—André Vigneau, 1920s

The 1960s were characterized by a titanic hunger for traces of lost authenticity. Fertile markets developed for natural foods, crafts, and such back-to-nature activities as hiking and caring for houseplants. This popular longing for the "real" helped spawn a vitriolic kill-the-mannequin movement. Written about in trade papers and in the popular press, "anti-mannequinitis" asserted the obsolescence of the old display style. Many stores stopped using mannequins altogether; instead, display heads recommended a combination of furniture, props, and platforms. A 1965 article in *Women's Wear Daily* reported, "The abolishment—an eventuality reported in these columns last month—culminates a gradual de-emphasis of mannequins that has been in effect for the past two or three years." Written histories of the mannequin give special attention to the period of their unprecedented disfavor. E. Stephen Barker writes that Robinson's, a California department store, may have been the first to "exile" its mannequins: "They revamped their fashion floors and, taking a cue from the exciting little boutiques of Europe, created myriad little settings of the swinging merchandise. Styles were small, short, colorful and petite and lent themselves to the

Patina-V's "dressable chair," a mannequin alternative. Courtesy of the manufacturer.

boutique [presentation style]. They were shown airborne with a pin here, a wire there, to create a look of motion. Yes . . . this was the sad story of the 'anti-manikinitis' disease. Stores all over the country followed suit and took the dummies down to the basement. They would never see the light-of-day again!"[1]

The etiology of the disease was complex. During the late 1940s department stores opened huge numbers of suburban branches, and with the tremendous surge in the building of malls during the 1950s and 1960s, the supply of mannequins (primarily for interior displays) could barely keep up with the demand.[2]

Manufacturers devoted little energy to developing new designs during the 1960s and were unprepared for the youth revolution that caused fashion—as it had during the 1920s—to radiate upward from the styles of the youngest women. Movement- and body-conscious fashion changed people's ideas of what the body looked like and was capable of. The once-elegant older figures suddenly seemed stiff and desperately out of step with the new, stripped-down body in motion. So did figures whose arms had been arranged to show off the latest appliances for the well-equipped suburban home. A Rootstein press release describes the display world of 1966, when the company created the influential Twiggy mannequin: "The display mannequins of the early '60s were production line stereotypes with frozen doll-like

*Fashion gets its inspiration
from the young, 1969
Henry Callahan window.
Photo by Nick Malan Stu-
dios. Courtesy of Saks Fifth
Avenue.*

faces and rounded joints: their proportions were unreal
—17 inch waists were common—and their shoes were
forever sculpted to their feet. It was not even thought
necessary to change mannequins more than once in
a while: most display manufacturers launched new
ranges only at eight year intervals." As Barker put it,
mannequins held "the same old do-nothing-for-the-
merchandise poses that dated back to before the war,
when the motto seemed to be 'Don't disturb the merchandise.' "

The inadequacy of the era's mannequins was emphasized by the revolution in fashion modeling, both photographed and live: "Fashions [were] modeled by kids
who literally danced down the runways," Barker recalled. "But at the back of the store, [buyers] saw their

finds on static, do-nothing manikins."[3] Display directors who had earned their reputations from the display
of the human figure challenged the anti-mannequin
movement. Henry Callahan at Saks Fifth Avenue took
"a dim view of anyone who dismisses such a useful
tool."[4] But critics thought mannequins actually de-
tracted from sales rather than enhancing them, and
some stores banned the figures against the wishes of
their display directors. Dan Arjé, an outspoken foe of
anti-mannequinitis, who was directing display at Bonwit Teller, admits that to their detractors mannequins
"seemed to be old-fashioned, fuddy-duddy." Indeed,
mannequins seemed so archaic during the 1960s that
they were preferred to live, costumed interpreters at
the living-history museum Plimoth Plantation, where
"mannequins had the 'aura of antiquity,' while the local
people seemed terribly 'modern' and were perceived as
such by the visitors."[5]

Rootstein's industry-shaking innovations cured anti-
mannequinitis, yet by the 1970s display people demonstrated a renewed interest in abstract forms and architecturally inspired constructions—"mannequin
alternatives"—that could show off the new oversized,
unisex clothing. The result was a fierce debate over the
relative merits of realistic and abstract representation in
mannequins.

The *Buyer's Guide* for the industry publication *Visual
Merchandising & Store Design* lists three kinds of mannequins: abstract, realistic, and stylized (semirealistic).
It also includes various forms in which no attempt at
anthropomorphization has been made. Forms are partial bodies designed to display individual pieces of apparel; pants forms, for example, are representations of
hips and legs but have the body sliced off at the waist,
where they are flat. Mannequin buyers make several
important choices at the start. Do they want male or female adult mannequins, or children? Do they want a realistic, a semirealistic, or an abstract mannequin? Might
a mannequin alternative be the best choice?

The choices of gender, age, and style are largely
governed by the merchandise to be shown. Children's

A mannequin dancing on pointe shows how heavy "movement" can look in fiberglass, 1969. Photo by Nick Malan Studios. Courtesy of Saks Fifth Avenue.

clothing has probably never been stretched onto a man's frame in window display, and although the unisex look has permitted men's clothes to be shown on female mannequins, the reverse has remained unacceptable.[6] The style choice may also be affected by the natural pendulum swing of preferences between realistic and abstract mannequins, a pattern as apparently self-perpetuating as cycles in fashion preferences.

The abstract mannequin, according to industry spokesman Martin Pegler, is "a highly stylized, usually non-featured mannequin devoid of wig and/or make-up details. Though based on human measurements and proportions, the shape and sculpting is not realistic and strives instead for a decorative and non-objective effect." Abstract mannequins are "ageless, non-ethnic,

non-specific, and can be finished in a variety of decorative colors or metallics."[7] A rather flexible boundary separates realistic and semirealistic mannequins; the most prominent differences are usually in the heads. Realistic mannequins take wigs and makeup, whereas most semirealistics have sculpted hair, which requires less maintenance. Eyes of semirealistic mannequins may also be sculpted rather than painted on. Still, the proportions of a semirealistic mannequin are more realistic, less evidently interpretive, than those of abstract figures. Mannequin alternatives are usually more architectural and more abstracted from the human form even than abstract mannequins, while maintaining proportions that allow a single garment or an entire ensemble to be displayed, though usually not "filled out" as they would be on a more humanlike form.

Once the gender and age of the required mannequin have been determined, the choice of style is usually left to the personal aesthetics of display directors—and directors have expressed emphatic opinions on the pros and cons of each type. A display person's preference for a given representational approach to human form and character is key to understanding that director's theory of how mannequins work on—and sell to—the customer.

The primary argument still advanced in favor of the realistic female mannequin is that of all figure types it most readily permits the customer to imagine how a particular garment would look on her. This process is in part a matter of identification and projection: the customer both sees herself in the mannequin and sees the mannequin's ideal body instead of her own imperfect one. Women have been trained, perhaps by exposure to retail modeling, to project their own bodies and personalities onto that of a figure wearing a garment they desire. A handbook instructs would-be models that the customer looks at "gown after gown with the utmost discrimination before deciding which one 'will do things' for her appearance. In other words, she buys with an intense personal interest, visualizes herself supplanting the mannequin in each costume with more or less realism."[8] A 1937 article identified a "school" whose members—Macy's, Altman's, Bonwit Teller, and Best's, among others—held that "without reproducing a complete human being you can't really show clothes that human beings are going to wear."[9] That school of thought is as vocal as ever.

The principle of identification goes beyond the relationship between the individual customer and the particular mannequin, for the realistic mannequin can be used not only to represent the ideal customer of the store but also to convey in human form the store's "personality." Nellie Fink of Adel Rootstein asserts that in an age when every store sells the same merchandise, the realistic mannequin is the only personal way to represent the image of the store; the mannequin must supply the part that the merchandise once played in making the store unique.[10]

Human form edging toward furniture form. Courtesy of Patina-V.

Michael Southgate of Adel Rootstein emphasizes the dramatic power of realistic mannequins. Abstract mannequins, he says, are essentially "merchandisers," fixtures without human interest: "A good mannequin is selling all the time, and a merchandiser . . . is just hanging there. You can feel, touch—but you could never identify that shape as a human shape, because it's all laid flat. And a great deal of clothes don't look good flat; they need a body inside to come to life." Southgate speculates that an abstract mannequin—one, for example, with a head lopped off—is attractive to visual merchandisers who are "frightened of an ordinary mannequin," who might not have the technique to dress and maintain it. "I think the good people tend to want a realistic figure," he muses; "there's more drama there. . . . And I find with our own mannequins, some of the ones with stylized faces and hands, they look wonderful as statues, but the moment you put the clothes on, they don't look so hot. They look better naked."

Street theatre artists almost exclusively used realistic mannequins—and these were almost without exception Rootsteins, partly because of the company's advances in achieving lifelikeness. Japanese visual merchandiser Toshi recalls first seeing American street theatre windows in 1971 and recognizing them immediately as theatre because they were "exciting" and "dramatic." At the same time, Toshi remembers, they were easy for the shopper to understand precisely because of their reliance on realistic mannequins, which permitted shoppers both to see how the clothes should be worn and to imagine how they might feel if they wore the clothes themselves.

The overriding preference for realistic figures changed in the early 1980s, when many display directors became interested in architecturally inspired abstract figures that would complement their store designs. As a result of the success of such abstracts as Pucci's active-men figures, a more architectural approach to the human body came into vogue. At the same time, the definition of visual merchandising expanded beyond window dressing to include store planning and the development of sophisticated merchandising strategies. Ralph Pucci said in 1986 that "there will always be a need for realistic mannequins for certain kinds of merchandise, but it will get slimmer and slimmer in the future."[11] Michael Southgate maintains that abstract mannequins and mannequin alternatives became more popular among visual merchandisers because "they don't interrupt the basic store design." When the surface of the body has been finished to blend in with the walls and floor, mannequin design becomes an extension of store fixture design.

The fresh surge in abstracts' popularity was partly economic. The retailing downturn of the 1980s left display departments with dramatically smaller budgets. Staff cuts included people skilled to wig, make up, dress, and maintain realistic mannequins. Budgets for buying new mannequins were reduced, so directors of display departments and mannequin buyers for large chains had to find figures that would serve in a variety of different settings and with many kinds of merchandise, that would require minimal skill to work with, and that would last a long time. As Martha Landau put it, budget-conscious stores favor abstracts because they "never go out of style."[12] And, unlike realistics, abstract mannequins can often be presented without shoes— a significant saving for small boutiques that don't ordinarily stock them. Finally, abstracts are ageless and lack ethnicity, making them both adaptable and politically safe.

Toshi has said that the growth of mass merchandising altered the basic creative problem for display people. Visual merchandisers who once occupied themselves with how to dramatize the material must now discover how to organize the sheer quantity of things on the market. This shift accounts for the increased emphasis on store fixtures and geometric layouts rather than on dramatizing the individual outfit. Once abstract mannequins took over, Toshi believes, display art showed less sensitivity to the clothing. For Toshi, abstract mannequins are statements that the visual merchandising industry makes to itself, a form of "masturbation, internal satisfaction," as abstract mannequins are too sophisticated for the over-thirty shopper who can actually afford to buy the clothes they merchandise.

Yet prejudices just as strong prevail against realistic mannequins. Halston display man Victor Hugo found them sordid, evoking a reality he'd much prefer to forget. To Hugo, realistic mannequins "either look[ed] like prostitutes off Forty-Second Street or empty models." Cliff Bostock found evidence of the superficial values of the 1970s in the period's move toward extreme realism: "The contemporary mannequin, a gorgeous and super-realistic individual, may be the very emblem of society's celebration of decadence, whose objectives are extreme refinement of style and artificiality of content."[13]

Bostock's argument is at least as old as the headless dressmaker's forms, their shoulders topped with white paper cones, that were used for display in the United States in the 1840s. The prejudice against mannequins with heads is a longstanding one, surviving today in the preference of many display artists for abstract mannequins, onto whose enigmatic faces any personality may be projected—and which resemble neither the streetwalker nor the dreaded drag queen. A 1914 article in the trade paper *Merchants Record and Show Window* called the wax faces of the recent years a "gross libel on nature"; the writer took offense at the mannequin's pretension to reality, most falsified by the face.[14] The abstract mannequin's dressmaking origins is obvious: it shares with the form the ethic that as long as the body does what it is supposed to do, the head is "extra." At the same time, the focus of some abstract mannequins on the creation of an outrageous character—as consciously styled as the clothes it is wearing—shows how far this once purely functional tool has evolved.

Realism quickly appears banal to some. In the early 1980s, when Japanese-style clothing swept American fashion, abstracts began to display Asian facial features, filtered through the art nouveau or art deco styles that were also being revived in clothing. For the fashion designer Cathy Hardwick, however, even the stylized suggestion of ethnicity was too specific: "I'm not the average American white, but I'm tired of ethnic mannequins. I prefer ambiguous faces, white porcelain finishes, short hair—a nothing kind of look." Andrée Putman created a sort of "failed ethnic" mannequin; the abstract figure metamorphosed during the sculpting process: "It started being absolutely Chinese, then black, then very much like a South American, and ended by being anything."[15]

Many fashion designers, like costume curators, prefer abstract mannequins to realistic ones because they focus attention on the clothing itself rather than on the "character" wearing it. In his own boutique, Halston preferred abstracts to show his clothing, and maintained that, as his display designer Victor Hugo put it, "if you promote make-up and wigs you should have a mannequin with a face and wigs; but we sell clothes, so we should just suggest a body."[16]

Some display directors prefer an abstract mannequin precisely *because* they believe that the customer relates better to a realistic one. Relating better, they reason, may also mean brewing all the other emotions that one person may feel for another—not all of them positive or sales-inducing. Edward T. Cranston, a prominent manufacturer of abstract mannequins and a leading innovator in their design, found that customers' preferences for one face over another can be capricious at best. There will be certain realistic children's faces that you'll adore, Cranston said, others you'll just want to "smack." And he finds the margin for error even smaller with a woman's figure: "Let's face it: all women aren't beautiful. That's —the birds! They're not! Say you do something [in a mannequin] that isn't quite beautiful; people criticize it. [Yet] if you do something that is too pretty, she's 'too pretty.'" Guy Scarangello concurs: "It's funny—You know, you think of mannequins sometimes only as a form to display the merchandise. But it's more than that: People really think of them as people, as the ideal person, because that's the ideal body underneath there making that thing look dynamite. . . . Even the face of a mannequin becomes very important to them; I mean, they can be turned off by a face, or violently opposed to a face."

A few display directors, in contrast, have preferred to use abstract mannequins for dramatic reasons, believing that they permitted greater identification on the part of the viewer. Hugo found greater expressive freedom with the "sprayed-out" silver and white mannequins that Halston had purchased for his shop than he would have with mannequins in set positions. Although he often showed the mannequins performing everyday actions, Hugo discovered great versatility in the abstracts. According to Lynne Lapin, "A faceless mannequin allows for more drama as it permits the viewer to place herself in the mannequin's place. There is no face on the form, allowing you to think it might be whomever you wish it to be. In this way, reality is actually enhanced rather than diminished." And some display people give moral reasons for their choice of an abstract. Manufacturer Mary Brosnan notes that "the abstract trend in mannequins' faces started with the idea proper in a boutique that the mannequin shouldn't force its own personality on customers."[17]

The choice of a realistic or an abstract mannequin may ultimately depend on how the designer assesses the consumer's intelligence and imagination. In general, Toshi prefers realistic mannequins for the American market, except for inexpensive juniors' clothing; teenagers alone, he feels, have enough imagination to project their own identities onto an abstract figure. Colin Birch took the opposite view, prescribing abstracts in all situations but the display of clothing for juniors. Birch reasoned that because teenagers lack a fixed sense of their developing identities, display needs to provide strong, realistic images and a complete picture of the social world available to those who wear the featured clothing.[18]

Mannequin designers have expressed wonder at the paradox that an abstract mannequin may convey the greatest effect of realism of all. Andrée Putman told the *Washington Post* that her new mannequin for Pucci conveyed a surprising sense of reality: "Though abstract, she looks more like the real person than the make-believe dolls with fake everything. . . . It seems very paradoxical that something that is so different and abstract, with only one eye, with wet hair, like out of the shower, should look so real. . . . It is far from real and yet it is the most realistic of all." Putman's assessment of the startling realism of an abstract figure is echoed in a review by Harold Chester: "Paradoxically, the most lifelike mannequins are often the most disquietingly corpselike, while figures such as the sinewy Art-Deco models distill a vital energy through distortions of human forms."[19]

The Transfigured Body

The first abstract mannequin is reputed to have been presented to an unenraptured audience at the 1911 Salon d'Automne in Paris. Perhaps inspired by photography, the mannequin was a cubist figure, its surface a defracting myriad of tiny broken mirrors. In 1925, V. N. Siégel of Siégel & Stockman manufactured the first modern stylized mannequins, "abbreviated renditions of the human form, with expressions that seemed to mask feelings and retain a certain aloofness." The concept had been suggested by the director of the Paris store Galeries Lafayette. The mannequins were to be inspired not by live models but, revolutionarily, by fashion drawings. Siégel explained the rationale behind his designs: "The old mannequin, too realistic to respond to the abstract form assumed by architecture and decoration, could no longer fit into the window display with its effective and sober luxury as it is now conceived. This basic conviction prompted me to make an appeal to a new form of expression in order to bring about a timely rejuvenation and modernization."[20] Beginning with the 1911 cubist figure, the model from which sculptors of abstract or stylized mannequins worked has been not a live person but an artful representation of one.

Often the idea for an abstract mannequin has involved imposing a form onto the human body. Creative director George Martin said that the essential idea of the abstract mannequin is "to take the human body and to put some geometry into it." For Martin, trained as

"Astral." Courtesy of Gem-ini Mannequins.

an architect, this meant primarily either rounding or sharpening the body's planes, literally a geometrically influenced process of layering on. When Patina-V develops a new line of abstract mannequins, one pose is used to "set the style" for the rest. This basic pose often takes three times as long to create as any of the others, but it gives the sculptor and the creative director the opportunity to view the body in three dimensions so they can "finalize the stylization of the body."

Geometric stylization is one primary type of abstraction; another is reconstitution. L. Frank Baum had already boasted in 1898 of the many ways he had found in the harsh economic climate of the period to fabricate humanlike figures out of unaccustomed materials. His *Show Window* included an illustration of "a very clever make-up of a man formed entirely from Manila twines and ropes" that bore a startling resemblance to later illustrations of the Cowardly Lion in *The Wizard of Oz.* Surrealists later showed special interest in the refabrication of human forms out of novel materials: "Fantastic figures made of twisted tree branches, pieces of colored rags, and glittering beads roamed about many a Fifth Avenue window."[21]

A visitor to the influential 1925 Paris Exposition, where abstracts were featured prominently, returned to America questioning the taste of these creatures' purveyors, as well as that of the "modern" design characteristic of all the displays there: "Walk into most of the Exposition buildings and you will see sausagey furniture distorting itself to look 'different,' loud tapestries on gaudy fabrics, tricksy things of all kinds. Why should the very mannequins in the *pavillons* of the fashionable shops be made to appear as if they had kept a four-thousand years' vigil in Tut-ankh-Amen's tomb? . . . Everything has to strike the visitor by its unexpectedness, nothing by its charm."[22]

Art deco became the dominant style of 1920s mannequins. Like Frederick Kiesler and other artists and thinkers of the decade, Siégel saw display as the vehicle for the most modern and forward-thinking expressions of the day, and his company produced the first documented androgynous mannequins in 1929. They "resembled aliens with luminescent eyes—the earliest bald-headed, androgynous figures"; they had a "vacant sadness to their faces."[23]

By the 1930s a dialectic developed between a lifelike mannequin that satisfied the demand for realistic display and a stylized mannequin that seemed to reflect the spirit of the times. Nicole Parrot has noted that "paradoxically, it was just at the time when [the more architectural] mannequins were becoming part of the scene around them by changing colour to match their surroundings that they began to exist in their own right." Parrot wrote that the two types of mannequin "represented the widespread antagonism between two visions of the world, two irreconcilable mentalities. The former clung to the decorous, reasonable, bourgeois model, appreciative of plush drawing-rooms and traditional villas; the latter lived in a spare decor with plain furniture in Le Corbusier's buildings that were full of light."[24]

The 1937 Paris Exposition featured mannequins by Robert Couturier, who was attempting to create "tragic silhouettes that were intentionally devoid of any of the pleasantness, the gentleness, that usually go with elegance. Their defensive, frightened gestures, their featureless faces, their badly balanced bodies, recalled the inhabitants of Pompeii surprised by a cloud of ashes rather than the habitués of the Faubourg Saint-Honoré or avenue Montaigne." Couturier's plaster and oakum figures were finished to look as if they had been made of terra cotta and were designed to be "in complete harmony with the decor."[25] An architectural aesthetic governed the body and created a notion of mannequins as sculptural objects.

The designer of the realistic mannequin operates under many constraints. Bodies must be of certain proportions, sizes, and apparent weights, and must adopt poses that convey only particular types of moods and attitudes. By contrast, the designer of the abstract mannequin or the mannequin alternative not only is less constrained by these criteria, but may graphically distort certain elements of the figure to suit his or her own aesthetics.

Clothes must look appealing when displayed on the mannequin, but the seven-foot figure and the hulking muscular shape become legitimate possibilities.[26]

Lester Gaba, a veteran of the 1920s obsession with stylized figures, made perhaps the most impassioned "plea for realism" in the next decade. Unwilling to call what he had seen at the 1937 Paris Exposition "mannequins," he referred to them pointedly as "statues" that were "exciting for the reason that they were not made to wear clothes. They are seven feet high and in order to show fashions on them, the Parisian Couturier made *special* clothes for them, and in some cases actually went to the exposition grounds and draped clothes on them on the spot. Fancy trying to show a $59.50 fur trimmed cloth coat on a seven foot abstraction." Reviewing the years it took to get over "what I would call 'The Dark Ages' of window display," Gaba urged display people, long titillated by new designs in mannequin bodies, to choose the figures "which American shoppers understand, and reward with sales." The same year, the display man Dana O'Clare wrote that the audience's eyes "should be made to open in pleased surprise, [because] a startled blink doesn't go far toward arousing an urge to buy."[27]

Futuristic abstracts are part of a history—prevalent since the futurist movements of the early twentieth century—of associating people with machines. The trend has continued in the work of such sculptors as Richard Stankiewicz, for whom "parts of machines stirred recollections of parts of figures, or the reverse."[28] The 1927 film *Metropolis* summed up early twentieth-century angst about the coming of the machine age and the possibility that people may come to be nothing more than imperfect machines. The ruthless inventor Rotwang has "created a machine in the image of man, that never tires or makes a mistake. . . . Now," he declares, "we have no further use for living workers." Lotte H. Eisner wrote of the film that "the inhabitants of the underground town are more like automatons than the robot created by . . . Rotwang. Their entire person is geared to the rhythm of the complicated machines [that they operate]: their arms become the spokes of an immense wheel, their bodies set into recesses on the façade of the machine-house represent the hands of a gigantic clock. The human element is stylized into a mechanical element."[29] Anthropomorphized embodiments of corporate identity were developed around the turn of the century partly as a product of the fascination the machine held for many artists and painters, even as many people were concerned with the reduction of man to machine. A familiar example is Bibendum, better known as the Michelin Man, which was created in 1898 and still exists as the cuddly personification of a major manufacturer.

Marsha Bentley Hale has noted the influence of the Memphis school of design on abstract and semi-abstract mannequins: "Memphis is a blend of Bauhaus and the Fifties with bold colours (some) and the clean graphic quality of cartoon-land plus a dash of space-age added in; cubist bodies, featureless androids with and without moulded hair, half-heads, no-heads sometimes with an interpretation of a muscular body—torso forms with the feeling of a painting by the Italian artist Di Chirico."[30] The futuristic abstract is also in part a by-product of parallel design solutions in other fields. Because fiberglass made mannequins virtually indestructible, the visual merchandising industry had continually to update its designs—or to declare previous ones outdated—to sell more mannequins.

Adrian Forty postulated that a "a basic grammar or repertory of design imagery" can be reduced to three essential ways of styling a commodity to make it appear fresh and eminently buyable. All three styling techniques were developed during the late 1920s and early 1930s, in the beginning days of radio, and at least two had to do with positioning the object in relation to time. In the antiquarian approach, the radio was encased in what looked like an antique cabinet, which imbued it with the comfort of nostalgia. A second strategy was to deny the radio by hiding it in something else entirely. The third technique, which worked better as people became less apprehensive about the new technology, was to "place it within a cabinet designed to suggest that it belonged to a future and better world."[31] Abstract mannequin design capitalized on advances in the post-Twiggy realistic figure: in Forty's terms, the abstract did not reflect the 1970s, as many have said about the realistic mannequin of that period, but rather created its own chronology by playing havoc with ours. The abstract mannequin relates not only to what is happening on the street in art-world currency, but plays against current trends in realism.

Until the 1970s most stylized mannequins were rehashes of designs from the 1920s and 1930s; sometimes manufacturers used the old molds outright. Around 1970, however, the first futuristic abstracts began to appear. Gemini Mannequins produced "Focus One Abstracts," which looked like creatures from outer space. Swiss manufacturer Jacques Schläppi became famous for its abstracts, which were well suited for showing off the unisex looks of the early 1970s. Parrot called the new abstracts "a new race of mannequins, smooth creatures with ill-defined features and egg-shaped heads," figures that "seem to have been created to evolve in the nude."[32]

Abstract mannequins flourished during the 1980s, the period just after the death of street theatre, when display budgets crashed and display evolved—or devolved—into "visual merchandising." As display people assumed responsibility for store planning and design, mannequin manufacturers placed greater emphasis on mannequins' architectural dimension, typified for some in the industry by the figures' foundry finishes. Ralph Pucci, who entered his father's business in 1976, regards mannequins as "a touch of reality, a touch of fantasy, and a touch of the architectural element of the store." Gaba would never have perceived all mannequins this way: realism yes, artistry yes, but not the linkage of the body with its environment (though Colette's "Living Environment" was a precursor to that element of the Pucci approach). In some cases, the active human body even seems to have supplanted more orthodox architecture in the world of display. A pair of chiseled abstracts, one male, one female, from Patina-V's "Sublime" collection, lean back against back, their buttocks, shoulder blades, and sliced-off crowns of heads meeting in flat planes. The figures are bookends—or paired pillars.

Display directors of the 1980s, like Jim Mansour, saw and used mannequins in relation to the interior designs

"Sublime," by Patina-V.
Courtesy of the
manufacturer.

of their stores. Guy Scarangello ordered a cream finish or a striated marbleized effect on his Pucci mannequins for the Gucci stores, whose color scheme—or "color story"—is a light-beige bird's-eye maple, with white and brown marble floors; that the mannequin reflects the decor of the store helps to bring out Gucci's "Italian" character. More recently, abstract mannequins have been offered both in solid lacquer finishes and in a selection of finishes inspired by building materials. A color card issued by the manufacturer Flat Friends features four faux stone finishes (to give the impression of agate, "Verdi Pompeii" marble, or two different types of granite), as well as copper, brass, aluminum, "copper-burnished," and "natural cork" finishes.

The differences between abstract figures of the 1980s and realistics go beyond the surfaces. Whereas the realistic mannequin—typically "caught" in motion: dancing, walking, or slouching—appears to act on its environment and to be situated comfortably within it, the abstract mannequin or alternative internalizes and re-presents the object world as a function of its own "body." The New York–based display props manufacturer George Dell makes human-sized torsos that are poised—cut off at the hips—on top of tables, like a photograph in Heribert Brehm's "Half Series." One of Brehm's shots features a nude woman who appears from the hips up as if emerging from the top of a desk; she snaps photos, which fall from her Polaroid. Another features a "secretary" leaning over her desk, her prominent buttocks clothed in sheer black fabric; the desk substitutes for the rest of her body. Robert Benzio portrayed a more modestly clad body emerging from furniture in a 1983 window series; in one scene, a stately mannequin appears, from the waist up, her torso planted atop a mantelpiece, her shoes and handbag placed gingerly on the floor in front of the fireplace.

Patina Arts also manufactures dressmaker's forms that have been coupled with tables, and these pairings are always explicitly underscored, both in the company's brochures and in its showroom. One form is poised atop a curved stand patterned after the lyre motif that replaces the "head" of the form. A companion piece, a half-torso, is connected by a pole to a clear glass table, which in turn is supported by a matching lyre-motif stand. One of the charmed pair is more human-looking; one is more like furniture with a human inspiration. Because they are always mated, each partakes of the qualities of the other. In Patina's brochure a bright pair of high-heeled shoes appears on the clear glass table, at the base of the half-torso. They look like an offering, like something to eat. The mannequin alternative incorporates actions of the body into its design, indicating both a being (the half-torso) and an action performed on its environment (the offering, presented on the glass table). The human province of action has been incorporated into design.

The likening of the human body to furniture is a rich theme for abstraction. Furniture, particularly chairs and sofas, is in a sense a negative of the space occupied by the human body in a seated position and may thus be thought of as a body representation. For Patina-V's Fall 1990 NADI Market show, George Martin promised "furniture you can dress," a project that was about "creating a body that's sitting down, that looks like a

"Soigné," one of a number of Patina-V's products that explicitly paired mannequins and furniture. Courtesy of the manufacturer.

piece of furniture." "ACH-1" is a sculpture in which a flat material with the surface texture of corrugated cardboard has been molded into the Z-shape of a chair. This creation is half-furniture, half-mannequin. The back of the chair curves concavely forward ever so slightly, like a person slouching, and the back has been molded to suggest the contours of a human torso: The top is wide, like human shoulders; there is a "waist" of sorts, and as the chair widens to its seat, a distinct pair of "hips" swell out. A tiny ball rests on top of a futuristically antennaed "neck." In its conception, the sculpture was both mannequin alternative and furniture. Martin reasoned, "When you're sitting down like this, you're really taking the shape of a chair, so why not make a chair that you can merchandise?" In Martin's formulation, we no longer design chairs to fit the positions that the human body takes in repose; instead, by seeing the artifacts of life we learn the human character and deduce the behavior that gives those artifacts meaning. The realistic mannequin sits; the abstract mannequin alternative apes a human body.

Precedents and parallels exist in both display and surrealist art for linking body and apparel with furniture. Elsa Schiaparelli treated pockets in a 1936 "desk suit" as drawers. Magritte had presented the body as casket. For the Surrealist Exposition of 1938, Kurt Seligmann created "L'Ultrameuble," a three-legged stool made out of three mannequin legs, fairly attired in hose and dress pumps. The tradition survives: in 1985, for example, Karl Lagerfeld showed a chair-shaped hat.

Years before the debut of Patina Arts' dressable chair, the display man Jim Mansour had substituted chairs for mannequins, dressing them instead. Guy Scarangello reports having presented chairs themselves "almost as dresses . . . [They] became clothing almost." At the same time the art world was doing related work, using environments and furniture as suggestions of human gesture and body stance. Vito Acconci created *People's Wall* in 1985, a fabric-covered wall with cutout profiles of people shown sitting, reclining, and walking. The work was displayed so that museum visitors could actu-

Designer Andrée Putman's mannequin, a merchandising drawing card for Barneys New York. Courtesy of Simon Doonan.

ally extrude themselves through the people-holes in the walls, assuming the positions demanded by the cut-outs.[33] Acconci's works demonstrated the negative-space aspect of furniture. Ronald J. Onorato writes that Acconci's body furniture was an extension of his body art. It gave the spectator-participant the opportunity to have contact with the traces of where the artist had been. In Acconci's body-furniture work, "We step into the artist's shoes, lie in his shadow, or sit in his place."

Scott Burton's furniture, which stood on its own as a reflection of the humans that would inhabit it, played an integral role in such performance pieces as the *Behavior Tableaux* of the 1970s. Critic Brenda Richardson described Burton's 1971–74 work *Pastoral Chair Tableau* as "found second-hand chairs . . . situated in stage-like arrangements." For Richardson, bodily meanings and spatial meanings are inseparable in Burton's work: "All objects, and especially objects familiar from daily use in a personal environment, are charged with meaning and memory. The wordless drama of the chair tableau projected its eloquence through these 'persistent meanings' and through the 'body' language, conveyed in the specificity of each spatial interval, of these inanimate objects."[34]

Constructions such as Patina-V's blur the line between human representation and architecture in display and may challenge our ideas about just what sort of response is demanded of the viewer. A 1987 editorial by *Visual Merchandising & Store Design* editor P. K. Anderson registered the confusion of the industry as the lines between mock-furniture and mock-architecture intersected:

> When is a mannequin not a mannequin? We found ourselves pondering that question on more than one occasion while sorting through the products received for our special mannequin section. And we continue to be perplexed. There are abstract forms made out of pipe or wood or wire that seem to bear striking resemblance to fixtures in substance and function. But because they remotely resemble the human form, we're inclined to call them "mannequin alternatives." What are these creatures? . . . Even with fixturing systems, figures have become integral to the mechanics of presentation. . . . Where do you draw the line between fixturing and many mannequin alternatives in today's market? After some lengthy discussion, we determined that if you can dress the "object," then it qualifies as a mannequin alternative —no matter what it's made out of or what it looks like. And if you can't dress it, then it must not be a mannequin. . . .
>
> To further confuse matters, think about this: . . . If mannequins = displayers and displayers = fixtures, then mannequins = fixtures. Funny how the circle is a wheel.[35]

This entire "mannequin issue" dealt with the preponderance of mannequin alternatives. Ysla Design offered a dressable ladder with broadened "shoulders" and a

"Invisible mannequin" display by Henry Callahan, 1964. Photo by Nick Malan Studios. Courtesy of Saks Fifth Avenue.

tiny ladder "neck" at the top, intended to display shirts and jackets. By contrast with the abstract mannequin, Martin Pegler notes, the mannequin alternative may require even more skill of the display person than would a traditional realistic, calling upon him or her to pin, pad, plump, drape, fold, and fly garments.[36] For the less of a body the manufacturer provides, the more the display artist must suggest.

The Disappearing Body

Jean Baudrillard proposed in his essay "The Precession of Simulacra" that "to dissimulate is to feign not to have what one has. To simulate is to feign to have what one hasn't. One implies a presence, the other an absence. But the matter is more complicated, since to simulate is not simply to feign: 'Someone who feigns an illness can simply go to bed and make believe he is ill. Someone who simulates an illness produces in himself some of the symptoms,' [according to the lexicographer Maximilien-Paul-Emile Littre]. Thus, feigning or dissimulating leaves the reality principle intact: the difference is always clear, it is only masked; whereas simulation threatens the difference between 'true' and 'false,' between 'real' and 'imaginary.'"[37] The simulation of the human body—fragmented, complete, or represented through absence—confronts us directly with our uncertainty over the boundary between the real and the imaginary. For even if what were to replace the invisible body in display were actually present, it might not be the realistic mannequin, the sign of a person, but rather an abstract mannequin, a mannequin alternative, or a sign for another kind of creature altogether. As we encounter body fragments and suggested bodies in display, we are likely to question our own reality.

Variations on or distortions of the realistically sculpted head are the most typical alterations introduced in abstracts by manufacturers and by display people themselves. A 1970s window by Simon Doonan shows a male figure standing tall and well-armored against the cold in his winter coat and muffler. On his neck rested a rather ripe-looking pumpkin; the figure held his head gallantly in one arm. Again, surrealist aesthetics are certainly a major influence, as are headless warrior figures from literary sources.

Abstract treatments of the head, however, can be traced at least to the fifteenth century, when artists of the "grotesque" emphasized "unnatural, biomorphic mergings of plant, animal, and human features." In the sixteenth century, Giuseppe Arcimboldo painted faces made of fruits, vegetables, fish, tree roots, and insects, among other natural objects.[38] These art movements partook of the most heretical revisionism toward the Western psyche possible: the head was not the center of being or of human consciousness, but merely an object, and a common one at that. Mannequin manufacturers and display artists top realistic and abstract bodies with fruits or vegetables, abstract geometric shapes, poodles' heads, light bulbs, antlers, or fish bowls with live fish

E. T. Cranston's Glove Holder, designed to appear to arise out of the display case. Courtesy of E. T. Cranston-Almax (USA).

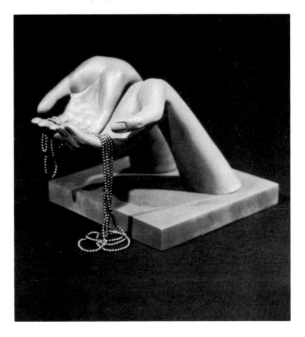

Mannequins with Corinthian capitals for heads. Courtesy of Carol Barnhart.

swimming about inside. Both parody and serious effort within the mannequin-as-architecture tradition can be seen in the manufacturer Carol Barnhart's 1987 mannequins, whose necks are bowed by top-heavy, antique-gold Corinthian capitals. Another architecturally inspired technique is to lop off part of the already-chiseled face of the abstract mannequin, as if the face were a found archaeological relic, of no more significance "historically" than the rest of the body (which has somehow remained intact).

New York audiences are familiar with mannequins whose heads have been replaced by bouquets of flowers, sheaves of wrapping paper, balloons, or bizarre or cartoonlike masks. At Esprit during the 1980s, it was a matter of corporate principle to alter the head of the mannequin, using only the company's own merchandise or packaging: "One of the trademarks of Esprit manne-

quin styling is the way they are finished with unique head treatments—handbags, belts, shopping bags, socks, shorts, shoeboxes, scarves and shirts are all candidates. . . . This adds color, texture and humor to the displays."[39] Heads may be multiplied as well as replaced, sending the same message—that bodies and selves are as alterable as fashion itself. A 1949 Bonwit Teller window by Gene Moore shows a mannequin in the enlarged center box of a grid of thirteen smaller boxes, each holding a stylish hat. The mannequin is elegant as ever for those days, except that she has two heads. Moore recalls: "I wanted to show a woman who loved hats so much she grew an extra head to wear them."[40]

Throughout display history "operated-upon" bodies and the presentation of body parts have been among the favorite devices of display manufacturers and directors. Since the reign of the studio system in Hollywood, glamour and fragmentation were closely linked in the public mind. Stars were associated with particular

Head replacement options, by Goldsmith. Courtesy of the manufacturer.

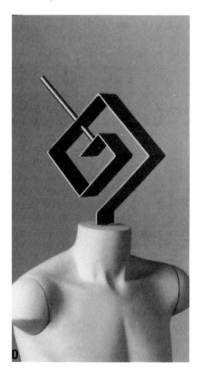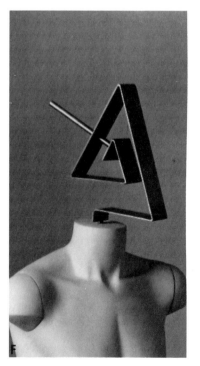

Mannequin with head of bouquet and antlers, 1959. Photo by Nick Malan Studios. Courtesy of Saks Fifth Avenue.

"parts," roles that placed the actors and their characters in a social and personal schema. In our own time, the fragmentation of the represented human body aligns with notions of defracted and borrowed selfhoods. The fitness boom of the 1980s may also be responsible for the popular insistence on the body as moldable, divisible, and separable from the self. As Alan M. Klein notes in his study of bodybuilding culture, "The view of the body as distinct from the self, and the view of the body as partible (separated into distinct parts), works to enable the bodybuilder to establish a sense of self-mastery. Body parts are specialized, named, acted upon, all in the name of fashioning a championship physique. . . . Days of the week are devoted to exercising one or another body part, even named after that part—e.g., 'Tuesday is a leg day.'"[41]

E. T. Cranston-Almax is perhaps the leading chopper and slicer among mannequin makers. Building on the use of pants forms and other "partial mannequins" to merchandise individual pieces of clothing rather than complete outfits, Cranston-Almax has developed provocative combinations of realistically sculpted body fragments that are intended to be mounted on a store's wall, slightly above eye level. A 1990 Belt Displayer shows a twisted torso, whose top is a diagonal slice starting in the midst of the curve of one breast and whose bottom is a horizontal slice just above the pubis. The Belt Displayer was ostensibly designed to show sashes bound around the waist, but as is made clear in the Cranston-Almax showroom, nonapparel cords can be wrapped package-style around the vertical and horizontal dimensions of the form to suggest bondage and erotic violence. A Panty Displayer, also flattened to be mounted on a wall, provides an analogous view from behind. Ladies' rears are prominently displayed in a row—one bare, the next with panties, another with garter belt, and one with both undergarments. The Earring Displayer, painted a neutral chalk white, features a semi-realistic half-head, shown in profile. Like the Belt Displayer, the Earring Displayer is sliced on a diagonal on top and appears to emerge from the wall. The design

seems to ask, If you don't need the hair to show the earring, what do you need it for?

Cranston-Almax also makes nearly complete bodies that are sliced not to *present* a body fragment to the viewer, but to leave one behind. These figures appear to melt through walls. The Handbag and Accessory Displayer is a complete mannequin from head to just below the buttocks—complete, that is, on the right side of its body, where a shapely arm rests on one hip, setting the shoulder in the perfect position for carrying a shoulder bag. The left half of its body appears to be on the other side of the showroom wall, or in another dimension. Cranston-Almax carries the going-through-walls illusion to the extreme in a collection of semirealistic mannequins that premiered in 1990. Some are designed to stand up fully, others to recline or sit or touch each other. "Jessica" is designed to emerge from the wall, a drawn-up knee at just the right position to throw a foot on the shoulder of a standing mannequin. These seemingly whole mannequins appear to have left behind parts of their bodies. In one, the left arm never quite makes it through the wall; neither does the right leg below mid-thigh.

This collection of wall displayers partakes in a novel way of the traditional display motif of breaking the boundary of the display space; it is a variation on window display's attempt to suggest that something is happening beyond either the temporal or the spatial frame of the window box. But the collection also reflects the interest in the disappearing body in display and the use of the fragment to suggest on the one hand the whole figure and on the other the dissolution of the whole human body.

Robert J. Leydenfrost wrote, echoing many others, that "showing only part of the mannequin creates a natural curiosity in the onlooker." The withholding of part of the body helps create a sense of "mystery" in the window, a theme discussed again and again in manuals on display. The use of fragments also has a source in contemporary sculpture, where, according to Albert Elsen, "there has been a growing tendency to link the

Henry Callahan window linking glamour with both consumer abundance and bodily fragmentation, 1958. Photo by Nick Malan Studios. Courtesy of Saks Fifth Avenue.

partial figure and figural part to specific as well as anonymous or imaginary persons and to the artist's contemporary urban environment—more specifically to those aspects of the city we associate with used industrial objects and the artifacts of fashion, from department store mannequins to knees revealed by mini-skirts that determine the contemporary feminine look." In 1966–68, Claes Oldenburg created *Knees.* A case stood on its side and opened to reveal a pair of sculpted leg fragments, presented from mid-thigh down to mid-calf. In 1969 Elsen noted the power of contemporary costume to refashion notions about the body: "The miniskirt, far more than Rodin, has made the British public partial-figure conscious."[42]

Gene Moore's mastery of "sliced-out" display is unmatched for delicacy and bite. His frequent use of medical imagery and his delicate Valentine's Day windows at Tiffany & Company suggest the fragility of the human condition with particular poignancy. The 1987 Valentine window, in which diamond jewelry has been laid simply on the floor, focuses attention on a giant, lustrous heart, encased in a wooden frame as if for shipping and marked "Fragile." The packed heart is being lifted by a crane, only part of which we see in the window. Although the heart is the double scallop–shaped symbol of love rather than an anatomically correct representation, its size, richness of color, and explicit fragility make us think of the anatomical heart and sigh over the fleetingness not only of love but of life as well. This heart's sufferings are both emotional and physical. Asked about the portraits of human vulnerability he depicted in his windows without ever using whole mannequins, much less showing them in relationship, Moore responded that the creatures he hints at are "like me."

Gilbert Miller said, "The partial figure has in many ways more expressiveness than the whole figure."[43] In his tiny shadow-box windows at Tiffany, Moore preferred to use body parts, most frequently hands, suspended by wire in mid-air, to suggest the action of the human body upon its environment. A 1957 jewelry window shows two delicately formed hands cracking an egg

over a hibachi. What spills from the egg is not yolk and white, however, but a diamond necklace—our eyes catch it before it hits the pan. Moore wrote that "the original thought was just of a diamond necklace inside an egg."[44] But for Moore it is essential, even if there is no literal mannequin in the window, to show "the hand that *did* that"—to lend a human presence. He edited the window to make the merchandise the object of an evident human action, rather than merely the object of the spectator's glance.

Many windows suggest human presence by show-

Jessica and friend emerging from wall, a popular treatment at the Macy's flagship store. Courtesy of E. T. Cranston-Almax (USA).

*"Torso." Courtesy of
Patina-V.*

ing evidence of an action already performed. A 1984 Tiffany window for crystal stemware has as its centerpiece a broken glass lying on its side, a hammer placed forcefully next to it. Critical to Moore in this kind of window—his way of humanizing it—is the chance to show that someone has been there, or is about to come.

During the 1970s, the Upper East Side boutique Fiorucci staged a maelstrom of events in its windows. Some environments were staged to appear as if they were inhabited and acted upon by their inhabitants, though human presence was for the most part just implied. The performances in Fiorucci's windows lasted

only a few hours. The rest of the time the windows were left empty, leaving viewers to speculate about the absence of live performers and what their role in the window might be. The store's art director, Philip Monaghan, wanted passersby to wonder what the environment was doing in a display window. Gacci, an illustrator who specialized in celebrities' shoes, and the set designer Calvin Churchman created an accurate rendition of a 1950s kitchen and served up such shoe-pun specialties as "Shoe-Fly Pie" and "Swiss on Pump." When Gacci had other work to do, the window stood, sans merchandise, as an art environment for the passersby. Windows generally stayed in for between two weeks and a month. Monaghan said that these window environments—where the performer's absence was as much of a self-conscious performance device as a character's presence might have been—were the most important display innovation the store had introduced.

If, as some display directors and manufacturers seem to suggest, we can perceive furniture and environments as objects of human action, the next step is to anthropomorphize the negative spaces of the body, viewing garments as ghosts or shadows of a performative human form. Display artist Maggie Spring cast shoes in the designer boutique Charles Jourdan as if they were dramatic figures. Spring set shoes in place, "pretending people are in them."[45] In some displays the shoes were shown, Gene Moore–style, in relation to an action performed or about to be performed on them. Some shoes were presented as if someone had just stepped out of them, others as if a wearer were about to arrive, still others as if they were currently being inhabited. "Another thing I do: I make them totally still, they're not doing anything," Spring said. "They're just there," which "gives the feeling that something is going to happen to the shoes, an element of mystery—somebody's going to take them, want them, or make them something else."[46]

One Christmas, Spring did a series of windows, each of which told a story centered around a fireplace. One window showed the leg of Santa Claus—a female Santa

Claus—as she apparently went back up the chimney. Her Charles Jourdan boot distinguished her. The rest of the shoes in the display were set around the fireplace as if there were people in them watching the ascent. Spring's shoes were often cast as voyeurs, surrogates for the viewer who stood just outside the windowpane. In one window, shoes "pose[d] as tourists viewing the ruins at Pompeii." At other times, Spring's shoes were themselves the participants, doing activities appropriate to shoes and feet: standing in line, dancing, parading, and chasing. "The shoes do occasionally become personae in a fiction," wrote Ruth Miller Fitzgibbons, "as in one head-less bride's wedding, in which they trailed her veil like tiny attendants. In others, white shoes paid tribute to the Bicentennial in statuesque parade-rest; boots lined up like wallflowers at a holiday dance; high-heeled sandals played the part of 'timidity' in a cat and mouse game."[47]

As with most workers in contemporary display, Spring was recycling old material, if perhaps unconsciously. Lester Gaba had written advice to a typical display director in 1952 that suggested the very kind of shoe-as-character displays that Spring specialized in:

Question: My store sells shoes, only—and I'm down to my last shoe idea. Can you help?

Answer: Have you tried lowering a curtain to calf height, showing only a parade of legs and feet— with each "woman" leading a dog on a leash? . . . Or lower the curtain still further so that only feet and ankles are shown (a) stepping on an accelerator, (b) pushing down a piano pedal, (c) resting on a shoe-shine stand, (d) crushing out a cigarette, (e) standing on a bathroom scale, (f) walking on grass—in front of a "Keep off the grass" sign.[48]

When anti-mannequinitis swept the display world, the flying and pinning of clothing as if in motion made it seem to have a life of its own. Following Henry Callahan's virtuosic invisible-people displays at Saks during the 1950s and 1960s, Timothy Fortuna stuffed, wired, and positioned full suits of clothes for his 1977

displays at the New York menswear boutique Jean-Paul Germain to suggest entire invisible figures in action:

The invisible men's clothing is first semi-stuffed with brown craftpaper, the pants and shirt stuffed separately and then joined together by pinning. A heavy wire coathanger is clipped with wire cutters and curved slightly to form the armature for the shoulders. Heavy wire is attached to the coathanger armature and suspends the figure from the ceiling. The length of wire is determined by whether the figure will be standing or seated. Heavy wire holds the weight and the fine invisible wire supports detailed definitions. After a general positioning of the figure is achieved, the form is stuffed with more tissue paper for subtle positioning and shape.

Fortuna's scenes took place at a restaurant, a card table, a moped ride, and a park in autumn. The poker game window represented "three invisible men . . . at a table playing cards. They held actual poker hands, had their shirt sleeves rolled up and collars opened. One figure stood outside of the game as a voyeur of another's hand. Customers would enjoy checking the players' hands to find out who was winning." In the restaurant window, a cigarette was suspended "in the air where an invisible hand would ordinarily be holding it." *Visual Merchandising* commented on the windows, "There is a wise old adage applicable to the retail and display business, which says, 'Clothes make the man.' Imagine, if you will, a visual representation of this adage: an invisible man. . . . How do we know if he's a Clark Kent or a Superman? By his attire, of course, since that is what meets the eye. What this invisible man is wearing tells a story about what kind of man he is, or aspires to be, and the store or boutique from which this man purchases his clothing greatly influences the image which he projects."[49] Just as the hyperreal mannequin bends around to become a form of abstraction, the invisible—or "conceptual"—man is where abstraction reaches all the way back to meet realism. Even in the absence of a human body, we stage and read the bare suggestions of a figure as representing a naturalistic whole.

Reflexivity in Display

British display director Simon Doonan, who since 1985 has directed display at Barneys New York, has brought a consistent reflexivity to display styles, staging mannequins in ways that refer directly back to their own manufacture and to the window frame. Doonan's windows both challenge the common notion of the spectator's identification with the mannequin and deal explicitly with the theatricality and dream-value attributed to contemporary shopping. Although Doonan himself had done street theatre–like stagings while directing display

at a Los Angeles boutique called Maxfield Bleu in the late 1970s and early 1980s, the bulk of his work incorporates the most extravagant visions of abstraction. Doonan treats realistic mannequins not as characters in a drama but as props. Often he stages them in scenes together with abstract mannequins, with photographed bodies, with their own shadows, and with cartoon figures, pointing up the artificiality of the window staging and of the position of being outside the glass with one's nose pressed up against it.

A number of the four hundred windows Doonan created at Maxfield Bleu were representational—based, as street theatre windows often were, on local events. One controversial window, frequently cited in feature stories on Doonan's work, was staged during the coyote scare in southern California and showed a stuffed coyote making off with a baby while the mother nonchalantly watered the lawn. Other late 1970s windows played on

Television-headed mannequin by Simon Doonan for Maxfield Bleu, Los Angeles. Courtesy of the artist.

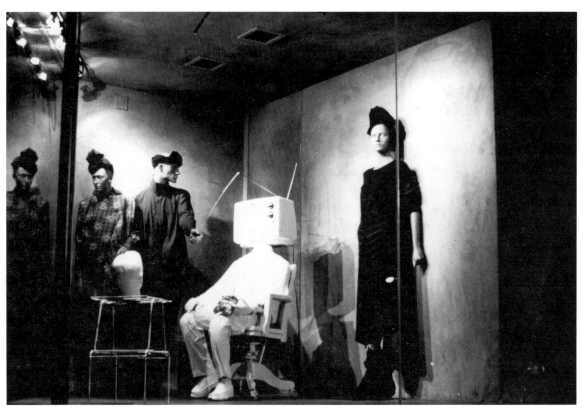

the shock tactics popular at the time. Though Bob Currie never got to display his funeral window in New York, Doonan did a two-window series at Maxfield showing a funeral procession with a mannequin encased in a coffin as a child strewed calla lilies over her breast and a man looked on. The funeral windows were part of a narrative that got a new layer after a week. A couple was shown having a fight; later the woman hanged herself. Says Doonan, "In L.A., people are quite irreverent about stuff like that."

Certain subjects that Doonan tried, however, were censored by his audience. A Nativity scene, complete with the kings, shepherds, and Mary on a donkey, provoked one passerby to throw cinder blocks through the window. A window that showed mannequins "juggling scruffy, badly stuffed cats" also elicited a negative reaction: "Somebody came and threw a big tray of ravioli down the front of the whole window. I guess some people are very sensitive about animals." Perhaps because he occasionally shocked his public, Doonan believes the displays helped to "put [Maxfield's] on the map."[50]

Although budgets for Maxfield's displays were exponentially lower than those at Barneys, they were concept-rich. Having inherited the store's disparate—mismatched, really—collection of old stylized mannequins when he was hired, Doonan exploited them for what they were. His challenge was to use the ragged mannequins to encourage passersby to buy at the store and at the same time to poke self-conscious fun at figures that, in the superrealistic 1970s, were "dummies." In his hands, the macabre, surreal, sometimes halfcracked faces and bodies were presented frankly. A female mannequin whose face was pocked with holes and scars and botched repairs—and she was armless, too—was displayed without shame, wrapped in a tartan blanket, looking brazenly out onto the street. Doonan highlighted these crumbling bodies even more during sales, when he would lavishly display mannequins without arms or in some other state of decomposition as though they were standing in line to be clothed and limbed.

Pratts and other street theatre artists explored the range of things that could be done to and with a bodily defined character. They found a wealth of material in stories of the body that shocked by presenting subjects whose graphic details many viewers considered inappropriate to polite company, even less so to shop windows: pregnancy, drug overdose, nervous breakdowns. Doonan, too, deals with ordinarily covert experiences, but his treatments are more subtle and variegated. Doonan's figures depend less on how one is expected to present oneself physically in public than on standards for emotional role-playing. A "Twelve Days of Christmas" series for Barneys in 1988 depicted gift-giving gone sour: "My basic idea was to take the traditional idea of the song to its lunatic conclusion. It sort of reminds you of when people have a vendetta against someone and send them things like 12 aluminum ladders on approval or have ready-mixed concrete delivered to people they don't like."[51] The "Five Golden Rings" window showed two mannequins ("fashion victims") covered between shoulders and chin by scads of shiny gold rings, their heads drawn out from their bodies like giraffes'.

Christmas windows in other New York stores may have soft-pedaled promotion of specific merchandise in favor of expressing general goodwill, but they certainly didn't make fun of materialism. Doonan put it plainly: "In America . . . Christmas is a one-day affair that's really about shopping." No need for sentimentality. In "The Twelve Days of Christmas," the "recipients of Yuletide gifts appear to be befuddled or disgruntled. In one, a cross-eyed mannequin, done up in red silk taffeta and surrounded by 12 bongo drummers drumming, has been pushed to the edge. 'She simply can't take it anymore,' Mr. Doonan said."[52] His 1987 windows, based on a "decaying palace theme," also dealt with unconventional emotionality.

Doonan's iconoclasm also complicates his relationship with his viewers. Some of his windows have appeared simultaneously to educate and to make fun of his customers. In one, a blowup of an old tailoring manual

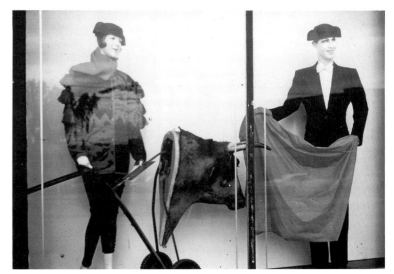

Abstract mannequins in bathroom setting in window of Maxfield Bleu, Los Angeles. The sensational environment is quite street-theatrelike. Courtesy of the artist.

Doonan's bullfighting window for Maxfield Bleu, Los Angeles. Courtesy of the artist.

shows how to fit a suit. In another, a reprint of a complicated footwork pattern for a ballroom dance covers the pane through which we see a mannequin. And a display of ties includes a step-by-step drawing showing what to do with them. The viewer who fails to read these displays with a sense of humor may become the object of their scorn.

Although most New York display directors of the 1980s appeared to be consciously rejecting the street theatre aesthetic, creating all manner of minimalist, architectural displays, Doonan retained some of the street theatre feel. Like Candy Pratts, he refused to accept mannequins as sent by the manufacturers. Whereas Pratts had altered mannequins to achieve greater flexibility and realism in poses, Doonan distorted, reshaped, and hybridized mannequins, thereby increasing their strangeness. Many of his windows featured—à la L. Frank Baum—human and animal forms that had been sculpted out of everyday materials, or whose original fiberglass form had undergone material alteration.

As in street theatre, Doonan told stories whose central figure was not a character per se but a type of body. Street theatre windows, like body art of the 1960s and 1970s, had taken as their subjects bodily processes and life-cycle events, pushed to their most graphic physical conclusions. Mental states could only be deduced from the portrayal of these physical events. Where an orthodox window might suggest a soft abstraction like introspection, a street theatre window depicted the painfully concrete flip side, suicide; instead of blessed motherhood, street theatre showed childbirth, with muscle. In Doonan's work, the body still takes center stage. It is still acted upon, but has ceased to be the agent of its own actions. Rather, the hand of the artist is the sole agent. One window shows a tiny neoclassical sculpture, a nude male whose body has been "attacked" by an army of menacing screws which stick out all over the form. A life-size figure looks on.

In treating the figures as objects of interest in their own right, Doonan overturns that fundamental dictum of display aesthetics, that displays follow from the merchandise. Although Doonan has said that "the merchandise is a springboard for the windows," his displays typically feature formal repetitions that derive from the mannequins or other figures rather than the merchandise. A window for Maxfield Bleu is backed by a stylized, painted blowup of the already stylized 1930s-style face of an antique male mannequin. The repetition in the painting of the oval cheeks, the shining forehead, and the diminishing hairline of the mannequin draws attention to the features of the figure rather than to those of the merchandise. The mannequin itself is the subject of the display.

In a series of 1987 Barneys windows, Doonan displays swimwear on mannequins that are backed by larger-than-life-size black-and-white prints of athletes striking active poses and wearing black cat suits. The positions of the athletes mimic those of the mannequins rather than referring to some structural feature of the garments. The dynamism of the photos is absorbed not so much by the merchandise as by the figures that wear it.

By making the body of the mannequin a formal element in his display, Doonan also overturns a hierarchy that would place human beings—much less humans-as-consumers—at its apex. A series of 1987 windows pairs surreal-looking female mannequins with other kinds of creatures. In one, a sashaying semirealistic mannequin looks over her shoulder to find a poodle that matches her chalk-white finish *and* her high topknot. Lanky abstract sculptures in a second window are interspersed among their wild-haired human counterparts; the juxtaposition emphasizes the structural similarity between the animate and the inanimate.

Doonan's attention to the interaction between the figures was also adapted from street theatre. Many windows feature some kind of contact, often almost a recognition scene, between one figure and another. Again, the contrast between the ways Pratts and Doonan used interaction is important. Pratts focused attention on the action or situation being enacted between two characters, who were frequently posed in specialized, activity-centered positions. This action often took place in time, with the window being a moment "sliced" from a longer strip.[53] Doonan's figures also stand in relation to one another, but the relation is neither naturalistic nor activity centered. Doonan frequently stages an abstract mannequin who mimics the pose of a realistic one, or a mannequin whose pose mirrors that of a gigantic photographic cutout on the back wall. A March 1987 window juxtaposes a semirealistic female mannequin, presented in profile, with an enormous profile photograph by George Mott of a heavily muscled male sculpture with an intense stare. The creatures face each other, as if engaged in some kind of primal, cross-species recognition.

Doonan's windows frequently give an air of other-worldly contact. A Barneys window features four gray-white Andrée Putman mannequins that were commissioned specially for the store. Each wears career clothing, suits or daytime dresses, in black, white, or red, and all stand in identical poses—balancing straight on the right leg, the left knee turned coyly inward, the left arm extended slightly to the side. These four mannequins are placed in a flat row facing front. Just behind them, staggered to fill the gaps in the front row, are four identical mannequins—only these are black and nude. They are shadow figures, visual reinforcements for the front row.

In creating windows that show interaction among multiple realities, Doonan aligns himself with body artists and other performance artists who treat art as a mixture of lived, documented, and imagined worlds. John Baldessari, for example, "made an unannounced visit for 15 minutes to an instructor friend's art class. After his departure, a police artist was called in, and the students were asked to describe him, as they would any suspect, so that a 'wanted' sketch could be drawn. A photo documents the body artist standing next to his completed portrait."[54]

Doonan's penchant for juxtaposing multiple realities may well have come from his eight years of practice with that cast of odd and mismatched mannequins at Maxfield Bleu. Even once he had a fully unified cast of mannequins at Barneys, Doonan found ways to show in his windows the contacts between more and less substantial bodies, as in his 1989 Detective series, which featured not only the shadow of a mannequin-detective cast high against the wall, but also a black cutout figure that had been pasted there.

Not all of Doonan's recognition scenes portray full bodies. A 1988 window juxtaposes a haughty female mannequin in a red suit with an enormous fragment of a head, like a classical sculpture seen through a microscope. She is clearly modern; it is apparently a relic, the shard of a world valued for history's sake. Behind them both a stylized, almost cartoonlike abstract landscape in single-point perspective trails off. This backdrop shares neither period nor style with either of the other items in the scene. The three worlds represented ironize one another by forcing us to see each through the lenses of the others.

Doonan has used photographs and language as additional media in which he can play out these alien contacts. Doonan says that using words in his displays, like the proverbs or jokes written especially for the windows by the comedian Joan Rivers, involves the sense of hearing. Doonan believes that the viewer not only hears the words while reading them but even hears them in different voices—the words are often displayed in a variety of fonts within cartoon bubbles emanating from the mouths of figures.

The windows that Doonan commissioned from artist Duane Michals for Father's Day, 1989, combined photographic images on the subject of fathers and sons with poetry that Michals wrote shortly after the death of his own father. The artist was known for "pairing his dreamlike images with handwritten narratives." The poetry was painted, in Michals's "inimitable penmanship," directly on the windowpanes. "Dear Father," one window read, "How I wish we could have been friends and done all of the things that fathers and sons are supposed to do together." Doonan remembered, "People didn't stop telling me how much they loved those windows. They cried and laughed and kept going back to look at them." Michals commented, "There's this ideal

*From Doonan's Detective
Series, 1989. Courtesy of
the artist.*

notion that kids do all these things with their fathers, but my own experience was mythical."[55] The juxtaposition here is not only among photograph and word and dressmaker's dummy, but also between the usual stance of the show window as emblem of a fulfilled dream and Michals's ironic and heart-wrenching memorial to a lost one.

Mannequin Abstraction and the Theatrical Avant-Garde

Italian futurists were fascinated with bodily dissection and reconstruction, as well as with the notion that inanimate objects could be construed as theatrical agonists. In "The Futurist Cinema," F. T. Marinetti urged the creation of "filmed dramas of objects," in which objects would appear "animated, humanized, baffled, dressed up, impassioned, civilized, dancing—objects removed from their normal surroundings and put into an abnormal state that, by contrast, throws into relief their amazing construction and nonhuman life." The futurist manifesto writer also called for "show windows of filmed ideas, events, types, objects, etc.," and for "filmed unreal reconstructions of the human body."[56] In its insistent anthropomorphic treatment of the inanimate object, futurism is a close relative of the aesthetics of window display.

Symbolism worked from the opposite direction, stripping individuality and psychology from the human figure. Early twentieth-century stagings of works by such playwrights as Maeterlinck and Hauptmann tried to efface the actor, much the way invisible-people displays withhold the presence of the mannequin's body. Figures in symbolist drama were frequently staged behind an obscuring scrim, which would iron out differences in their faces and carriage and make them seem like puppets. Movements were also generalized and made more mechanical, and actors intoned their lines instead of speaking. Symbolist actors appeared more like phantoms than presences.

Oskar Schlemmer and his colleagues at the Bauhaus promoted using the body itself as a design medium and so paved the way for exploring the theatrical meanings of bodily abstraction. Schlemmer's creation of dances for students at the Bauhaus combined futurism's desire to bring life to objects with symbolism's impulse to downplay the aura of co-presence of actor and spectator.

Schlemmer's ideas are central not just to a perspective on the abstracted body. They also make it possible to view the realistic body as potential design material. Although Schlemmer certainly did not perform surgery or mutilate the bodies of his dancers directly, he designed costumes for the "ballets" performed at the Bauhaus that distorted the natural shapes of the body and imposed instead geometric shapes on top of them, anticipating the manipulation of the human form into furniture or the mannequin alternative. For Schlemmer, "the transformation of the human body, its metamorphosis, is made possible by the *costume*, the disguise."[57]

Schlemmer outlined four possibilities for costuming the dancer in a way that did not simply display the body but drastically reshaped it to express the fundamental Bauhaus design question—the relation of person and space. The designer might treat the body simply as architecture, enclosing its various parts in the cubical forms that best fit them, creating what he termed "ambulant architecture." Another choice might be to express through costume the "functional laws" of the body-space relation by demonstrating the ways in which individual body parts may move in space. The result is "the marionette." By taking that idea a step further, the designer might express through costume how the entire body moves in space and the volumes it fills in such motion: "Here we have the various aspects of rotation, direction, and intersection of space: the spinning top, snail, spiral disk," which would create "a technical organism" defined entirely by what it can achieve spatially through movement.

Schlemmer called the fourth approach "the metaphysical forms of expression symbolizing various members of the human body: the star shape of the spread hand, the ∞ sign of the folded arms, the cross shape of the backbone and shoulders; the double head, multiple limbs, division and suppression of forms," combining to produce "dematerialization." The dematerializing costume abstracts body configurations—not just single limbs, digits, or expanses—into patterns that need not reflect on the original body. In a sense, the dematerializing costume is an inverse of Schlemmer's first type: rather than encasing the body within arbitrarily cubical volumes, it uses the body as an apparently arbitrary occupant of essential forms, whose symbols have been painted onto the outside of the costume.

In Schlemmer's 1922 ballet *Figural Cabinet I*, bodily fragmentation was the central theme: "The bodies look for heads, which are moving in opposite direction across the stage. A jerk, a bang, a victory march, whenever there is a union of head and body: the Hydrocephalus, the Body of Mary and the Body of the Turk, Diagonals, and the Body of the 'Better Gent.'" Not only is the body as a whole capable of redesign, but a director-designer need not accept the body wholesale but merely those parts that he or she chooses as givens.

In planning his 1922 *Triadic Ballet*, Schlemmer presented the idea that there is no essential or single meaning that the body has in space. Its changing relation to space itself is the defining element of its meaning. The realistic becomes abstract as Schlemmer plans to "dress one . . . two . . . three actors in stylized padded tights and papier-mâché masks. The effect of the tights and the masks together is to regroup the various and diffuse parts of the human body into a simple, unified form." The body, which Schlemmer sees as being in need of regrouping, is reconceived as a simpler form. Through the redesigning process, each individual part, if it must be referred to, seems more fragmented than before. Schlemmer's cohort at the Bauhaus, Laszlo Moholy-Nagy, referred to each body part as if it were independent of a live performer: "If we . . . provide the masks with mustaches and glasses, the hands with gloves, the torsos with stylized dinner jackets, and if we add to their various ways of walking also places to sit down (a swivel chair, an armchair, a bench), . . . the result is what we call 'gesture dance.'"[58]

The Bauhaus encouraged the association of the inanimate and the human by the treatment of both as design material. Mannequin displays treat design objects anthropomorphically. Stagings of both abstract and realistic mannequins imply that our own relation to the physical world is not simply that of subject to inanimate object. Our very bodies are as much acted-upon as they are actors. Display windows suggest our receptivity to—indeed, our hunger for—such transformation.

Conclusion: Breaking Glass

This book has been about window dressing, façades—the surface and most literal emblem of retail, whose own substance has come to be viewed with some suspicion. So wherefore window display?

Because mannequins are not humans but have some startling resemblances to them, we can learn a great deal by watching audiences watch them. The staging of mannequins behind illusion-preserving glass calls forth cultural associations with high art, death, and voyeurism. Mannequin displays provide multiple windows into the workings of the psyche and the machinations of social life: as psychodynamic agents in the development of identity, as necessarily distorted mirror reflections of the viewers, as idealized versions of a gender type, or as stylized merchandising representations. At the same time, the form explores the meaning of the mannequin as a comment upon the incestuous relation between art and commerce and upon the role of the viewer in constructing personal value.

The perspective of performance theory has helped clarify some of the issues of persona, audience, and agency that are raised by the representation of human characters and situations in a format that demands audience participation. Mannequin displays share and further some of the most radical twentieth-century movements in the theatre—the need for an active audience, the questioning of human ascendancy over the in-

Gene Moore window for Bonwit Teller. Courtesy of the artist.

animate, the notion of character as a demonstrated rather than assumed being, the antipsychological sense of character defined by the outside dimensions, the theatricality of the body itself, and the idea that the self and the body are both the subjects and the objects of action, rather than mere instruments.

Theatre is a form of practical social philosophy played out over time. It shows us how we create a sense of self through experiences of self-representation. Window displays highlight both the dramatic nature of gazing and the value for identity construction of concoctions of selves.

In his ethnographic study of the bodybuilding subculture, Alan Klein remarks the centrality of mirroring "in both the clinical notions of narcissism and the institutions of bodybuilding." Conducting fieldwork in four élite West Coast gyms, Klein observed the frequency with which bodybuilders "spotted" themselves in the mirror; typically, half would glance at the mirror within a thirty-second period. Bodybuilders, he found, use their reflection as a training partner: "In performing difficult sets (with heavy weights or a long string of repetition), one has a tendency to look at one's mirror image and transfer the labor and/or pain to the image in the mirror. This transference works almost as if the mirror image were helping you, the real person, lift the weights." Mirroring is admitting a "view of oneself reflected back through another person"—or by way of a human image. For historian Anne Hollander, the mirror "is the personal link between the human subject and its representation." It enables everyday people to "mak[e] art out of facts," as they attempt to "mold the[ir] reflection into an acceptable picture, instantaneously and repeatedly. . . . Behind the reflecting surface is something waiting to be born."[1]

A special case of self-conscious body and body-image manipulation, bodybuilding may have been the 1980s' answer to body art. "Gender narcissism" is Klein's term for the "nonerotic appreciation of one's gender," the view of members of one's gender as an "extension" or representation of oneself. Although Klein related gender narcissism primarily to the bond between the male bodybuilder and his cohorts, the term is well applied to the relationship between the female pedestrian-gazer-buyer and the mannequins designed and staged to attract her. By the late nineteenth century, the shop window was beginning to function, like the mirror, as a tool of gender narcissism and an important "site of identity construction," particularly for women, who, "parading up and down the streets, . . . examined the goods displayed as well as their own reflections in the plate glass windows and the mirrors cannily placed to pander to their vanity. They stopped to discuss the merchandise and the quality of the displays with their friends, their loitering in public space legitimized by its association with consumption."[2]

For Walter Benjamin, the shop window was the paradigmatic icon of modernity as "dream world," and the prototypical look of the city was summed up by window vision—both by the view from behind a window, such as that of a moving train or car, and by the peering into the shop window from streetside.[3] The class of women pedestrian-gazer-buyers—*flâneuses*—became possible only once women were free to embark unaccompanied into urban/window vision. And the harnessing of buying to looking was based on an elaborate "system of selling and consumption which depended on the relation between *looking* and *buying*, and the indirect desire

to possess and incorporate through the eye." As Anne Friedberg writes, "The department store may have been, as Benjamin put it, the flâneur's last coup, but it was the flâneuse's first."[4]

The Difference the Window Makes

Benjamin wrote in the *Passagen-Werk*, his enormous mass of notes taken between 1927 and 1940 on the Paris Arcades, that urban Europe's erection of "glittering showcases" as temples to progress during the nineteenth century was prompted by an essentially deceptive motive: "The City of Mirrors—in which the crowd itself became a spectacle—[Paris] reflected the image of people as consumers rather than producers, keeping the class relations of production virtually invisible on the looking glass' other side." In such a "phantasmagoria," the displayed object became divorced not only from its actual use value, but from its exchange value, becoming socially valuable only for the degree of "enthrallment" it could produce in the spectator.[5]

The simplest explanation of how the window works on its public is as façade, as representation of what the passerby might expect to find inside the store. At a deeper level, and implicit in the overtones of the word "façade," hums the suggestion of false self-representation. The window may present a grandiose image of who the customer considers herself to be; it may also stand as an image of how the world is supposed to work. One common display theory holds that during hard times the windows should project high spirits. An extreme example of this impulse was seen in the windows that Parisian shopkeepers created under Nazi occupation. These bright and busy windows were designed to convey the image of business-as-usual, even though the shop behind them might be completely empty.

Yet both levels of the façade theory unrealistically ignore the spectator's active role. The "Lazy Hardware" window that Marcel Duchamp and two other artists created in 1945 to promote a new edition of André

The mannequin, the mirror, the glass, 1973. Photo by Nick Malan Studios. Courtesy of Saks Fifth Avenue.

Breton's essay *Arcane 17* demonstrates that responsibility isn't so easily assigned. Famous in the lore both of window display and of literary gossip, "Lazy Hardware" implicates the viewer in a charged relationship with a mannequin that Duchamp arranged so as to exploit the problems of viewing a figure through a glass in daylight.

To his mannequin's right thigh Duchamp attached a faucet; he draped her in "a short, bright white apron, rather skimpily cut to show a good deal of leg." In her arms he placed a copy of Breton's book, which she held "as if either to read it or present it to the spectator." The display was originally designed to appear in Brentano's window, but it was moved to Gotham Book Mart after the League of Women denounced the sexual imagery of a photograph that had been contributed by Roberto Mattà. Duchamp's mannequin was headless, and, based on measurements of the Brentano's windows, the artist placed her at a height that would permit "the reflection of the spectator's head in the window glass [to] take the place of the mannikin's missing head." At Gotham Book Mart, the bright white apron was specially illuminated from above, adding another dimension: the brightness from the mannequin's pelvis would overpower the reflection from the spectator's head. Charles F. Stuckey concluded that this kind of concourse between spectator and figure was what Duchamp referred to when he wrote that window display was a kind of "coition through a glass pane."[6]

Duchamp had influential predecessors. Eugène Atget's photographs of Paris shop windows in the second decade of the century—the first well-known photographs treating this subject matter—played upon the way the daytime patterns of light and the spectator's shadow on the pane partially obscured the view of the window. Atget's window shots blend the direct and reflected images of those inside and outside the pane of glass. Atget's photographs show the faces of staff peering out from within the store, and sometimes even the photographer's own reflection is visible in the window pane.

Duchamp integrated window display into his role as artist more than other visual artists who worked in display. He once urged others to think of him not as a painter but as a *fenêtrier*, a window-maker. His interest in windows began as early as 1913, when he became fascinated with a chocolate-grinding machine whose workings were displayed in a confectioner's window. That year, he began work on his *Chocolate Grinder* paintings. He also scribbled some notes to himself about the workings of a shop window:

> The question of shop windows.
> To undergo the interrogation of show windows.
> The exigency of the shop window.
> The shop window proof of the existence of the outside world.
> When one undergoes the examination of the shop window, one also pronounces one's own sentence.
> In fact one's choice is round-trip.
> From the demands of the shop window, from the inevitable response to shop windows, my choice is determined.
> No obstinacy, ad absurdum, of hiding the coition through a glass pane with one or many objects of the shop window. The penalty consists in cutting the pane and in feeling regret as soon as possession is consummated.
> Q.E.D.[7]

For Duchamp, as for others in the display world, the glass provides a necessary barrier between the world of the spectator and the world of the display. They can only co-penetrate with the glass between them.

Duchamp focused on the fourth wall of window display—the simultaneous barrier and invitation to penetration that the glass presents—but others have argued that window is defined by its other box boundaries, its frame. Typical of those in her industry, visual merchandiser Robin Lauritano spoke of the window as a "little world." Self-consciousness about the frame can be detected quite early in American display. In 1930, Frederick Kiesler wrote,

The Window is a framed picture.

The display window has to paint the picture for the public. [The display artist's] canvas is space, his pigments merchandise and decoration, his brushes light and shadow.

There are two ways of making the frame of the plate glass a contributing featuring of the show window:

1. Develop it into importance.
2. Omit it entirely.[8]

Kiesler was interested primarily in the visual effect of emphasizing or omitting the metal frame surrounding the glass, but his words also suggest that the arsenal of the display artist includes the ability to couple separate worlds—of spectator and of window space. Later display men—like Duchamp—suggest that this coupling can take place not only visually but also socially and psychologically.

Working in windows has a singularly abstract quality, demanding the capacity to execute an idea from one perspective while imagining it from the spectator's point of view, rotated 180 degrees. Gene Moore spoke of his sensation of working as if in a mirror. "I wonder now how it came out looking so well from the front, when I was working backwards," Moore once said after installing a window that consisted of a taut maze of strings from which wine glasses were suspended every which way. "I guess I must see the way you see in a camera, which is upside down." Moore is a devoted protégé of display man Jim Buckley, who compared creating a window display to painting a picture through the rear of the canvas.[9]

And a three-dimensional picture at that. Patina-V's creative director George Martin develops mannequin poses from fashion photographs, but he has a model re-create the pose in the studio to see whether it works three-dimensionally. For Martin, the most successful mannequins can be staged and viewed from several angles. Even Kiesler pointed out that "every good piece of sculpture cannot be looked at from one side only, but from all around."[10]

Robert Currie took the abstraction of window work one step further. He said that he could never tell what he had in the window simply by looking at it, and he used the glass as a reference when installing windows at Bendel's. Just as a ballet dancer or a weightlifter often checks placement and line in a mirror rather than by physical sensation or by looking directly down, Currie checked his displays against the nighttime reflection of the windowpane. Currie said that when he checked his work in the reflection, he never perceived himself as being in the same picture as the mannequins he was staging; the realities remained visually and psychologically separate.

For Currie, the window itself was the most magical part of display. The glass "creates a layer that creates the fantasy. It distorts it—minutely, but it distorts it. I think if you were to look at a display without glass, you would be disappointed. It would be like . . . walking through a department store." The glass both distorted the image behind it and kept the viewer away, rendering whatever lay behind it "untouchable." As one display director noted, "mannequins are much more precious under glass." Moore took the image a step farther, regarding the scene behind the windowpane as a vision of "that other world."[11]

Display artist Toshi contrasted the functions of the window and the store interior. The window "presells" an item, he said, whereas the interior of the store "reassures" the customer in his or her choice. The opportunity to touch the merchandise is a vital part of that difference. So is the opportunity inside the store— apparently irresistible—to touch the mannequins. Adults are "fond of caressing mannequins that strike their fancy, and children love to roughhouse with them." One reason that only older, less valuable mannequins are used in interior displays is that they are often stolen or tampered with.[12]

That glass obscures the image during daylight was remarked early in American display. A 1937 article noted that the sun's glare both distorts and conceals; if the glass were to reflect too much back to the customer, she would be looking at herself in the window rather than at the window's contents. "Invisible glass" was posited as a solution, albeit one with its own drawbacks. According to Gene Moore, windows are installed at night in order to get the reflection from the glass; working in daylight, an artist gets no feedback from the glass and must constantly be dashing outside to check the view, a time-consuming addition to an already painstaking process. Even when Moore installed a window in the early-morning hours, he frequently returned to the store after work to make sure that the window worked under moonlight, fixing the windows the next morning if necessary. Many window artists regard display as a night art, yet the window is seen by a much larger audience in the day, in less than peak form.

As seen by daylight, however, the window display may be the emblem of the prototypically modern gaze. Friedberg finds *window shopping* the most appropriate metaphor for a peculiarly modern way of seeing whose current endpoint is the cinema (but which may be closely related to virtual reality as well). Friedberg's "mobile and virtual gaze" depends both on the power of the viewing subject to be in motion with respect to the object and on the illusory nature of that object:

> The *virtual gaze* is not a direct perception but a *received* perception mediated through representation. . . . [It] travels through an imaginary *flânerie* through an imaginary elsewhere and an imaginary elsewhen. The *mobilized gaze* has a history, which begins well before the cinema and is rooted in other cultural activities that involve walking and travel. The virtual gaze has a history rooted in all forms of visual representation (back to cave painting), but produced most dramatically by photography. The cinema developed as an apparatus that combined the "mobile" with the "virtual." Hence, cinematic spectatorship changed, in unprecedented ways, concepts of the present and the real.[13]

In some sense, the cinema's ability to make the absent present and apparently real—far more effectively than could the nineteenth-century panorama or the re-created natural disaster—has eroded the uniqueness of window display, which itself had gone the mirror one better. Indeed, the movies seal the relationship between looking and paying for the experience, their ticket price a parallel admission of the dollar value of visual identification. The popularity of film, a more versatile and sensational forum for virtual gazing, is responsible in part for the demise of window display, as well as for a decreased sensibility for theatrical experience. Retail history itself suggests how the singular theatricality of mannequin displays may have been displaced.

The End of Window Display

As Gene Moore resigned from Bonwit Teller in 1962 to focus full-time on the windows next door at Tiffany, he gave Walter Hoving, the president of both stores, an impossible ultimatum: "I want the main floor to be devoted entirely to display. I want there to be no limitations as to window size. The windows should be totally flexible as well as refrigerated and heated [to accommodate the use of perishables]. And I want to be able to use fire, air, and water in my displays."[14] What seemed ridiculous and impracticable at Bonwit Teller, however, began to make sense for other stores. Although temperature change and the use of fire were hardly mainstays of store design in the 1960s, retail was swept by a demand for increasing adaptability and for a re-envisioning of the spectator's experience of display. Over a twenty-five-year period, these changes may help to presage the end of window display as such, even given its own moves toward increasing theatricality.

Perhaps inspired by developments in experimental theatre and encounter groups, presenters of fashion shows and events in the 1960s abandoned what a J. C. Penney's spokesperson termed the "you sit and we show you" approach, which was essentially a lecture format. By late in the decade Penney's was trying to maximize audience involvement by abandoning the old stage and runway system and displaying models on boxes of various sizes placed around the room. In August 1968, Gimbels held an open house in its New York flagship store, promising thirty thousand shoppers under twenty-five years of age "The Night of Your Life." The first floor featured a body-decorating and leg show, the second a for-men-only Fad Show. On other floors there were lucky drawings, Beatles poster giveaways, dance demonstrations, and magic tricks. During the same month, Dayton's sponsored a College Night, with fifteen bands, graffiti and karate workshops, and fashion news presentations. *Stores* magazine reported the events as part of a new trend in merchandising, designed to reach a media-drenched customer: "Whether it's open house for the super-consuming young, an all-out sound-and-lights happening that just so happens to be in a store, or a Broadway-caliber revue where the costumes are for sale rather than show, retailers hard-bent on imagery have tuned in to show business tactics as the latest means to reach the already over-stimulated consumer."[15]

The promotion director for *Mademoiselle* magazine said, "The store should be a theater of ideas—yet completely integrated with what's going on in terms of selling." Stanley J. Goodman, president of the May Department Stores Company, observed, "Almost the worst crime the store can commit is to bore the customer, and it must be remembered that with her increasing sophistication she bores easily." A Penney's spokesman of the late 1960s added, "The entertainment facet of fashion will become basic—but it won't be entertainment per se. It has to be fun to shop." By this time, theatrical events in stores were referred to as "fashion happenings," which could signify "shows on the floor, on counter tops, even on overhead display ledges."[16]

The fashion shows and fashion merchandising techniques of the 1960s set the stage for the public to perceive shopping as theatre. Wolfgang Haug cites the publication late in the decade of a Swiss retailer's book, *The Key to the Consumer,* which emphasized the need to make the consumer a "participant" and urged that shopping be arranged as an entertainment that in-

vites and engulfs the shopper. Merchandise, the guide stressed, should not be displayed according to traditional classifications but should be grouped together thematically. The store must become a "theatrical total work of art which plays upon the public's willingness to buy."[17] Display, long considered the best form of advertising because it let the customer touch and see the goods at the exact moment of the sales pitch, now took the further step of allowing the customer to interact with the merchandise.

During the seventies shopping was reinvented as pure entertainment. Where street theatre had demanded the viewer's participation to construct the event, theatrical merchandising constructed the shopper as an indispensable player in an ongoing panoply of environmental experiences. At The Limited, display director Jim Mansour staged mannequins in a participatory rather than presentational relationship with the customers, showing them "undressing" in dressing rooms, standing in line at the sales counter, or sitting on a sofa: mannequins "had always been put on platforms, and made to be mannequins. Or put in windows. I grounded them, and made them people in the store." As the concept of the role of the mannequin in merchandising evolved, so did the experience of the customer.

Bloomingdale's is credited with bringing the innovations of the boutiques to large-scale retailing. Under Marvin Traub's much-praised direction, Bloomingdale's "was the first major store to recognize that department stores could be collections of small stores within a store, that the excitement of the boutiques could be reproduced on a larger scale." One Bloomingdale's customer described "the dazzle of the Manhattan store at Christmas" as "the closest you can ever come to being in a pinball machine."[18] One part of the strategy was, in Traub's words, to be "true to the merchandise," a restatement of the mainstream tradition in American display. But even if the style and function of the merchandise govern how it is to be presented, resonances grounded in the focal point of a display can radiate well beyond the domain of the store.

Under Traub, Bloomingdale's refined this approach to create networks of displayed goods, with each item relating to items in other merchandise categories. The infinitely attractive and closed system was designed to suck the shopper in. Bloomingdale's believed "that merchandise should be tied together in unified themes, rather than being forced to sink or swim on its own. The retailer's function is not simply to stock and sell products, but also to package and promote them with great style and appeal. So when Traub says 'be true to the merchandise,' he demands that a display of English bone china be presented in a replica of a London townhouse or a country cottage in Surrey. And when Cuisinart food processors are promoted, play French ballads, hire a Parisian chef and demonstrate the preparation and cooking of ratatouille." As Bloomingdale's broke away from its traditional dependence on "mannequins, racks, and static settings," it moved into more fluid media for communicating excitement and the entertainment value of shopping, putting "new emphasis on sound, color and movement." A *Time* story called Bloomingdale's "the adult Disneyland." A profitable ethic for marketing, the Bloomingdale's strategy promoted excitement more than price, and customers paid a premium for it.[19]

By the 1980s, few stars were left in display—and those who remained were executives in charge of centralizing and supervising national display operations. Centralized store planning has contributed to the decay of window display, and so, ironically, has the increasing theatricalization of store interiors. The greater theatrical savvy of the industry is drawing its energy, like heat on a sunny winter day, from the windows into the store.

As a store bent on innovation in merchandising, Bloomingdale's has become a leader in centralized display. The Visual Presentation department provides day-to-day style direction to all the branch stores by means of detailed visual merchandising manuals that are prepared in the New York flagship store. One design coordinator in the central office writes directives for display ideas executed in women's ready-to-wear; another writes directives for menswear, junior's, and children's wear; a third directs branch presentation of home furnishings. A fourth design coordinator handles special projects. Coordinators make regular visits to the branch stores and conduct meetings with branch visual merchandising managers to maintain the visual standards they have established in New York. The flagship store's interiors are designed by a different team, which allocates one designer to oversee visual direction on each floor.

Severe restrictions discourage branches from deviating from established guidelines. In a 1986 memo to the branches under his jurisdiction, visual director Colin Birch demanded that all design projects of whatever scope be submitted to his approval. Central Design was to be consulted immediately should any design mandate that came down from Birch's office prove impracticable for a branch. Above all, Birch ordered, "Do not allow the Display Managers or Store Managers to change a design directive without Central Design approval." Other documents demonstrate a similarly proprietary—even abrasively custodial—attitude of the Central Design staff toward branch visual merchandisers. In a speech Birch summarized his impressions from recent branch store visits and reviewed his inspection routine:

> When I enter a store, immediately I expect to be impressed by your efforts, their overall impact which delivers the message welcoming and interesting me to look for more.
>
> I then proceed quickly to expect to find increasing quality visual impact and coverage. All this time I focus and search for detail [and look at] your execution standard and at the same time, I notice faults.
>
> It takes me a few minutes to analyze whether I have a success or failure of visual presentation in this store even without delving into details.
>
> We then walk and I expect you to proudly present your product. I listen to your problems, reasons and intentions. I understand *all* your problems but do not accept them when I have seen other stores who have

succeeded under the same budget, direction and staff and timing.

I consider you all very skillful, capable and creative presentation experts who can produce the best in the country.

We are not getting the best in the country yet, so I am giving all the opportunity now to show me your strength which I believe can produce Ecco L'Italia to be Bloomingdale's biggest, best and most unforgettable country promotion!![20]

Robin Lauritano, Bloomingdale's display director, affirmed that there has traditionally been animosity between Bloomingdale's central and branch staff. Central staffers complained that the branch people always needed their direction and yet, even after being given elaborate directives, could never "get it right." The branches' low budgets—the result of higher revenues at the flagship store—also make them a target of Central staffers' ridicule. And because branch stores are limited in their access to unusual materials or props, Central must act as the cosmopolitan center, ordering exotic fixtures for all the branches. The differential in artistic freedom and resources between Central and branch stores probably makes any antagonism mutual.

As centralized control is curbing creativity, the increased reliance on theatrical techniques inside stores represents another threat to window display as an art form. If customers know that they will always find entertainment inside the store, window displays become superfluous.

The in-store "event" is designed to draw the crowds and keep them inside the store long enough to do some serious financial damage. Birch, during his tenure in the eighties, was Bloomingdale's best-known director of "country event" promotions, generally semiannual events that focused on the lifestyle of a trendily "exotic" country to promote its clothing and other consumer objects. Major country events were scheduled in the fall, with smaller promotions in the spring. Besides drawing customers during peak buying periods, the events built store loyalty and encouraged "multiple sales"—related items suggestive of the featured country and designed to be used together. For a Japan promotion, Birch's staff produced a modernistic interpretation of a torii gate, which would typically stand at the entrance of "temples and shrines where the faithful go to pray." At Bloomingdale's, too, the torii gate was an invitation to submit to a higher power—the consumerist urge. Bloomingdale's torii gate "loom[ed] above the main floor concourse, . . . lighted from above with red neon."[21]

Interaction with Japanese merchandise and artifacts was supplemented by the opportunity to see "real Japanese" at work (at life?) right in the store. Bloomingdale's featured performances by artisans in origami, calligraphy, fan painting, bonsai, and sushi. With the presentation of craft performances, Bloomingdale's mimicked innovations of such living history museums as Plimoth Plantation, where static exhibits had been replaced by costumed interpreters who, instead of talking about them, actually performed seventeenth-century tasks. Should Bloomingdale's customers wish to translate product into practice, an ample array of "ancient Japanese grooming tools [and] aids" was available for sale, supplemented by "instructions for their use."[22] To *buy* at Bloomingdale's was to *be*—or, at least, to try on for size.

Other country events were at least as lavish, and concentrated on the preparation and "authentic" serving and eating style of native foods. The store began the trend toward a multisensory definition of display, and taste and smell joined the list of other senses that videotapes and exhibits, hands-on workshops, and visual splendor reached.

Bloomingdale's display directors make extensive research trips, bringing back lifestyle merchandising ideas from the countries they will be promoting. In the spring of 1989 even California was treated as a "country" for promotional purposes. The introductory text to the manual prepared by the New York Visual Presentation staff for "California: The New International Style" read: "California—The Golden State is compromised [*sic*] of 12 spectacular regions—each region with a character of its own, each influencing the worlds of design, taste, and style internationally. From the lush vineyards and giant redwoods of the North Coast to the cosmopolitan diversity of the San Francisco Bay Area; from the unparalleled grandeur of the High Sierra to the sandy beaches of San Diego county and the sprawling metropolis of greater Los Angeles, home of Hollywood's brightest stars, Bloomingdale's celebrates the Golden State and all of its diversity."[23] That diversity was not celebrated for its own sake, however; in the later pages of the manual it became the setting for various in-store shops, some already existing, others short-lived but highly profitable venues created specifically for the promotion. Women's ready-to-wear was styled under six labels—Wave, Wilshire Boulevard, Venice Beach, California Dreaming, Zuma Beach, and Spa. Wave was the new name for the juniors' clothing shop, Wilshire Boulevard the theme for the existing women's dresses collection.

Even first-floor accessories departments carried emblems of the "country" theme. Branch hosiery departments were urged to create a feeling of free, worldly movement by placing "in-motion" mannequins on high ledge walkways—"ladies who shop walking dogs, etc., with addition of surfers, bicycles, people moving, shopping, beach, street skateboards, etc."

Each department highlighted both the way the prospective customer should be cast under the glow of the new promotion and the way the department, particularly the mannequins, should be styled. To transform a Tahiti Plage environment into Zuma Beach, raffia and hibiscus were removed from the swim forms and mannequins, and zinc was applied to noses and cheekbones. In the California Dreaming shop, both mannequins and customers were restyled: "Rich hippies rub shoulders with beach boys and starlets while driving Suzuki jeeps through the Hollywood Hills chatting on cellular phones, this focal will incorporate mannequins, jeep and phones." The Year of the Dragon promotion called for dark-haired adult female mannequins with either a French twist or a high top knot. Infants' and children's

mannequins were also to be made to look "Chinese," girls' hair braided, boys' cropped.

Both mannequins and customers were defined in terms of their material interests. For Wave, the design manual predicted, "the California promotion will introduce the 'new age' surf girls into the B-2000 department. She is into crystal jewelry, pouches, hippie beads and platform surf sandals. The junior highlight will consist of neon, surfboards, fixturing and mannequins." Under the direction of Bloomingdale's active-fashion office, special garments may be designed to complete the look of a department and the characterization of the customer. For the Spa shop, "Nancy Heller creates a collection of cotton knit active wear ideal for Nautilus or Nantucket, and lush linen separates with crest emblems for the posh, pedigreed, and prosperous." For a 1989 France promotion, Josephine Baker–inspired dresses were created for the Casino de Paris Night Glamour shop. For a 1988 China Year of the Dragon promotion, Norma Kamali provided Suzie Wong dresses for the Enter the Dragon shop. The manufacturer Ultra Pink "developed an exclusive collection of t-shirts and Mao jackets emblazoned with Chinese Worker's Poster motifs that will be merchandised with heavy drill pants and worker's caps."

In such a retail environment as this, designed to star—rather than fascinate—the shopper, what place has window display? The popularity of the street theatre windows may have provided the most powerful impetus for theatrical merchandising, but interiors are now wiping out the windows as theatrically dynamic areas.

Malls, too, as tightly and centrally controlled interior public spaces, may satisfy the desire for multisensory experience knitted tightly with acquisition, a mode of experience expressly connected with theatricality by the mall-management term, "The Retail Drama." William Kowinski enumerates the staggering range of experiences that malls may offer:

> You can get anything from diamonds to yogurt in the mall; you can attend college classes, register to vote,

A 1959 interior, before live people, in strongly thematized shopping environments, usurped the theatricality of mannequins. Photo by Nick Malan Studios. Courtesy of Saks Fifth Avenue.

go to the library, see topless dancers and male strippers, give blood, bet, score, and meditate, and get a room or a condo and live there. Someday it may be possible—if it isn't already—to be born—go from preschool through college, get a job, date, marry, have children, fool around, get a divorce, advance through a career or two, receive your medical care, even get arrested, tried, and jailed; live a relatively full life of culture and entertainment, and eventually die and be given funeral rites without ever leaving a particular mall complex—because every one of those possibilities exists now in some shopping center somewhere.[24]

The early department stores were not far from this in their exhaustive dedication to serving the object-oriented needs of consumers, though many of the activities they promoted were more conventionally wholesome. With the growth of a service economy, the mall promises to become even more an encapsulation and simulation of daily life, interactions within them more stringently routinized by centralized mall managements. And these interactions will have a theatrical dimension, just as workplace performances do.

What we gain in the new participatory commercial interiors is a sense of our own role-playing in the cultural marketplace of commerce.

What we may miss are the challenges pressed upon our own reality by illusionistic presentations of a figure caught as if in a moment of performance.

Notes

Much of the material for this book was gathered in interviews. For ease of reading, interview citations are unmarked in the text. Details of the interviews appear in the References list, alphabetized by interviewee's last name.

Introduction

1. Miller 1984:18.

2. These were Lancôme, Prescriptives, Estée Lauder, Chanel, Christian Dior, and Elizabeth Arden. For a couple of weeks before the promotion, women could sign up at their favorite cosmetic counters. Each woman paid $25 for the glamour of a window makeover, but the fee was entirely "redeemable in product"—and anyone who bought even a fraction of the products that go into an elaborate makeover spent considerably more than that. Only women who already frequented the cosmetics counters would have known about the promotion; these women know that they can often receive makeovers "free" (but for the weighty social obligation incurred by having someone work intimately and concentratedly on one's face) inside the store—but no glamour there.

3. I am indebted in this discussion to Edward Braun's *The Director and the Stage.*

4. Braun 1982:99.

1: Spawning an "American" Display

1. Ewen 1988:33. See also p. 25, where Ewen relates this loosening of the relation between form and substance in the material world with the popularization of photography, which allowed "a new reality, shaped by the flourishing of dematerialized surfaces, [to] take hold."

2. Benson 1986:13.

3. Hendrickson 1979:30–32.

4. Benson 1986:13; Orvell 1989:xvii.

5. Orvell 1989:28, 42–43.

6. Buck-Morss 1989:85.

7. Hall 1986:15–16.

8. Haraway 1984:25, 57.

9. Liberman 1979:8.

10. Carlin 1899:335.

11. The distinction between the earlier style of display—which focused on visibility—and the more atmospheric stagings is still around today in the contrast between museum and commercial display. Lighting a costume for museum exhibition is like early photographic presentations of fashion: the garment is flooded with light that has little character of its own, to point up the details of the garment without distracting from it. By contrast, contemporary commercial displays and fashion photography feature dramatic or atmospheric lighting.

12. Benson 1986:44, 102–103.

13. Fjellman 1992:39.

14. Mowry 1963:15; Ewen 1988:46.

15. Friedberg 1993:57.

16. Ewen 1988:83.

17. Fox 1984.

18. *Fortune* 1937:91; Parrot 1982:90; *Time* 1938:37.

19. Gaba 1952:15–16.

20. Gaba 1937:13.

21. Fashion magazines also found a provocative way to combine text and image that may have inspired later display attempts at visual puns, as well as surrealist work in other genres.

22. Martin 1987:218.

23. Leach 1989:100; Martin 1987:14–15.

24. Martin 1987:9.

25. Museum of Modern Art 1990:5.

26. Kiesler 1930:66–67.

27. Wallace 1981:63.

28. Buck-Morss 1989:255–256; Fox 1984:79.

29. Ignatius 1949:94; M. Anderson 1989:117.

30. Ashell 1961:7.

31. Matthews 1948:52.

32. Ewen 1976:43, 56, 76.

33. Leach 1989:102.

34. Arjé 1990.

35. Gaba 1939:42; Kiesler 1930:27. Even before the Great Depression, display had a history of using inexpensive materials, a strategy that is still associated with periods of belt-tightening. In 1898 L. Frank Baum observed with evident glee that "it has become the fashion to make forms of different classes of goods"; he constructed a Manila Man out of manila twines and ropes (Baum 1898:157). These from-scratch reproductions of the human form are conceptual ancestors to the contemporary abstract mannequin.

36. Ewen 1976:46–47.

37. Moore and Hyams 1990:49.

38. Kiesler 1930:110.

39. Hall-Duncan 1979:77.

40. Hall 1986:16.

41. Moore 1951:n.p.

42. Hall-Duncan 1979:217.

43. Turbeville 1978:n.p.

44. Fraser 1977b:63.

45. Hall-Duncan 1979:201.

46. The other was in the years just after World War II, when windows were "reported weekly in columns and hundreds of people strolled along Fifth Avenue to 'do' the windows" (Wood 1982:156).

47. Gramke 1977:29.

48. Moore and Hyams 1990:61, 55.

49. Fortune 1937:91.

50. Fuersich n.d.

51. Wood 1982:xi-xii.

52. Miller 1984:20.

53. Gray 1976:52.

54. With the growth of chain stores and the economic demise during the 1980s of those department stores that had attained the status of cultural landmarks, however, New York's position in the national display world is not likely to hold. Industry observers, who travel not only to fashion shows but to display industry markets worldwide, anticipate that New York's reputation for innovation may pass. Michael Southgate commented in 1990 that "in fact, New York seems to have lost a great deal of ground, because it's become very conservative and other places are doing more experimental things." Southgate found that, by contrast with Europe, where the major cities show much more display sophistication than the suburbs, in the United States "the standard overall is very high."

55. *Women's Wear Daily* 1986:31. Laying the shoes on the floor saves a display artist from having to drill a hole in the sole of the shoes for the mannequin's support rod to go through.

56. *Retail Attraction* n.d.:30.

57. In Germany (admittedly not in the fashion vanguard), abstract head treatments seem to be the rage, and mannequins "are treated only as props, [with] a strong streak of the carnival" (Southgate 1990b).

A comparison of Japanese display styles with American would be a worthwhile study, tracing whether increasing theatricality portends a greater dependence on tangible interior displays and events and reduced emphasis on windows. Display was regarded in Japan as a foreign concept, "fancy and unnecessary," until shortly after World War II. The sudden onset of enthusiasm for the practice, however, was followed by a long popularity, as for many elements of American style. In the mid-1970s, Makoto Nakamura called Japan "a display designer's paradise" because of the hunger there for new display ideas (1975–76:518). The contrast between Japan's blossoming retail economy and America's sagging one in the 1980s and early 1990s also provides a basis for a comparison of display strategies. Writing in 1990, Holly Brubach noted the amplified presence of Japan at the European fashion shows, sounding a bit stampeded over as she remarked that "the Japanese have taken our place as the world's No. 1 consumers" (1990:77).

In 1981 the Japanese display artist Toshi observed that displays in his country never aim to sell specific merchandise, but rather the store's image. That may account for why street theatre could not have happened at the same time in Japan as it did in New York. Toshi explained, "If you put one of your bizarre windows in Japan, like some of the ones here that are trying for shock value, people would take it as reflecting the image of the store and would say, 'Wow, what is this store all about. What are they trying to do?'" (quoted in Undercoffer 1981a:85).

Another distinctive feature of Japanese display is the cultural insistence on a multilayered reading. "They teach you in Japan that everything has to have a cultural philosophy to it," Toshi says, adding that Japanese consumers demand some kind of "twist" from every display (Undercoffer 1981a:85; Toshi 1990). One of the definitions of "display" that the celebrated Japanese display artist Haruhisa Hattori explicated in

How to Understand and Use Display is "to reveal the inside of something" or "to make something known" (1988:12).

It is reductionistic and inaccurate, however, simply to dismiss American display as superficial or knowable, while calling Japanese display mysterious and needing to be unlocked. Toshi aired his belief in a 1990 interview that the Japanese merely took up the styles of American visual merchandising and adapted them to their own needs as another trend. As in Colin Birch's Britain, Toshi maintains that the Japanese don't see window display as a sales tool, but merely as another fun—and most important, *new*—thing to try. In Toshi's estimation, display in Japan remains at the level of decoration. Michael Southgate might agree: he sees the Japanese as being skilled in handling only the tiniest and most expensive items (jewelry, e.g.) in display, while showing less imagination or technical expertise in handling more basic items (1990b).

Two points, however, evoke further interest here: One is Hattori's insistence on the necessity for windows to instigate a "friendly" or "hospitable" relationship with the viewer, a point of view that the American display artists I interviewed agreed with upon reflection but which never appears in writings about display in the United States. According to Hattori, "When friendliness is experienced it has the ability to excite the soul of the receiver. Such friendliness usually has its roots in sympathy. It seems as if humans offer sympathy on such occasions as when an interesting object is offered for comment, [or when a piece] of unusual information is passed across and when a covered object is presented in gift-form" (1988:16). Hattori writes that friendliness can be construed as a form of hospitality: "This is because hospitality is the art of expressing good-will and respect. . . . A place of business is also a place where guests are received. The act of hospitality certainly cannot be overlooked there. In this way hospitality also plays a very important role" (1988:16).

There is no suggestion from the American display community, aside from a stray comment by Gene Moore in his book on Tiffany—or the sudden, industry-wide change of heart, come Christmastime—that window display is a social transaction. This contrast deserves further investigation, preferably by assessing the role that display plays in urban Japanese life. Is it linked with advertising, other forms of fashion presentation, and avant-garde art movements, as it is in the United States? To what degree has Japanese display lifted American values along with techniques?

Another key to such a cross-cultural comparison in Japanese display is the movement through the 1980s toward multimedia presentation and to the theatricalization of the department store to a degree that may have surpassed even Bloomingdale's.

Susan Chira describes the two strains of visual merchandising at war in contemporary Japan. One is exemplified by the more traditional store Hankyu, whose advertising slogan is "Authentic," the other represented by a new kind of "post-department store" called Seibu, whose slogan is "Mind Theater." "Puppets dance and television sets flicker in Seibu's windows," Chira writes, "while mannequins in gray and black suits stare silently from the Hankyu branch. Seibu blasts music that keeps the decibel level at a Tower Records pitch, while Hankyu shoppers are greeted with soft Muzak and the chirping voices of young women. Seibu has devoted an entire floor to services such as vacation home bookings, life insurance, home loans for women and other credit information; Hankyu has reserved most of its space for merchandise." At Seibu, the emphasis is on technology and sensory stimulation: on the busy first floor, "over the din floats a voice saying, in the peculiar English so chic in Japan, 'These are the feelings; this is the quality of life'" (Chira n.d.:1). Seibu's move into the realm of theatricality in merchandising and in everyday life was made possible by grass-roots, low-tech work in the form of New York's street theatre.

58. The advertising industry has long been characterized as a clan of male producers creating images for hungry female consumers. These women were portrayed by the industry as standing in need of "expert" advice—both because they couldn't be expected to know how to consume enough goods on their own and because, in the advertisers' perception, they responded to such corporate personas as Betty Crocker, created in 1921, who seemed to talk directly to them.

59. Benson 1986:5, 23, 37. Benson notes, however, that early twentieth-century department store managers frequently "longed for male customers because they perceived them as personally preferable to women. . . . '[Men] do not "shop" in the sense that a woman does. A man goes into a store with a specific purchase in mind, which he makes as expeditiously as possible and then gets out.' The irony was considerable: while they were trying to create a female style of shopping, they found a male style of making discrete purchases personally more appealing and less disruptive of store operations" (p. 99).

60. Senerius 1976b.

61. O'Clare 1937:15.

62. Wood 1982:140–141.

63. O'Clare 1937:14; *Retail Attraction* n.d.:31; Wood 1982:151.

64. Harper 1987a:27.

65. Baum 1898:103; Leydenfrost 1950:10; Kiesler 1930:72.

66. *Fortune* 1937:91.

67. Wood 1982:137–138; Kiesler 1930:21.

68. *Fortune* 1937:91.

69. Friedberg 1993:118.

70. Tompkins 1989.

71. Babuscio 1984:41; Sontag 1982:105–108, 114.

72. Babuscio 1984:45.

73. Bronski 1984:186.

74. Voguing, a dance style closely associated with transvestite and transsexual life, originated in the drag balls of black and Hispanic Harlems. The style involves stringing together a series of poses imitated from high-fashion models and stars, particularly of the 1940s and 1950s. Madonna's song and video "Vogue" broadened awareness of the style.

75. Dorfles 1970:221.

2: Performance/Art

1. Perreault 1989.

2. Moore and Hyams 1990:67.

3. Moore and Hyams 1990:70.

4. Moore and Hyams 1990:69.

5. Weinstein 1989.

6. Weinstein 1989.

7. Scherer 1989.

8. Goldman 1980:30.

9. The mannequin sculptors are noticeably absent. By contrast with the more capricious situation in the art world, it seems that in mannequin manufacture the person farthest from the hands-on physical process invariably gets the most credit. Lowell Nesbitt, for example, an art-world sculptor with an international reputation and the creative director for a 1990 Pucci collection, had the entire grouping named after him. The names of career mannequin sculptors, on the other hand, are rarely revealed to the buying public.

10. Orvell 1989:223.

11. Hall 1986:93.

12. Knight 1982:E-4.

13. Perreault 1989:109–110.

14. *Candy Wholesaler* 1980.

15. Birch 1986a.

16. Birch 1986c.

17. Miller 1984:74.

18. Fraser 1977:66.

19. Oldenburg 1967:39, 83.

20. Perreault 1989:110.

21. Hershman 1990.

22. Blum 1977.

23. Bourdon 1976:85; Minton 1973:11; Lyons 1976.

24. Bourdon 1976.

25. Deitch 1981; Gumpert and Rifkin 1981:15.

26. Brandenburg 1981.

27. Städtische Galerie Nordheim 1985.

28. Frauenmuseum 1988; Gumpert and Rifkin 1981:17.

29. Jones 1991.

30. National Cash Register Company 1959:9.

31. Hammond 1935:164.

32. The vast majority of robot mannequins are women; the feminine pronoun will therefore be used generically.

33. New York Times n.d.

34. Marx 1984:92.

35. Indeed, the reality behind the window may be more compelling than that on the streets. Everett has watched two rubberneckers collide on the sidewalk just under her nose as they gaped at her mystifying form.

36. LePage 1979:B1.

37. Parrot 1982:121.

38. LePage 1979:B1.

39. LePage 1979:B1.

40. Audiences vary in their response to a performance. Everett finds that Soho audiences are particularly severe in their scrutiny. Accustomed to seeing live people in windows, they are determined to find "mistakes" in her performance and are vocal if ever she makes any. (She can often read their lips.) Everett also finds that women more clearly register their surprise once they are certain she is real than do men, who, she says, try to pretend they can't be fooled. Audiences of all kinds regard her work as artistry, coming into the store and asking her during her breaks where she acquired her technique and what her "influences" are; a self-taught performer, Everett laughs at these questions.

41. Viewers are clearly inspired by the robot mannequin's theatricality to try to participate in the drama. Ironically, the vital illusionism and the actor-audience separation provided by the glass pane seem to be dramatically significant: robot mannequins performing inside malls, more physically accessible, seem to invite more poking than co-performing.

42. Schechner 1973:78.

43. Mathews 1988:11; P. Anderson 1988a:26–27.

44. Wood 1982:3, 162.

45. Everett remembers with particular fondness and pride the time an informal troupe of six young black breakdancers spotted her window and used it as a backdrop for their act, positioning themselves between her and her gathered audience. Allowing them for a few minutes to steal her audience, Everett began to toss in a few moves of her own—still within the robot style. The street dancers noticed her and challenged her with their movements. And so a true jam began, which won Everett

the admiration of the audience and of the dancers. Everett saw her role-playing as a robot mannequin as fundamentally akin to that of the breakdancers, whose performance "isn't human either."

46. Gaba was not the first to make public appearances with his mannequin. In the second decade of this century expressionist painter Oskar Kokoschka commissioned the making of a life-size doll in the likeness of his lover, Alma Mahler. According to sculptor Nathan Cabot Hale, "The story was that Kokoschka took it all around, to restaurants and coffee houses, and sat it in the chair next to himself for a period of a couple years. He also used it in some of his paintings" (N. Hale n.d.).

47. Gaba 1952:11–12.

48. Haden-Guest 1972:244.

49. Rogers 1987:57.

50. Dolezal 1981:6.

3: "Coition through a Glass Pane"

1. Haug 1986:45.

2. Mulvey 1975.

3. See Partington 1992.

4. See Mulvey 1975; Partington 1992:156; Dolan 1988:13.

5. Freud 1955:220.

6. Freud 1955:241.

7. *Visual Merchandising* 1979e:40–41.

8. Freud 1955:233, 226.

9. Hoffmann 1982.

10. Films International of America n.d.

11. Collins 1988:261.

12. Dolezal 1981:9–10.

13. Nemy 1983:K7; Chadakoff 1990.

14. Taylor 1977:38.

15. O'Brien and Oliver 1946:86.

16. Nemy 1983:K7.

17. Hile 1937.

18. Gaba 1952:11–12.

19. Burggraf 1981:84; Ingrassia 1984.

20. Collins 1988:263–4. In 1897 Stanley G. Hall remarked in *A Study of Dolls* that "the cases of fear of dolls are almost always of large dolls" (Stewart 1993:124). A provocative study of the impact of scale on temporal perception was done at the University of Tennessee in the early 1980s. People were asked to move scale figures around in 1:6, 1:12, and 1:24 "lounge" environments, to imagine themselves as these figures, and to report when they felt they had had thirty minutes' worth of "experience" in those spaces. There seemed to be a relation between scale and time in the study: the smaller the figures used, the more quickly did the subjects feel that the allotted amount

of time had passed (described in Stewart 1993:66). Perhaps the fascination associated with the perception of mannequins—often significantly larger (at least in height) than human scale—is based on a similar effect: here, the *suspension* of time.

21. Dunstan n.d.; Bostock 1979:15.

22. E.g., see Snead 1990.

23. *Smithsonian* 1975.

24. Snead 1990; Dolezal 1981:6.

25. Collins 1988:261.

26. Haden-Guest 1972:241.

27. Quoted in Schickel 1985:336.

28. O'Brien and Olivier 1946:86.

29. Benson 1986:9.

30. *Fortune* 1937:96.

31. Other kinds of "decency" concerns may be raised, however. Gene Moore suffered attacks from industrial purists who felt he acted disrespectfully by half-burying some of Tiffany's diamonds in dirt in a 1957 display: "A representative of the De Beers Syndicate, the group that controls the diamond market, called to register a complaint about my treatment of those precious stones. Diamonds, he told me, were not made to be put in dirt. 'Where do you think they come from?' I asked him. And, anyway, they're washable" (Moore and Hyams 1990:84).

32. *Visual Merchandising and Store Design* 1989:81.

33. One notable exception is the street theatre movement of the mid-1970s.

34. Mansour 1990.

35. Parrot 1982:153.

36. Hess 1978:176.

37. Notably, they rarely seem to become politically engaged in the relation between the whole form of mannequin displays and the display of live women in culture, at least not to the extent that Lynn Hershman did in *25 Windows*.

38. Scarangello 1990.

39. Lague 1989:50.

40. Moore and Hyams 1990:206–207.

41. Bloomingdale's n.d.; Landman 1987.

42. Hammond 1935:161.

43. Moore and Hyams 1990:121; Goldman 1980:19.

44. At work here is a principle akin to J. L. Austin's idea of a performative utterance, in which anything you say is something you simultaneously accomplish by saying, as in "I christen thee" or "I congratulate you."

45. Moore 1990.

46. Southgate 1990b.

47. Pegler 1980:53. Gene Moore spoofed this industry-wide ethic to his own advantage when he posed mannequins wear-

ing boxing gloves in the Bonwit Teller window in honor of the fiftieth anniversary of neighbor and competitor Bergdorf Goodman. The Bonwit mannequin "said" cattily to the Bergdorf mannequin, "Happy birthday. You don't look a day over 50, dear." Moore gloats, "The boxing mannequins attracted much attention. One afternoon I ran into Andrew Goodman, Bergdorf's president. He wasn't pleased. 'You're some smart fellow. It's our anniversary, and Bonwit's is getting all the publicity because of your windows.' All I could do was wish him a happy birthday" (Moore and Hyams 1990:45).

48. Cranston and Bunch 1990.
49. Taft 1926:222.
50. Marchand 1985:356–357.
51. Gutman and Alden 1985.
52. *Visual Merchandising* 1979a:42.
53. Hughes n.d.
54. Matthews 1948:17, 52–53.

4: Realisms
1. Orvell 1989:xv, 85.
2. M. Hale 1983:49.
3. In Rutledge 1986:61. The fashion doll was used in earlier centuries to convey French fashions, in miniature form, to the rulers of neighboring countries.
4. Quoted in Hale 1986:39.
5. Parrot 1982:46.
6. M. Hale 1985:45.
7. Bostock 1979:21; M. Hale 1985:45.
8. O'Brien and Olivier 1946:27.
9. Hammond 1935:161.
10. This practice sometimes produced disastrous results. Martha Landau reported that a top display director of the 1950s would use the same face and makeup palette and style on every mannequin in a bank of windows but would vary the pose, often by taking the torso and "matching" it with different legs. "Sometimes you did pretty well," she recalls, "and sometimes you didn't. You had to be careful that you didn't wind up with a deformed cripple" (Landau 1990).
11. O'Brien and Olivier 1946:26.
12. *Advertising Arts* 1933.
13. *Life* 1937.
14. *Advertising Arts* 1933; Stubergh 1983:2. Stubergh saw the Imans figures for the first time at the age of four, when they were exhibited at the 1915 World's Fair in San Francisco.
15. *Fortune* 1937:92.
16. Parrot 1982:114; O'Brien and Olivier 1946:86.
17. Paraphrase of Parrot 1982 in Chester 1983a:11.
18. Moore 1990.

19. M. Hale 1983:49.
20. Landau 1990; Charles J. Onorato quoted in Burggraf 1981.
21. Adel Rootstein quoted in Ingrassia 1984:22.
22. Hyde 1986:H4. Rootstein is given credit for bringing the suggestion of movement to contemporary mannequins, but in the late 1930s Lillian Greneker developed mannequins whose movable, accordion-pleated waists made body attitudes more varied and natural (Cook 1990).
23. Adel Rootstein *B:*4; Ingrassia 1984:22.
24. Ickeringill 1968:55. Multiculturalism in the mannequin industry was associated with greater acceptance of ethnicity in the wider culture. For example, the Barbie doll, which was invented in 1959, gained a black friend, Christie, in 1968, the same year Luna appeared. Since then, Miko, a Eurasian friend, and Theresa, a Hispanic friend, have been added to the lines, as have black and Hispanic Barbies. In the mid-1980s, Barbie began to be issued in four different lines, corresponding to wardrobe and pose choices. These were Lead Glamour, Trend, Music, and Swimsuit (Bender 1989:27).
25. Lee-Potter n.d.
26. Pegler 1978:48.
27. Marlowe 1980:135.
28. Fraser 1977a:18.
29. "Classic Drama" may well have been the first older-woman mannequin of Filoso's generation. Recall, however, the wide array of types that were "enmannequined" in the 1930s.
30. Ingrassia 1984:22.
31. This went against the whole history of mannequin design, which had practical as well as aesthetic bases. Dan Arjé recalled that manufacturers had to observe certain modesties of pose to facilitate the dressing of the mannequin. The legs could not be placed too far apart if the display artist was going to get a straight skirt over them, and the arms could neither be too contracted nor too extended for most jackets.
32. Burggraf 1981; Haraway 1984:34.
33. Oestricher 1978.
34. Burggraf 1981.
35. *New York Sun* 1941; *New York Sun* n.d.
36. Takahama 1983:B4.
37. Gellers n.d.
38. Ingrassia 1984:22; Barker n.d.:118.
39. Collins 1988:264.
40. Hammond 1935:166.
41. Pegler 1978:47.
42. Marlowe 1980:18.
43. Collins 1988:264.
44. Scarangello 1990.

45. Chester 1983a:10.

46. Pegler 1978:47. Disco in turn owed much to a gay aesthetic. The discos of the period were amalgams of gay culture, dress-up, role-playing, and self-expression.

47. Triggs 1992:25.

48. Sharpsteen 1987:26.

49. Brubach 1990:79.

50. Harper 1987b:31.

51. Ingrassia 1984.

52. Paraphrased in Dolan 1988:35.

53. Stewart 1993:57.

54. Thomas 1976:306; Bright 1987:165.

55. Bright 1987:229.

56. Finch 1973:402.

5: Street Theatre

1. Miller 1978:41; Stevens 1979:2–3.

2. Fraser 1985:259.

3. Ingrassia 1984:22.

4. *Visual Merchandising* 1979d:55; Burggraf 1981.

5. Dolezal 1981:6.

6. Massey 1948:133,27; *Fortune* 1937:92.

7. Kent 1976:82.

8. Kent 1976:85; "What's Going On Behind That Plate-Glass Window?" 1977.

9. Stedelijk Museum 1974:n.p.

10. Tucker 1981:10–11; Onorato 1987:10.

11. Kirshner 1980:3, 17.

12. Seiberling 1976a:49–50; Kozloff 1975:36.

13. Kozloff 1975:34, 37.

14. Fuersich n.d.

15. Higgins 1979:182.

16. Brecht 1964:92.

17. Lapin 1976:53–54.

18. Nando Miglio, an Italian creator of fashion "events," took the action to the streets when he staged a 1987 event in honor of the twentieth anniversary of the New York boutique Charivari: "We brought 15 mannequins out on the sidewalk and arranged them as if they were waiting for cabs. They wore Byblos fall/winter fashions (cashmere coats, furs, etc.) and their faces were wrapped in woolen 'gauze' to represent winter. People could actually touch them. The response was wonderful" (Harper 1987b:27).

19. Coleman 1977:11–13.

20. Marchand 1985:60; Seiberling 1976a:52.

21. Weiss 1990:E6.

22. Seiberling 1976b.

23. Kent 1976:82; Lague 1989:51.

24. *House and Garden* 1976:12.

25. Bethany 1985:64.

26. Kanner 1987:13.

27. Miller 1984:18.

28. Orvell 1989:35, 240.

29. Kent 1976:83. As ever, precedents exist in display history for ideas that seemed novel in their own generation. Lester Gaba had proposed in 1952 showing off housewares by using a mannequin "in formal evening dress whipping up an after-theater supper in her kitchen" (Gaba 1952:69).

30. Bethany 1985:64; Fitzgibbons 1977:92.

31. Seiberling 1976b.

32. Wood 1982:155.

33. Besides, Bloomingdale's was (and remains) a union shop, with union regulations preventing the display director from entering the windows, so Pratts's hands-on experience was extremely limited. Pratts would direct the windows from the street, tapping on the glass and indicating how changes should be done.

34. Bob Currie and Candy Pratts have also said that their choice of realistic mannequins over abstracts was partly a matter of simply having a better "feel" for one kind of form over the other.

35. Heinemann 1976.

36. Gray 1976:42, 54.

37. Posner 1980b:38F; Kent 1976:82.

38. Taylor 1977. This style of posing held fast in display, even after the death of street theatre. Colin Birch, a display director at Bloomingdale's during the 1980s, posed mannequins so that they "rarely looked at passersby, almost as if their own worlds were more exciting" (P. Anderson 1988b:43).

39. Higgins 1979:179–181.

40. Lapin 1976:56.

41. Yaeger 1976:1.

42. Heinemann 1976.

43. Seiberling 1976b.

44. Gramke 1977:30–32.

45. Josephson 1976; Gramke 1977:29.

46. Saarinen 1965:16; Bethany 1985:62.

47. Moore and Hyams 1990:33, 101.

48. Moore and Hyams 1990:135–137.

49. Moore and Hyams 1990:33–34, 162.

50. Goffman 1979:26.

51. These are often traditionally "feminine" poses: reclining, gazing in a mirror, stretching languidly.

6: The Abstract Mannequin

1. Wood and Rosenthal 1965:85; Barker n.d.:117.

References

Sources listed below that are not cited in the Notes contributed to the development of this book and are provided for readers who wish to investigate the subject further.

Adel Rootstein Display Mannequins. 1989. "Ross." Press release. Adel Rootstein company archive, London.

———. 1984. "Classy Lady Long Legs." Press release. Adel Rootstein company archive, London.

———. 1982. "Runway Geo." Brochure. The Mannequin Museum, Los Angeles.

———. 1980. "Body Gossip." Brochure. The Mannequin Museum, Los Angeles.

———. 1967. "Luna." Brochure. The Mannequin Museum, Los Angeles.

———. 1966. "Twiggy." Brochure. The Mannequin Museum, Los Angeles.

———. *A.* "Adel Rootstein Display Mannequins." Brochure. The Mannequin Museum, Los Angeles.

———. *B.* "The Adel Rootstein Story." Undated press release, ca. mid- to late 1980s. The Mannequin Museum, Los Angeles.

Advertising Arts. 1933. "Gaba Girls." November, p. 30.

Alderson, William T., and Shirley T. Payne. 1985. *Interpretation of Historic Sites.* Nashville: American Association for State and Local History.

Anderson, Marie P. 1989. *Model.* New York: Doubleday.

Anderson, P. K. 1988a. "Life Imitates Art." *Visual Merchandising & Store Design.* January, pp. 24–27.

———. 1988b. "Colin Birch: 1949–1988." *Visual Merchandising & Store Design.* August, pp. 42–43.

———. 1987. "Perspectives." *Visual Merchandising & Store Design.* September, p. 4.

Arbus, Diane. 1984. *Diane Arbus: Magazine Work.* New York: Aperture.

Arjé, Dan. 1990. Interview with author. New York. November 25.

Ash, Juliet, and Elizabeth Wilson, eds. 1992. *Chic Thrills: A Fashion Reader.* Berkeley: University of California Press.

Ashell, Ben. 1961. "Blue Print for Successful Fashion Shows." Unpublished manuscript. Fashion Institute of Technology, Vertical Files on "Fashion Shows."

Autié, Dominique. 1982. "Artificial Bodies or the Naturalist's Chamber." Introduction to Nicole Parrot, *Mannequins,* pp. 9–32.

Babuscio, Jack. 1984. "Camp and the Gay Sensibility." In *Gays and Film,* ed. Richard Dyer. New York: New York Zoetrope.

Balavender, Robert. 1991. "Spring/Summer '91 Fashion Trends from Paris." *VM + SD.* January, pp. 26–31.

Barker, E. Stephen. N.d. "Manikins: The Original Visual Merchandisers." Chapter 12 of a photocopied manuscript, pp. 113–22. The Mannequin Museum, Los Angeles.

Baudrillard, Jean. 1983. "The Precession of Simulacra." In *Simulations,* trans. Paul Foss and Paul Patton. New York: Semiotext(e).

Baum, L. Frank. 1906. *The Art of Decorating Show Windows and Interiors.* Chicago: Merchants Record.

———. 1898. *The Show Window.* Chicago: Show Window Publications.

Behr, Edward. N.d. Photocopy. The Mannequin Museum, Los Angeles.

Bell, Jane. 1976. "Art in a Department Store's Windows." *St. Louis Post-Dispatch.* November 21.

Bender, Karen E. 1989. "Barbie Turns the Big 3-0." Photocopy, pp. 26–28. The Mannequin Museum, Los Angeles.

Benson, Susan Porter. 1986. *Counter Cultures: Saleswomen, Managers, and Customers in Department Stores, 1890–1940*. Urbana: University of Illinois Press.

Benzio, Bob. 1974. "Speaking Out; Seeking Out." *Visual Merchandising*. May, p. 18.

Bethany, Marilyn. 1985. "Making Scenes." *New York*. April 1, pp. 60–65.

Birch, Colin. 1986a. Memo to Marvin Traub. Colin Birch Collection. Fashion Institute of Technology. February 26.

———. 1986b. Memo to Marvin Traub. Colin Birch Collection. Fashion Institute of Technology. March 7.

———. 1986c. Memo to Marvin Traub. Colin Birch Collection. Fashion Institute of Technology. March 31.

———. 1986d. Memo to Stephen Toon. Colin Birch Collection. Fashion Institute of Technology. April 22.

———. N.d. Speech notes, ca. 1985. Colin Birch Collection. Fashion Institute of Technology.

Bloomingdale's. 1989a. California "country event" book. Bloomingdale's collection.

———. 1989b. France "country event" book. Bloomingdale's collection.

———. 1988. China "country event" book. Bloomingdale's collection.

———. N.d. "Standing Room Only." *Bloomingdale's Face*. In-house publication, ca. mid-1970s. Robert Hoskins' private collection.

Blum, Walter. 1977. "A Museum Without Walls." *California Living* magazine, *San Francisco Sunday Examiner and Chronicle*. April 3.

Blumenfeld, Erwin. 1981. *My One Hundred Best Photos*. New York: Rizzoli.

Borcoman, James. 1984. *Eugène Atget, 1857–1927*. Ottawa: National Gallery of Canada.

Bostock, Cliff. 1979. "It's a Mannequin's World." *The Atlanta Journal and Constitution Magazine*. October 14, pp. 15 ff.

Bourdon, David. 1976. "Folies-Légères: Busting Out of Bonwit's." *Village Voice*. November 8, p. 85.

Brandenburg, Peter von. 1981. "Art Objects by Justine of the Colette Is Dead, Co." In *Colette (1970–1980)*, p. 65. Exhibition catalog. Milan: Giancarlo Politi.

Braun, Edward. 1982. *The Director and the Stage: From Naturalism to Grotowski*. New York: Holmes & Meier.

Brecht, Bertolt. 1964. *Brecht on Theatre*, ed. John Willett. New York: Hill and Wang.

Bright, Randy. 1987. *Disneyland: The Inside Story*. New York: Harry N. Abrams.

Bronski, Michael. 1984. *Culture Clash: The Making of Gay Sensibility*. Boston: South End.

Brubach, Holly. 1990. "Retroactivity." *The New Yorker*. December 31, pp. 74–81.

Buckley, Tom. 1975. "About New York: More Than Pins and Needles." *New York Times*. May 2.

Buck-Morss, Susan. 1989. *The Dialectics of Seeing: Walter Benjamin and the Arcades Project*. Cambridge: MIT Press.

Burggraf, Helen. 1985. "New York Fashion Designers Trim Frills From Shows." *Crain's New York Business*. December 9, pp. 3, 25.

———. 1981. "Mannequins: The Retailer's Silent Salespeople." *California Apparel News*. October 30.

Butler, Judith. 1988. "Performative Acts and Gender Constitution: An Essay in Phenomenology and Feminist Theory." *Theatre Journal* 40 (4): 519–531.

Calhoun, Catherine. 1989. "Barneys Puts Fashion Photos on Display." *Photo District News*. December, pp. 84–85.

California Apparel News. 1983. "Mannequin Experts Tell How Most Stores Err in Using Mannequins." The Mannequin Museum, Los Angeles.

Candy Wholesaler. 1980. "Candy's Magical Merchandising at Disney's Magic Kingdom." June.

Carlin, Eva V. 1899. " 'America's Grandest' in California." *Arena* 22 (September).

Carroll, Jerry. N.d. "Mannequins Are Getting New Figures to Show Off High Fashion." *San Francisco Chronicle*. Ca. 1988.

Chadakoff, Rochelle. 1990. "Molding Noticeably Human Shapes." *Newpaper Enterprise Association Fashion*. February 7.

Chapell, Caroline. N.d. Untitled manuscript on work of Leza Lidow. The Mannequin Museum, Los Angeles.

Chester, Harold. 1983a. "Mannequins: Models of Their Time." *Daily News Record*. March 11, pp. 10–11.

———. 1983b. "Pucci's Mold." *Daily News Record*. March 11, p. 10.

Chira, Susan. N.d. " 'Store Wars' on the Ginza." *New York Times*.

Churchman, Calvin. 1991. Telephone interview with author. New York. June 27.

Coleman, A. D. 1977. *The Grotesque in Photography*. New York: Summit.

Colette. 1991. Interview with author. New York. June 28.

Collins, Greg. 1988. "Body Doubles." *Gentleman's Quarterly*. April, pp. 260–300.

Cook, Joan. 1990. "L. L. Greneker, 95; Made Mannequins with Movable Parts." *New York Times*. February 6.

Cranston, Edward T., and Leonard Bunch. 1990. Interview with author. New York. November 6.

Currie, Bob. 1990. Interview with author. New York. December 18.

Currier, Richard. 1990. Interview with author. New York. November 12.

David, Yasha. 1987. Foreword to *The Arcimboldo Effect: Transformations of the Face from the 16th to the 20th Century*, p. 11. New York: Abbeville.

Davis, Dorothy. 1966. *The History of Shopping.* London: Routledge & Kegan Paul.

Decter Mannikin Company, Inc. 1990. "Young Americans." Sales letter. Collection of author.

———. 1989. "Possibilities Unlimited: The Max and Maxine Collection." Sales letter. Collection of author.

———. A. "The Profile Collection." Brochure. The Mannequin Museum, Los Angeles.

Deitch, Jeffrey. 1981. "Art Objects by Justine of the Colette is Dead, Co." In *Colette (1970–1980)*, p. 64. Exhibition catalog. Milan: Giancarlo Politi.

Devlin, Polly. 1979. *Vogue Book of Fashion Photography.* New York: Quill.

Display World. 1945. Advertisement for Mayorga Mannequins' "Welcome Home Mannequins." September, p. 71.

Dolan, Jill. 1988. *The Feminist Spectator as Critic.* Ann Arbor: University of Michigan Press.

Dolezal, Suzanne. 1981. "The World of Dummies." *Detroit Free Press.* May 24.

Doonan, Simon. 1991. Interview with author. New York. May 7.

Dorfles, Gillo. 1970. "Pornokitsch and Morals." In *Kitsch: The World of Bad Taste*, ed. Dorfles, pp. 221–223. New York: Universe.

Drapery and Drapery Times. 1923. "Realistic Wax Figures." March 17, p. 350.

Dreams That Money Can Buy. 1947. Film, dir., wr., prod. Hans Richter. Collection of Museum of Modern Art, Film Studies Center, New York. 80 minutes.

Dunstan, Keith. N.d. "We Have No Fat Models . . . " Newspaper article, source unknown. The Mannequin Museum, Los Angeles.

Eisner, Lotte H. 1984. Excerpts from *The Haunted Screen* reproduced as "On Metropolis" by Producers Sales Organization, Los Angeles. Collection of Museum of Modern Art, Film Studies Center, New York.

Elsen, Albert E. 1969. *The Partial Figure in Modern Sculpture: From Rodin to 1969.* Baltimore: Baltimore Museum of Art.

Everett, Diane. 1990a. Interview with author. New York. October 8.

———. 1990b. Videotape of various robot mannequin performances. Collection of author.

Ewen, Stuart. 1988. *All Consuming Images: The Politics of Style in Contemporary Culture.* New York: Basic.

———. 1976. *Captains of Consciousness: Advertising and the Social Roots of the Consumer Culture.* New York: McGraw-Hill.

Ewen, Stuart, and Elizabeth Ewen. 1982. *Channels of Desire: Mass Images and the Shaping of American Consciousness.* New York: McGraw-Hill.

Eynat-Confino, Irène. 1987. *Beyond the Mask: Gordon Craig, Movement, and the Actor.* Carbondale: Southern Illinois University Press.

Fashion Institute of Technology. N.d. Display and Exhibit Design department brochure. Ca. 1989.

Ferguson, Laura. 1986. "Andrée Putman In Black and White." *Visual Merchandising & Store Design.* June, pp. 118–121.

Films International of America. N.d. "Dreams That Money Can Buy." Catalog issued in conjunction with film of same name, ca. 1947. New York. Collection of Museum of Modern Art, Film Studies Center, New York.

Filoso, Robert. 1991. Interview with author. Los Angeles. January 9.

Finch, Christopher. 1973. *The Art of Walt Disney.* New York: Harry N. Abrams.

Fitzgibbons, Ruth Miller. 1977. "Windows of the World: The New Display Art." *Interiors.* January, pp. 92–95.

Fjellman, Stephen M. 1992. *Vinyl Leaves: Walt Disney World and America.* Boulder: Westview Press.

Florist. 1985. "Colin Birch/Bloomingdale's: Tops in Trendiness." November, pp. 64–65.

Font, Willo. 1990. Interview with author. New York. October 31.

Fortune. 1937. "Window Display." Vol. 15 (January), pp. 91–100.

Forty, Adrian. 1986. *Objects of Desire: Design and Society 1750–1980.* London: Thames and Hudson.

Foster, Susie. 1983. "Today's Mannequins Aren't Just Dummies." *Australian.* September 30.

Fowler, Elizabeth M. 1970. "Mannequins Limn Mores." *New York Times.* February 22.

Fox, Stephen. 1984. *The Mirror Makers: A History of American Advertising and Its Creators.* New York: William Morrow.

Fraser, Kennedy. 1985. *The Fashionable Mind: Reflections on Fashion, 1970–1982.* Boston: David R. Godine.

———. 1978. "On and Off the Avenue: Feminine Fashions." *The New Yorker.* June 19, pp. 61–65.

———. 1977a. "On and Off the Avenue: Feminine Fashions, The Fall Collections—I." *The New Yorker.* July 11, pp. 76–81.

———. 1977b. "On and Off the Avenue: Feminine Fashions, The Fall Collections—II." *The New Yorker.* July 18, pp. 63–69.

Frauenmuseum. 1988. *Colette: The Bavarian Adventure.* Exhibition catalog. Bonn.

Freud, Sigmund. 1955. "The 'Uncanny.'" In *The Standard Edition of the Complete Psychological Works of Sigmund Freud,* trans. James Strachey. Vol. 17, pp. 218–252. London: Hogarth Press.

Friedberg, Anne. 1993. *Window Shopping: Cinema and the Postmodern.* Berkeley: University of California Press.

Fuersich, Laurence. N.d. Open letter to *Views & Reviews* subscribers. New York: Retail Reporting Bureau, ca. mid-1970s. Collection of author.

Gaba, Lester. 1980. "Black Mannequins." Letter to the Editor of the *New York Times.* December 17.

———. 1952. *The Art of Window Display.* New York: The Studio Publications.

———. 1939. *Soap Carving: Cinderella of Sculpture.* London: The Studio Ltd.

———. 1937. "A Plea for Realism." *Merchant's Record and Show Windows.* September.

Gellene, Denise. 1989. "Forever Young: After 30 Years, Barbie Has More Clothes, Friends and Fans Than Ever." *Los Angeles Times.* January 29.

Gellers, Stanley. 1987. "Simon Says." *DNR/The Magazine.* March.

———. N.d. "The Sexiest Displays." Photocopied article from unknown publication, ca. 1977. The Mannequin Museum, Los Angeles.

Gewertz, Catherine. 1988. "The Mannequin as a Form of History." *Los Angeles Times.*

Gilbert, Richard. 1990. Interview with author. San Diego. July 29.

Goffman, Erving. 1979. *Gender Advertisements.* New York: Harper Colophon.

Goldman, Judith. 1980. *Windows at Tiffany's: The Art of Gene Moore.* New York: Harry N. Abrams.

Gramke, Pamela. 1980. "Mannequins: From the Beginning." *Visual Merchandising.* May, pp. 42–44.

———. 1977. "After Street Theater New York Windows Take Shape." *Visual Merchandising.* February, pp. 29–30.

Gray, Margaret. 1976. "If I Like, I Buy; But Don't Dictate to Me." *Visual Merchandising.* September, pp. 42–54.

Gumpert, Lynn, and Ned Rifkin. 1981. *Persona.* Exhibition catalog. New York: The New Museum.

Gutman, Jonathan, and Scott D. Alden. 1985. "Adolescents' Cognitive Structures of Retail Stores and Fashion Consumption." In *Perceived Quality,* ed. Jacob Jacoby and Jerry Olson, pp. 99–114. Lexington, Mass.: Lexington.

Haber, Holly. 1988. "Retail Display Devices Get Eye-Catching Innovations." *Women's Wear Daily.* February 16, p. 21.

Haden-Guest, Anthony. 1972. *Down the Programmed Rabbit-Hole.* London: Hart-Davis, MacGibbon.

Hale, Marsha Bentley. 1986. "Future Mannequins: Past and Present Tense." *Retail Attraction.* March–April, pp. 39–43.

———. 1985. "Lasting Expressions." *Visual Merchandising & Store Design.* November, pp. 45–49.

———. 1983. "Body Attitudes." *Visual Merchandising & Store Design.* August, pp. 47 ff.

———. A. "Body Art: Human and Mannequin Bodies as Canvas." Manuscript. The Mannequin Museum, Los Angeles.

———. B. "Leza Lidow." Manuscript, adaptation from live video recording by author. The Mannequin Museum, Los Angeles.

Hale, Nathan Cabot. N.d. Letter to Marsha Bentley Hale. The Mannequin Museum, Los Angeles.

Hall, Margaret. 1986. *On Display: A Design Grammar for Museum Exhibitions.* London: Lund Humphries.

Hall-Duncan, Nancy. 1979. *The History of Fashion Photography.* New York: Alpine.

Hammond, Albert Edward. 1935. *Men's Wear Display.* N.p.: Caxton.

Haraway, Donna. 1984. "Teddy Bear Patriarchy: Taxidermy in the Garden of Eden, New York City: 1908–1936." *Social Text* 11: 20–64.

Harper, Laurel A. 1987a. "Simon-Ized." *VM+SD.* June, pp. 26–30.

———. 1987b. "That 'Italian Maestro.'" *Visual Merchandising & Store Design.* September, pp. 27–31.

———. 1982. "Artfully Speaking: Mannequins Make the Move from Display to Sculpture." *Visual Merchandising & Store Design.* July, pp. 37–38.

Hattori, Haruhisa. 1988. *How to Understand and Use Display.* Tokyo: Graphic-sha.

Haug, Wolfgang Fritz. 1986. *Critique of Commodity Aesthetics: Appearance, Sexuality and Advertising in Capitalist Society.* Minneapolis: University of Minnesota Press.

Heinemann, Sally. 1976. "What's Going on in the Windows?" *New York Times.* November 24.

Hellemans, Alexander and Bryan Bunch. 1988. *The Timetables of Science.* New York: Simon & Schuster.

Hendrickson, Robert. 1979. *The Grand Emporiums: The Illustrated History of America's Great Department Stores.* New York: Stein and Day.

Hershman, Lynn. 1991. Telephone interview with author. New York–San Francisco. February 18.

———. 1990. Letter to author. December 11.

———. 1977. "The Windows of Bonwit Teller." Videotape. 12 minutes.

Hess, Thomas. 1978. "Store Windows." *Vogue.* January, pp. 128–85.

Higgins, Dick. 1979. "Postmodern Performance: Some Criteria and Common Points." In *Performance by Artists*, ed. A. A. Bronson and Peggy Gale, pp. 176–182. Toronto: Art Metropole.

High Performance. 1981. "Lynn Hershman: Non-Credited Americans." Summer, p. 36.

Hile, Hans H. 1937. "Lovely Annabelle: A Modern Fantasy of a Modern Maid." *Merchant's Record and Show Windows.* P. 17.

Hindsgaul Mannequins. N.d. "The Hindsgaul Story." Press release. P. 2. The Mannequin Museum, Los Angeles.

Hoffmann, E. T. A. 1982. "The Sandman." In *Tales*, ed. Victor Lange, trans. L. J. Kent and E. C. Knight, pp. 277–308.

Hollander, Anne. 1988. *Seeing Through Clothes.* New York: Penguin.

Hoskins, Robert. 1991. Interview with author. New York. July 18.

House and Garden. 1976. "Smashing Windows." August, p. 12.

Hughes, Alice. N.d. "Clear Cellophane for Models." Newspaper article, source unknown. The Mannequin Museum, Los Angeles.

Hugo, Victor. 1991. Interview with author. New York. February 13.

Hyde, Nina. 1986. "Designer Andrée Putman's Six-Foot Figure of Majesty." *The Washington Post.* September 14.

Ickeringill, Nan. 1968. "New Faces—Black—for Store Windows." *New York Times.* December 20.

Ignatius, Helen. 1949. "Formula for Fashion Shows." *California Stylist.* May, pp. 94 ff.

Ingrassia, Michele. 1984. "Rootstein's Real-Life Mannequins: They Changed the Way the World Looks at Fashion." *Los Angeles Times.* June 8.

Institute of Contemporary Art. 1982. "ICA Street Sights 2." Exhibition commentary. University of Pennsylvania. Collection of Lynn Hershman, San Francisco.

International Center of Photography. 1990. "Bazaar Years: A Fashion Retrospective." Exhibition on work of Man Ray. New York.

Interview. 1986. "Simon Doonan." January, p. 93.

Jan, Alfred. 1985. "Lynn Hershman: Processes of Empowerment." *High Performance.* December, pp. 36–38.

Jones, Alan. 1991. "Colette: Through the Looking Glass." Exhibition catalog/poster. New York: Rempire Gallery.

Jørgen Fuhr Design Center. 1990. "Dekofigure" mannequin alternative brochures. Collection of author.

Josephson, Nancy. 1977. "A Dramatic Climax." *Women's Wear Daily.* February 8, p. 24.

———. 1976. "The Prop Stopper." *Women's Wear Daily.* March 23, n.p.

Kammer, Nancy. 1977. "New York Opens Its Windows to Maggie Spring." *Visual Merchandising.* February, pp. 37–61.

Kanner, Bernice. 1987. "Window Dressing: Bloomingdale's Changing Faces." *New York.* August 17, pp. 12–13.

Kaufman, Joanne. 1987. "She's No Dummy: Rootstein's Model Mannequins." *The Wall Street Journal.* August 11.

Kent, Rosemary. 1976. "Drama Department: Comedy, Sex, and Violence in Store Windows." *New York.* May 24, pp. 82–85.

Kiesler, Frederick. 1930. *Contemporary Art Applied to the Store and Its Display.* New York: Brentano's.

Kirshner, Judith Russi. 1980. *Vito Acconci: A Retrospective, 1969 to 1980.* Chicago: Museum of Contemporary Art.

Klein, Alan M. 1993. *Little Big Men: Bodybuilding Subculture and Gender Construction.* Albany: State University of New York Press.

Klemesrud, Judy. 1969. "Bergdorf's Gives Boost to Fashion by Blacks." *New York Times.* May 21.

Knight, Christopher. 1982. "The Art Museum as Department Store." *Los Angeles Herald Examiner.* October 17.

Kowinski, William S. 1985. *The Malling of America: An Inside Look at the Great Consumer Paradise.* New York: William Morris.

Kozloff, Max. 1975. "Pygmalion Reversed." *Artforum.* November, pp. 30–37.

L. A. Feldman Fixture Company. 1920. Advertisement. The Mannequin Museum, Los Angeles.

Lague, Louise. 1989. "It's Not Just Window Dressing." *New York Times Magazine.* November 12, pp. 50–52, 72–73.

Landau, Martha. 1990. Interview with author. New York. November 7.

Landman, Beth. 1987. "Window Wonderland." *New York Post.* November 27.

Lapin, Lynne. 1976. "Bizarre Reality: An Approach to Display." *Visual Merchandising.* August, pp. 48–58.

Lauritano, Robin. 1990. Interview with author. New York. December 5.

Leach, William. 1989. "Strategists of Display and the Production of Desire." In *Consuming Visions: Accumulation and Display of Goods in America, 1880–1920*, ed. Simon J. Bronner, pp. 99–132. New York: W. W. Norton.

Lee, Sarah. 1991. Interview with author. New York. May 16.

Lee, Tom. N.d. *How to Put the WIN in Windows*. Fur Information and Fashion Council. Collection of the Fashion Institute of Technology, New York.

Lee-Potter, Linda. N.d. "She's New, She's Fantastic—She's For Me!" Adel Rootstein company archives, London.

Leopold, Ellen. 1992. "The Manufacture of the Fashion System." In *Chic Thrills: A Fashion Reader*, ed. Juliet Ash and Elizabeth Wilson, pp. 101–117. Berkeley: University of California Press.

LePage, David. 1979. "Live Manikins Intrigue Shoppers at Mall." *Los Angeles Times*. October 14.

Leydenfrost, Robert. 1950. *Window Display*. New York: Architectural Book.

Liberman, Alexander. 1979. Introduction to Polly Devlin, *Vogue Book of Fashion Photography: The First Sixty Years*. New York: Quill.

Lidow, Leza. N.d. "The Iron Maiden." Commentary on her own mannequin art. The Mannequin Museum, Los Angeles.

Life. 1937. "Life Goes to a Party with a New York Café Socialite Named Cynthia." December 13.

Lileks, James. N.d. "Hulking Hunks: New Male Mannequins Loom Larger." Knight-Ridder Newspapers. Ca. 1990.

Literary Digest. 1925. "Liking and Disliking the Paris Exposition." September 5, n.p.

Lynn, Carol. 1937. "Manikins, Models, Make-Up, Manners: Carol Lynn Gives Success Note in 'Modeling for Money.'" *The Literary Digest*. March 20, pp. 22–23.

Lyons, Harriet. 1976. "Store Windows: All Dressed Up and Going Way Out." *Ms.* November, pp. 32–34.

McCray, Rod. 1990. Interview with author. New York. October 17.

McFadden, Mary. 1987. Letter to Colin Birch. Colin Birch Collection, Fashion Institute of Technology. September 21.

Malanga, Gerard, ed. 1985. *Scopophilia: The Love of Looking*. New York: Alfred Van Der Marck.

Mansour, Jim. 1990. Interview with author. New York. October 15.

Marchand, Roland. 1985. *Advertising the American Dream: Making Way for Modernity, 1920–1940*. Berkeley: University of California Press.

Marcus, Leonard S. 1978. *The American Store Window*. London: Architectural Press.

Marinetti, Filippo Tommaso, et al. 1971. "The Futurist Cinema." In *Futurist Performance*, ed. Michael Kirby, pp. 212–217. New York: PAJ.

Markus, David. 1981. "Brehm's Better Halves: The Best Thing Since Sliced Bread." *American Photographer*. September, pp. 54–58.

Marlowe, Francine. 1980. *Male Modeling: An Inside Look*. New York: Crown.

Marsh, John L. 1976. "Drama and Spectacle by the Yard: The Panorama in America." *Journal of Popular Culture* 10: 581–592.

Martin, George. 1990. Interview with author. New York. November 14.

Martin, Richard. 1987. *Fashion and Surrealism*. New York: Rizzoli.

Martin, Richard, and Harold Koda. 1989. *Jocks and Nerds: Men's Style in the Twentieth Century*. New York: Rizzoli.

Marx, Howard. 1984. "In the Pink: The Galery of Wearable Art Exudes a Decidedly Feminine Flair." *Visual Merchandising & Store Design*. June, pp. 92–95.

Massey, Maria. 1948. *Principles of Men's Wear Display*. New York: Fairchild.

Mathews, Thomas F. 1988. "The Sequel to Nicaea II." Collection of The New Museum, New York.

Matthews, Clyde. 1948. *So You Want to Be A Model!* Garden City, N.Y.: Halcyon House.

"Meet Gregory: Stern and Silent Bodyguard Protects You 24 Hours a Day." N.d. Advertisement, source unknown. The Mannequin Museum, Los Angeles.

Melmed, Jerry P. 1976. "The Glass Is a Gas." *Visual Merchandising*. December, p. 69.

Merchant's Record and Show Window. 1937. "Are the Better Men's Stores Using More He-Mannequins?" September.

Metropolis. 1927. Film, dir. Fritz Lang. 95 minutes.

Meyer, Ursula. 1972. Introduction to *Conceptual Art*. New York: E. P. Dutton.

Miller, Nory. 1984. "Art for a Minute." *Industrial Design*. September–October, p. 16–75.

———. 1978. "Spaces for Selling: Psychology, Design and Show Biz in the Special World of Retailing." *AIA Journal* 67: 34–41.

Minton, James. 1973. "Trespassing at the Dante." *Artweek*. December 22, p. 11.

Moholy-Nagy, Laszlo. 1961. "Theater, Circus, Variety." In *The Theatre of the Bauhaus*, ed. Walter Gropius, trans. Arthur S. Weininger, pp. 49–70. Middletown, Conn.: Wesleyan University Press.

Monaghan, Philip. 1991. Telephone interview with author. New York–Columbus, Ohio. February 5.

Monterey Peninsula Herald. 1981. "Modern Store Mannequins Look Like Folks You Know." February 5. Photocopy. The Mannequin Museum, Los Angeles.

Moore, Gene. 1990. Interview with author. New York. November 2.

———. 1951. "A Star is Born at Bonwit's." *Display World.* July.

———. 1950. Introduction to Robert Leydenfrost, *Window Display.* New York: Architectural Book.

Moore, Gene, and Jay Hyams. 1990. *My Time at Tiffany's.* New York: St. Martin's.

Morris, Bernadine. 1974. "Fashions Were Part of a Colorful Show—People Were the Rest." *New York Times.* April 24.

———. 1972. "Career Girls Turn Models for Seventh." *New York Times.* September 22.

Mowry, George, ed. 1963. *The Twenties: Flapper and Fantasies.* New York: n.p.

Mulvey, Laura. 1975. "Visual Pleasure and Narrative Cinema." *Screen.* Autumn, pp. 6–18.

Museum of Modern Art. 1990. "High and Low: Modern Art and Popular Culture." Newspaper commentary and guide published in conjunction with exhibition of the same name. October 7, 1990–January 15, 1991.

Nakamura, Makoto. 1975–76. "Shiseido Cosmetics." *Graphis.* 31:518.

National Cash Register Co. 1959. "Making Your Windows Work for You." In *Better Retailing.* Dayton: n.p. Collection of Fashion Institute of Technology, New York.

Nemy, Enid. 1983. "Mannequins May Never Die, But They Do Get Redesigned." *The Register.* August 28. Photocopy. The Mannequin Museum, Los Angeles.

Newhall, Edith. 1989. "Father Figures." *New York.* June 12, p. 34.

Newton, Helmut. 1978. *Sleepless Nights.* New York: Congreve.

New York Sun. 1941. "New Manikins Shown: Fifth Avenue Models Have Life-like Faces." September 13.

———. N.d. "[Greneker] Creates New Method For Making Dummies."

New York Times. 1921. "Making Manikins for Display Uses: Process Used is Very Different From That Formerly Employed for Dummies." March 27.

———. N.d. "An Immovable Object Moves." Ca. 1987.

O'Brien, Anne, and Warner Olivier. 1946. "The Lady in the Window." *Saturday Evening Post.* July 20, pp. 26–86.

O'Clare, Dana. 1937. "The Eyes Have It." *Merchant's Record and Show Windows.* September, pp. 14–15.

Oestricher, Ralph. 1978. "Mannequins . . . Moods Through Makeup." *Visual Merchandising.* February, 36–37.

Oldenburg, Claes. 1967. *Store Days.* New York: Something Else.

O'Leary, Sean. 1989. "The High Cost of Being Right: Patent Protection in a Creative Industry." *Visual Merchandising & Store Design.* October, pp. 62–67.

Onorato, Ronald J. 1987. *Vito Acconci: Domestic Trappings.* La Jolla, Calif.: La Jolla Museum of Contemporary Art.

Orvell, Miles. 1989. *The Real Thing: Imitation and Authenticity in American Culture, 1880–1940.* Chapel Hill: University of North Carolina.

Parola, Robert. 1989. "Visualizing the Merchandise: Simon Says." *Daily News Record.* May 15, p. 26.

Parrot, Nicole. 1982. *Mannequins.* New York: St. Martin's.

Partington, Angela. 1992. "Popular Fashion and Working-Class Affluence." In *Chic Thrills: A Fashion Reader,* ed. Juliet Ash and Elizabeth Wilson, pp. 145–161. Berkeley: University of California Press.

Pegler, Martin M. 1988. "A Visual Marketer at the Cutting Edge." *Visual Merchandising & Store Design.* January, pp. 52–53.

———. 1980. "Alternatives." *Visual Merchandising.* May, pp. 53–54.

———. 1979. "A Mannequin Glossary." *Visual Merchandising.* March, pp. 56–59.

———. 1978. "Image." *Visual Merchandising.* February, pp. 47–48.

Perreault, John. 1989. "Through a Glass Darkly." *Artforum.* March, pp. 106–112.

PIC. 1941. April 29. Lillian Greneker Estate, The Mannequin Museum, Los Angeles.

Pierre Imans mannequin company. N.d. "Les Cires de Pierre Imans." Catalog. Ca. 1925. The Mannequin Museum, Los Angeles.

Popper, Frank. 1968. *Origins and Development of Kinetic Art.* Stephen Bann, trans. New York: New York Graphic Society.

Posner, Jack. 1980a. "Mannequins: Today and Tomorrow." *Visual Merchandising.* May, pp. 48–50.

———. 1980b. "Trendy Tableaux Mark Bloomies' Display: An Interview With Howard Meadows." *Visual Merchandising.* May, pp. 38E-F.

Pratts, Candy. 1991. Interview with author. New York. April 1.

Pucci, Ralph. 1990. Interview with author. New York. October 10.

Retail Attraction. N.d. "From Brum to Big Apple . . . and Big, Big Dollars." Ca. early 1980s. No. 5, pp. 30–31.

Richardson, Brenda. 1986. *Scott Burton.* Baltimore: Baltimore Museum of Art.

Robert Filoso Mannequin Inc. *A.* "Top U.S. Mannequin Designer Robert Filoso to Debut New Collection at WAVM." Press release. Robert Filoso Private Collection.

———. B. Press release for "Eye Spy" mannequin collection. Robert Filoso Private Collection.

Rogers, Michael. 1987. "Now, 'Artificial Reality.'" *Newsweek*. February 9, pp. 56–57.

Rutledge, Rebecca. 1986. "Rare Form." *Main*. December, pp. 61 ff.

Saarinen, Aline. 1965. "Window on Fifth Avenue." *Show*. April, pp. 16–20.

Sabol, Blair. 1977. "Let's Put the Living Back in Lifestyle." *Village Voice*. August 15, pp. 25–26.

———. 1971. "Fashion Shows Have Got to Go." *Village Voice*. April 1.

———. N.d. "The Fall Fashions Perform Themselves." *Village Voice*. Ca. mid-1970s.

Saks Fifth Avenue. N.d. "Saks Fifth Avenue Windows Feature 'Christy,' A New Mannequin." Press release. Ca. late 1970s. The Mannequin Museum, Los Angeles.

Scarangello, Guy. 1990. Interview with author. New York. October 19.

Schechner, Richard. 1985. "Restoration of Behavior." In *Theatre and Anthropology*, pp. 35–116. Philadelphia: University of Pennsylvania Press.

———. 1973. *Environmental Theatre*. New York: Hawthorn.

Scherer, Patrick. 1989. "Avant-Garb." *Art & Antiques*. January, p. 22.

Schickel, Richard. 1985. *The Disney Version*. New York: Simon & Schuster.

Schlemmer, Oskar. 1961. "Man and Art Figure." In *The Theatre of the Bauhaus*, ed. Walter Gropius, trans. Arthur S. Weininger. Middletown, Conn.: Wesleyan University Press.

Seiberling, Dorothy. 1976a. "The Art-Martyr." *New York*. May 24, pp. 48–66.

———. 1976b. "Windows: Whodunit First?" *New York*. May 24, p. 86.

Selz, Peter. 1981. "The Coloratura of Colette." Introduction to *Colette (1970–1980)*, pp. 8–17. Exhibition catalog. Milan: Giancarlo Politi.

Senerius, Pam. 1976a. "How Do You Make Display Live?" *Visual Merchandising*. May, pp. 28–54.

———. 1976b. "Is Display Passé?" *Visual Merchandising*. February, p. 23.

Sharpsteen, Bill. 1987. "A Day in the Life: Tanya Ragir, Mannequin Sculptor." *Los Angeles*. June, p. 26.

Sinderbrand, Laura, Harold Koda, and Richard Martin. 1989a. "Ancien Régime: Revolution in Fashion." Exhibition brochure. Fashion Institute of Technology.

———. 1989b. "The Historical Mode." Exhibition brochure. Fashion Institute of Technology.

Slade, Joseph W. 1989. "Pornography." In *Handbook of American Popular Culture*, ed. M. Thomas Inge, pp. 957–1010. New York: Greenwood.

Slesin, Suzanne. 1988. "He Really Does Windows." *New York Times*. December 8.

Smithsonian. 1975. "Inflation May Sometimes Be What's Needed." June.

Snead, Elizabeth. 1990. "Macho Mannequins Muscle Into Stores." *USA Today*. June 14.

Snow, Stephen. 1987. "Theatre of the Pilgrims: Documentation and Analysis of a 'Living History' Performance in Plymouth, Massachusetts." Ph.D. dissertation, New York University.

Sontag, Susan. 1982. "Notes on 'Camp.'" In *A Susan Sontag Reader*, pp. 105–119. New York: Farrar Straus & Giroux.

Southgate, Michael. 1990a. Interview with author. New York. November 30.

———. 1990b. Interview with author. New York. December 17.

Squires, Lloyd. 1991. Interview with author. Los Angeles. January 10.

Städtische Galerie Nordheim. 1985. *Colette*. Exhibition catalog. Mannheim.

Stedelijk Museum. 1974. *Dennis Oppenheim*. Amsterdam.

Steele, Valerie. 1985. *Fashion and Eroticism: Ideals of Feminine Beauty From the Victorian Era to the Jazz Age*. New York: Oxford University Press.

Steiger, Lucretia. N.d. "Realistic Mannequins: Did You See That Girl Move?" *The Daily Breeze* (Torrance, Calif.).

Stevens, Mark. 1979. *Like No Other Store in the World*. New York: Thomas Y. Crowell.

Stewart, Susan. 1993. *On Longing: Narratives of the Miniature, the Gigantic, the Souvenir, the Collection*. Durham, N.C.: Duke University Press.

Stores. 1969. "It's Lights, Camera, Action for Tuned-In Fashion Shows." June, pp. 13–15.

Stubergh, Katherine Keller. 1983. Letter to Marsha Bentley Hale. March 28. The Mannequin Museum, Los Angeles.

Stuckey, Charles F. 1977. "Duchamp's Acephalic Symbolism." *Art in America*. January–February, pp. 94–99.

Taft, William Nelson. 1926. *Handbook of Window Display*. New York: McGraw-Hill.

Takahama, Valerie. 1983. "The Mannequin Biz Isn't For Dummies." *Press-Telegram*. September 14. Photocopy. The Mannequin Museum, Los Angeles.

Taylor, Angela. 1977. "They Find Right Face—Then Create a Mannequin to Resemble It." *New York Times*. November 28.

Thomas, Bob. 1976. *Walt Disney: An American Original.* New York: Simon & Schuster.

Thompson, Mark. 1979. *Rubbish Theory.* Oxford: Oxford University Press.

Time. 1976. "Advertising: Wild Windows." July 19, p. 49.

———. 1974. "And Now, The Group." *Time.* January 14, p. 45.

———. 1938. "Avenue Art." December 5, p. 37.

———. 1937. "France: Success!" August 9, pp. 15–17.

Tompkins, Douglas. 1989. *Esprit: The Comprehensive Design Principle.* Tokyo: Robundo.

Toshi. 1990a. Interview with author. New York. December 13.

———. 1990b. Press kit. Collection of author.

Triggs, Teal. 1992. "Framing Masculinity: Herb Ritts, Bruce Weber and the Body Perfect." In *Chic Thrills: A Fashion Reader,* ed. Juliet Ash and Elizabeth Wilson, pp. 25–29. Berkeley: University of California Press.

Tucker, Marcia. 1981. "John Baldessari: Pursuing the Unpredictable." In *John Baldessari,* pp. 7–50. New York: The New Museum.

———. 1970. "PheNAUMANology." *Artforum.* December, pp. 38–43.

Turbeville, Deborah. 1978. *Wallflower.* New York: Congreve.

Undercoffer, Diana G. 1981a. "Free(Lance) At Last." *Visual Merchandising & Store Design.* June, pp. 83–86.

———. 1981b. "A Walking Tour of Henri Bendel." *Visual Merchandising & Store Design.* December, pp. 75–77.

Visual Merchandising. 1980. "What is Your Mannequin '10'?" May, p. 51.

———. 1979a. The Character of a Window: Ordering." March, p. 42

———. 1979b. "A Day in the Life: Maintenance." March, pp. 50–51.

———. 1979c. "The Eye in Image: Selection." March, pp. 44–45.

———. 1979d. "The Other Side of the Looking Glass: Directions." March, pp. 54–55.

———. 1979e. "The Other Side of the Window: Mannequins." March, pp. 40–41.

———. 1979f. "A Response to Light: Lighting." March, pp. 48–49.

———. 1977. "Invisible Men Haunt Boutique." December, pp. 76–77.

———. 1976. "The Next Best Thing . . ." June, pp. 38–40.

———. 1974. "Unisex." June, p. 54.

Visual Merchandising & Store Design. 1991. *Buyers' Guide.* February.

———. 1989. December, p. 81.

———. 1987. *Mannequins: The Possibilities.* September.

Waite, Derek. 1978. "From Showroom to Show Window." *Visual Merchandising.* February, pp. 40–41.

Wallace, Michael. 1981. "Visiting the Past: History Museums in the United States." *Radical History Review* 25: 63–96.

Warehousemen and Drapers' Trade Journal. 1883. Chapter 9, "A Guide to Window-Dressing." London. The Mannequin Museum, Los Angeles.

Warren, Virginia Lee. 1970. "Racial Bars Easing in Stores' Windows." *New York Times.* December 20.

———. 1964. "Beauty of Mannequins in Store Window Often Draws Its Pattern From Real Life." *New York Times.* September 16, n.p.

Webb, John. 1986. "Ecco L'Italia." *Visual Merchandising & Store Design.* January, pp. 36–39.

———. 1985. "Japan at Bloomingdale's: Classic Simplicity in a Modern Framework." *Visual Merchandising & Store Design.* January, pp. 38–42.

Weinstein, Jeff. 1989. "Consumerismo: I'll Be Your Window." *The Village Voice.* February 28, p. 35.

Weiss, Ray. 1990. "World-Class Windows: Simon Doonan Takes Great Panes With Barneys' Look." Gannett Westchester Newspapers. January 9.

"What's Going On Behind That Plate-Glass Window?" 1977. Author and publication unknown. The Mannequin Museum, Los Angeles.

Witt, Stacey. 1990. "Lowell Nesbitt's Homage to Humanity." *Visual Merchandising & Store Design.* May, pp. 146–151.

Wolf & Vine. N.d. "It's Easy to Be Brilliant." Brochure. Ca. 1960s. The Mannequin Museum, Los Angeles.

Women's Wear Daily. 1986. "New-Look Mannequins." September, pp. 20–31.

———. 1976. *Women's Wear Daily: 200 Years of American Fashion.* July 26.

———. N.d. Article on "The New Mannequins." Ca. early 1980s. The Mannequin Museum, Los Angeles.

Wood, Barry James. 1982. *Show Windows: 75 Years of the Art of Display.* New York: Congdon & Weed.

Wood, Jeff, and Richard Rosenthal. 1965. "Mannequins Passé at G-J: Callahan Takes a Dim View." *Women's Wear Daily.* June 1, p. 85.

Yaeger, Deborah Sue. 1976. "Chic Shops' Displays No Longer Are Just Window Dressing: Gimmicks and Realism Used to Project Sophistication; King Kong Goes Ape." *Wall Street Journal.* September 9.

Index

Gay sensibility in display, 29–31, 114

Gaze: of mannequins, 113, 171 n 38; relation to power, 46, 52, 91

Gemini mannequins, *128*, 130

Gender: association of men with production and women with consumption, 23–24, 27, 29, 167 n 58, 167 n 59; differences in mannequin design, 74, 91; of display workers, viii, 24; issues, viii–ix, 30, 41, 52, 59, 62, 63–64, 86–94, 153, 168 n 32, 168 n 40, 169 n 37; representation, 171 n 51. *See also* Colette; Gaze, relation to power; Hershman, Lynn

"Gender narcissism" (Klein), 154

Geographic quotations in fashion and display, 37

George Dell Display, 131

Gift-exchange or offer of hospitality, display as, 167 n 57

Gimbels, 65, 159

Glass: as barrier, 38, 40; plate, development of, 8; window, as aid to creation of illusion, 157, 158, 168 n 41, 173 n 11

Goldsmith mannequins, *137*

"Goodwill" windows, 16, 145

Gotham Book Mart, 155

Greneker mannequins, 18, 72, 75, 84, 86, *86*, 170 n 22

Grouping of mannequins, 97, 98, *99*, 109, 113, 119, 127

Gucci. *See* Scarangello, Guy

Halston, 101, 102. *See also* Hugo, Victor

Haring, Keith, 35

Headless mannequins, 156. *See also* Dressmaker's forms

Head treatments, 70, *86*, 123, 125, *131*, 132, 135, *136*, 137, *137*, *138*, 166 n 57

Henri Bendel. *See* Currie, Robert

Henry, Maurice, 62

Hershman, Lynn, 38–40, 103

Hindsgaul mannequins, *86*

Hoskins, Robert ("Buddy"), 110–14

Hugo, Victor, 20, 25, 110, 113–14, 125, 126, 127

Human-mannequin performances, *24*, 38, 47, 48, 59–60, 169 n 46

Idealization. *See* Body idealization of mannequins

Identification as selling technique, 49, 51, 67, 123, 126, 127, 158; Hershman's critique of, 40. *See also* Anthropomorphism and mannequins

Identity confusion as selling technique, 48, 49, 52

Ignoring the merchandise as selling and display technique, 16, 101, 106, 147. *See also* Street theatre displays

Insanity as subject of street theatre windows, 115, 145

Installation art, 38–39, 41, 43. *See also* Environment

Insulting the consumer as selling technique, 145

"Invisible people" displays. *See* Absent bodies in display

J. C. Penney's, 158–59

Japan, visual merchandising in, 17, 166 n 57

Jean-Paul Germain boutique, 143

Johns, Jaspar, 33

Kiesler, Frederick, 13

Kitsch, 31

Kokoschka, Oskar, 169 n 46

Kruger, Barbara, 34, *35*

Lagerfeld, Karl, 13

Lauritano, Robin, 156, 157, 160

Lee, Tom, 15

Lifestyle merchandising, 27, 97, 99, 101, 160, 161, 162, 171 n 29

Lighting, 8, 16, 165 n 11

Limited, The. *See* Mansour, Jim

Live elements in display, use of, 172 n 18

Live fashion presentation, changes in. *See* Fashion modeling, developments in

Live interpretation, in living-history museums, 122, 160

Loewy, Raymond, 27

Looking: as implicating the viewer, 2, 47; valorized during particular periods of cultural history, 9, 20, 101, 166 n 46

Lord & Taylor, 13, 47

Luna mannequin, 78, *78*

Macy's, 2, 13, 16, 26, 27, 124, *141*

Madonna, 1

Malls, shopping: growth of, contributing to demise of window display, 121; as multisensory environments, 162, *163*, 164

Manigault, Marc, 106

Mannequin, term applied to live models, 172 n 8

Mannequin alternatives, 13, 122, 123, 125, 129, 132,

Mannequins: as architecture, *131*; as image ideals, 74–75; presented as theatrical characters, 38, 39, 40; resemblance to models or to real human beings, 55, 82; as sculpture, 91, *93*, 125, 129, 157; as signs of store image, 67, 124, 125, 130; as used in persona-based performance art, 42, 43

Mansour, Jim, 25, 62, 91, 131, 132, 159

Martin, George. *See* Patina-V

Mary Brosnan mannequins, *83*, *98*

Masson, André, 62

Materials, novel, use of in display, 16, 21, 128, 147, 166 n 35

Maxfield Bleu, *32*, *65*, 144, *144*, 145, *146*, 148

Memphis School, 130

Meyerhold, Vsevolod, 4

Michals, Duane, 148

Middle age, representation of in mannequins, 75, 80, *81*, 123, 170 n 24

Miró, Joàn, 62

Mirrors and mirroring, 153–54, *155*, 157, 158

"Mistakes" as audience involvement technique, 44, *66*, 168 n 40

Mixed media in display, 144, 148, 160

Model-mannequin performances, 47

Model-mannequin photography, *50*, *56*, 82, 84

Modernism and modernization, 11, 13, 127, 128

Monaghan, Philip, 37, 142

Money, as subject of window displays, 116, *117*

Moore, Gene, 6, 18, 19, 21, *24*, 25, 33, 34, 47, 63, 64, 65, *66*, 67, 74, *75*, 103, 110, 115, *115*, 116, *117*, 119, 137, 141, 142, 157, 158, 169 n 47

Motion: of Audio-Animatronic figures, 60–61; "captured" in mannequin poses, *90*, 131, 162; implied, of mannequins, 1–2, 71, 82, *83*, 98, 110, 170 n 22; implied through staging of dramatic scenes in windows, 11–12; and perceived masculinity of mannequins, 91; of robot mannequin, 45, 47; as stock feature of *1960s* fashion, 121; suggested or captured through fashion photography, 17, 18; in window displays, 43. *See also* Stillness

Mott, George, 148